British-Islamic Identity

IOEPress *tb*

'This book is an excellent and systematic study of the experiences of third-generation Bangladeshis in the East End of London. It is an important resource that carefully and sensitively goes to the heart of the issues of identity, religion, belonging and citizenship facing a much-beleaguered community. The book will be of significant value to scholars and students of South Asian Muslim minorities in Britain today.'

Tahir Abbas, Professor of Sociology, Fatih University, Istanbul

'A compelling, insightful and refreshing book which challenges pre-held conceptions of young Muslims. Through the historical, theoretical perspective and the personal narratives of the participants, we are given a powerful account of the emergence of "British Islam", a fusion of their diverse, complicated and multifaceted identities. A compulsory read for all in education.'

Baljeet Ghale, Deputy Headteacher, Stepney Green Maths, Computing & Science College, London

'Away from the paranoid media hype over extremism and radicalization, the author has presented an outstanding analysis of the multifaceted complexities of identity that young Muslims face in Britain today. With extensive reference to academic work he provides a deep insight into the realities of our persona and how we can be perceived in society. A compelling read for anyone who truly wants to understand the young Muslim mindset and the external factors that play a part in shaping their view of the world.'

Harun Khan, Muslim Council of Britain

'A profound, though very particular, answer to the question of why so many offspring of Muslim immigrants in Europe adopt the identity neither of the sender country nor of their new homeland but instead embrace an Islamic identity. That this is a key question for Europe becomes more and more evident with each passing day. Aminul Hoque has provided those who seek a serious answer a full and thoughtful examination, based not just on study at his desk but on his experience in the street, with

Muslims, in this case third-generation British Bangladeshis, whom he has interviewed comprehensively. His findings that Islamic identity has supplanted a Bangladeshi identity because, typically of immigrant children everywhere, they wish to distance themselves from the old-fashioned, old-country ways of their parents but also because they do not receive a welcome from the new country. That Hoque's exhaustive research is consistent with my own, I consider an honour.'

Robert S. Leiken, Author of *Europe's Angry Muslims: The revolt of the second generation*

'A fine ethnographic study of older Bangladeshi teenagers and how they imagine, contest and deploy a British-Islamic identity in ways quite different from their parents and grandparents.Indispensable for teachers, youth workers, academics and policymakers.'

Dr Philip Lewis, Author of *Young, British and Muslim*, Department of Peace Studies, Bradford University

'This book is a timely and crucial study of British-Islamic identity and the way young (Bangladeshi) Muslims are living their lives despite a politicized Islamism and familiar majority-society hostilities. It should be required reading for every politician, educationalist and indeed every person who wants to live in a sane and civilized society.'

Professor Sally Tomlinson, Honorary Research Fellow, Department of Education, University of Oxford

British-Islamic Identity

Third-generation Bangladeshis from East London

Aminul Hoque

A Trentham Book

Institute of Education Press

First published in 2015 by the Institute of Education Press, University of London,
20 Bedford Way, London WC1H 0AL

ioepress.co.uk

British Library Cataloguing in Publication Data:
A catalogue record for this publication is available from the British Library

ISBNs
978-1-85856-603-0 (paperback)
978-1-85856-659-7 (PDF eBook)
978-1-85856-660-3 (ePub eBook)
978-1-85856-661-0 (Kindle eBook)

Typeset by Quadrant Infotech (India) Pvt Ltd
Printed by CPI Group (UK) Ltd, Croydon, CR0 4YY

Cover and internal photos ©2015 Asia Begum
Cover and back design by Atique Miah, www.atiquemiah.com

Contents

List of figures and tables

Glossary of foreign words, key concepts and terms

aaki	Brother.
abba	Father.
amma	Mother.
Bangladeshis	People who originate from the country of Bangladesh. There is much diversity in terms of language, class and caste in Bangladesh, and a pivotal divide between urban and rural culture. However, as the majority of British Bangladeshis originate from the Sylheti region of Bangladesh and all of the participants of this study are Sylheti, 'Bangladeshi culture' in this book refers only to a particular Sylheti rural Bangladeshi culture.
Banglish	The fusion of the English and Bengali language as a means of communicating with others.
Bengali	Has two meanings: the language spoken by Bangladeshis and people of the Indian state of Bengal; and aspects of their respective national/regional cultural identities. With reference to Bangladesh the terms Bengali, Bangla, Bangladeshi and Sylheti are used interchangeably.
bhai	A term of respect and endearment, meaning older brother.
Bidesh	Foreign country. Term mainly used by the first generation of settlers to refer to Britain.
British Islam	A fusion of Bangladeshi cultural norms, Islamic spirituality and ideology alongside a practical Western lifestyle. It is a dynamic culture that enables third-generation Bangladeshis to comfortably identify with and fuse the many segments of their multifaceted identities: national, linguistic, ethnic, racial, cultural, religious and gendered.
burka	Long and loose piece of outer garment covering the whole body, and also the head covering and face veil. Worn by many Muslim women across the globe. Although there are stylistic, geographical and cultural distinctions between the burka and the jilbab (below), the terms are used interchangeably as there is much

	confusion. Both overgarments are loose and denote the important Islamic concepts of modesty and privacy.
cotching	Modern urban language meaning 'socializing, relaxing'.
daadi	Grandmother.
dada	Grandfather.
Desh	Referring to Bangladesh as 'home'.
East London	A reference to the East End of London. 'East London' and 'Tower Hamlets' are used interchangeably.
Eid	There are two Eid celebrations per year. Eid ul-Fitr is celebrated at the end of the fasting month (Ramadan) and Eid ul-Adha, the festival of sacrifice, which entails ritual slaughter of sheep, goats and camels that are then distributed mainly to the poor. It celebrates the end of the annual pilgrimage to Makkah.
first generation	Bangladeshi migrants who immigrated to Britain predominantly in the 1950s and 1960s.
hadith	The stories, traditions and actions of the Prophet Mohammed (PBUH) and his companions.
halal	Permissible Islamically.
hijab	Has a trilogy of meanings: (1) to conceal, hide, cover and veil; (2) lowering the gaze when with the opposite sex – this applies to men as well, who must lower their gaze in the presence of unrelated women; (3) in recent times, hijab has also become the common name for the headscarf worn by Muslim women, pinned at the neck to reveal the face. According to Islamic scholarly thought, 'hijab' is given the wider meaning of modesty, privacy and morality.
inshallah	God willing.
jazakallah	Thank you.
jilbab	Refers to a long, flowing, baggy overgarment worn by some Muslim women. In some parts of the world such as Indonesia, the headscarf is called the jilbab, sometimes also referred to as the burka (see above).
kyaf a haal	How are you?
madrasa	Islamic education centre, usually a boarding school.
maya	Love.
niqab	A face veil.
PBUH	Abbreviation for 'Peace be upon him', always said after hearing or making reference to an Islamic prophet.

purdah	Protecting Muslim women from contact with men outside of their immediate family.
Qu'ran	Holy religious book for Muslims who believe that the words in the Arabic text of the Qu'ran are sacred, revealed to the Prophet Mohammed (PBUH) by God (Allah) over a period of 23 years in the seventh century CE.
sahabiyat	Full citizenship.
salaam alaikum	A greeting used by Muslims that translates as 'peace be upon you'.
saree	A long, draping dress worn mainly by the first and second generation of Bangladeshi women.
second generation	Children of first-generation settlers, most of whom were born in Bangladesh and came to Britain as young children in the 1970s and 1980s when family reunification took place.
sharia	Islamic law.
shisha	Smoking flavoured tobacco.
Sylheti	The language spoken in the Sylhet region, from where most British Bangladeshis originate. Sylheti is often referred to interchangeably with Bengali.
third generation	British-born children of second-generation Bangladeshis.
thobe	A baggy piece of clothing covering the whole body from neck to ankles. Usually worn by men.
ukthi	Sister.
umma	One global Muslim community (brotherhood and sisterhood).
wagwan	A form of greeting in slang, meaning 'how is it going?'
walahi	Arabic term meaning 'I swear (in God's name)'.
9/11	A reference to the 11 September 2001 terrorist attacks in New York.
7/7	A reference to the 7 July 2005 terrorist attacks in London.

Acknowledgements

This has been the most difficult part to write. There are so many people that have helped make this book happen and they need special mention. I am sure there are many others who have contributed immensely and whose precious names have escaped me. I have tried to manage this difficult task of appreciation by grouping them into family, friends and colleagues.

I would first like to thank the many members of my chaotic family. My champion, my hero, my role model, my inspiration, my father – Haji Shamsul Hoque – for unknowingly and silently encouraging me to be kind, fair and ask questions. His migrant story of sacrifice, struggle, upheaval, discipline and hard work has been a constant source of energy in moulding me and also the composition of this book. My mother, Ayatun Nessa, for her unconditional love and for her important role as super-granny – often babysitting my children while I toured the streets of East London as an ethnographer. My father-in-law and brother-in-law, Haji Abdush Shahid and Abdur Razzique, for constantly reminding me to complete this book simply by asking, 'How is the book coming along?' I am indebted to all my brothers and sisters who have always inspired and supported me, and to my nephews and nieces (far too many to list), whose complex stories of identity as British-born third-generation Bangladeshis shaped the foundations of this book.

I am blessed and grateful to have such a culturally diverse and global group of friends whose experiences and insight have contributed significantly to my conceptual thinking: the boys (Al, Amit, Arj, Chu, Chunder, Hazza, Lee, Imran, Rikka and Webb), for hours of endless banter, discussion and debate on the many issues and themes discussed in this book; and my Bengali brothers (Amz, Atique bhai, Azad, Foisol bhai, Gaff, Kal and Sel), who, without knowing it, contributed to my repertoire of cultural knowledge – often being the gatekeepers into a complex and often strange Bengali (Sylheti) world. Your support, humour, sarcasm, honesty and satire have helped me to cope with many knotty ideas. Thank you all for your unfailing friendship and for sometimes telling me how it is.

I have been extremely fortunate to have a group of colleagues at Goldsmiths and London Metropolitan University, at the London Borough of Tower Hamlets and at the BBC, who have been incredibly supportive of my work. First and foremost, special thanks to my supervisor, Dr Chris Kearney, who held my hand and expertly guided me through the PhD study upon which this book is based. I will remain forever indebted to Chris for the faith that he showed in me and will never forget our initial discussions in 2003, which inspired me greatly. Many others have mentored me through debate, reflection, inspiration, professionalism, friendship, encouragement and administrative support: Paul Fletcher, James Cook MBE, Shohidul Ahmed, Nadira Huda, Sheila Leighton, Peter Cunningham, Patrick Turner, Rosalyn George, Clare Kelly, Carrie Paechter, Anna Carlisle, Charmian Kenner, Mryna Felix, Coral McCarthy, Fran Acheson and Innes Bowen. Shaynul Khan, in particular, acted as an invaluable source of local knowledge about community, culture and religiosity among youth. Asia Begum, for her brilliant photography contained in this book – for capturing the mood, emotions and complexity of identity within a photo frame. Her devotion to visual sociology is self-evident in the pages that follow. Also, the hundreds of students, young people, journalists, teachers and social workers I have taught, trained and learned from over the years – thank you for your refreshing honesty in debating the ideas that inform this book. And thanks to the key group of people who have given their valuable time to read earlier drafts and give me really useful critical feedback: my *amigo fiel* Ben Stewart, Alex Irvine, Pete Steen, Filippo Artoni, Robert Leiken, Jean Conteh, John Hardcastle, Heather Mendick and Assia Ali.

The book owes a great deal to the expert and thorough editing skills of Gillian Klein. Gillian, thank you for your enthusiasm and humanity, and for sharing my vision. I am grateful also to the publishing team at Trentham Books and IOE Press who have helped me get the message of this book to a wider audience.

Finally, my enduring gratitude must go to the six participants of this study who entrusted me with intimate and sensitive details of their lives. They were generous with their time, courageous and truthful. Their narratives remain the heart of this project. I hope I have faithfully represented their complex stories of identity here.

But I owe the biggest debt to my long-suffering and neglected wife, Asia, whose faith in me, love, patience and encouragement have kept me going, and to my three little daughters, Safaa, Eva and Hannah, who have kept me in good humour throughout.

My love, respect, admiration and deepest gratitude to you all.

Aminul Hoque
London, 2015

About the author

Dr Aminul Hoque is a lecturer in the Educational Studies Department, Goldsmiths, University of London, and a visiting lecturer at London Metropolitan University. He gained his doctorate from Goldsmiths in 2011, and his research for it forms the basis of this book.

He has some 25 years of voluntary and professional experience in the youth, community and voluntary sector, including eight years as a street detached/outreach worker and youth engagement adviser for the UK charity Rathbone. In this work he has pioneered groundbreaking methods such as an innovative five-step model of working with the 'hard to reach', since replicated by community groups and other youth programmes across the UK. He has been a major contributor to national youth policy through involvement in research programmes such as the Nuffield Foundation's 2008 enquiry into young people who are NEET (not in education, employment or training). His work has been recognized by accolades such as a National Training Award in 2002 and the Philip Lawrence Award in 2005. In 2008 he was awarded an MBE for services to youth justice in East London.

As a journalist, his inaugural radio documentary *Islamic Pride* was shortlisted for the prestigious Sony Awards in 2004. His writing focuses on issues of multicultural Britain, identity, social justice, youth policy and race relations.

Born in Bangladesh, his family came to the UK when he was 3 years old. He considers himself a British-Bangladeshi and a Londoner. He is the proud father of three girls, a keen footballer and a passionate Manchester United fan.

Part One

Introduction

1

Introduction

> I really wanted to have white skin. I was scared. I hated being black or brown or whatever else. I wanted to be white just so I wouldn't hear things as 'go back to your own country, you don't belong here'.
>
> (Taiba, aged 17)

> I was born here. I am 100 per cent British. Where is it exactly that I am supposed to go back to?
>
> (Zeyba, aged 15)

This book is an in-depth ethnographic study of the lives and multifaceted identities of six third-generation British-born Bangladeshi teenagers from Tower Hamlets, East London. By adopting a narrative approach to the research, this book retells the complex stories of these individuals. I argue that they find it hard to be both British and Bangladeshi, and face difficult identity choices. Marginalized by some sections of mainstream British society due to ethnocultural differences, many are also excluded from the Bangladeshi community due to their adoption of a seemingly Western lifestyle. This tension around cultural and racial exclusion and a blurred meaning of nation, home and a sense of belonging is painfully echoed by Taiba and Zeyba. Born and raised in Britain with a commanding grasp of the mainstream culture and language of Britain, and situated in a community where her friends and family reside and to which she affectionately refers as 'home', Zeyba asks rhetorically, 'Where is it exactly that I am supposed to go back to?' This complex situation brings into sharp focus the question of identity or identities. Are the teenagers in this study:

- Bangladeshi?
- British?
- Muslim?
- A fusion of the three?

The central argument of this book is that this dual exclusion from both wider British society and Bangladeshi culture has forced many third-generation Bangladeshis to seek alternative identities.

In modern geopolitics, the emergence of Islam as a powerful mobilizing entity for its followers has led to the growth of religiously oriented identities in the younger generations across the Muslim diaspora. Numerous third-generation Bangladeshis from East London have syncretized their Bangladeshi culture with their Western socialization within an Islamic framework. The result is the construction of what I have termed a British-Islamic identity. This 'new Islam' is a strong modern public identity and represents both a critique of Western society and also of a 'backwards' traditional Bangladeshi culture (Basit, 1997; Kibria, 2006). Enabling the subjects to identify comfortably with their multifaceted identities, British Islam challenges traditional Bangladeshi norms, values and rituals and also contests the complex notion of what it means to be British. British Islam allows many to be British, Bangladeshi and Muslim all at the same time, thus occupying more of a sociopolitical rather than theological space in wider society. Importantly, British Islam is still a relatively new form of identity and is in its formative years. And not all third-generation Bangladeshis from East London are active participants of British Islam.

Furthermore, as a dynamic and complex postmodern identity, British Islam requires a constantly changing view of self, responding to rapid social, economic and technological changes in modern society. British Islam is a fluid response to this crisis. It is a hybrid concept negotiating the complexities of modern society and providing its members with the voice, visibility, belonging, representation and confidence to partake in the wider political process.

This book is appealing to a variety of audiences – young people, community, policymakers, teachers, academics, youth and social workers, students, politicians, media professionals and international audiences, among many others – as it explores the fluidity and complexity of identity within a disadvantaged and marginalized social group: young Bangladeshis from East London. The readers will gain in-depth insight into the experiences and aspirations of this group. Many will be able to empathize with the struggles of what it means to be a young person of immigrant-minority heritage living in an urban global city. Others will gain fresh insight into and perspective on many complex and misunderstood issues affecting this social group, and apply this insight positively to policy, practice and teaching pedagogy.

The recent growth and appeal of Islam across the globe, especially among young people, is the backdrop to the book. This has been controversial and has baffled communities, students, feminists, atheists, academics, media professionals and politicians alike. With its supposed link to terror, fundamentalism, extremism and the subordinate treatment of women, why would any British-born Western Bangladeshi be attracted to this religion? This book explores the appeal of a modern syncretic version of British Islam and, through self-narratives, outlines the diversity, complexity, appeal and attraction of Islam as a core component of what it means to be British, Bangladeshi and Muslim in contemporary society.

My starting point

No research or action happens without a reason or a purpose. I recount below some of the key historical events and memories that have contributed towards defining my own identity and that have led me to write this book. The story of why I have decided to examine third-generation British-born Bangladeshi identity is complex and needs to be located within its own context and time frame. Self-narrative and memory are important in our understanding of self and the construction of identity (Randall, 1995; Gubrium and Holstein, 2000). The identity question 'Who am I?' is a complex and highly subjective one (Woodward, 2004: 8) so it is important to tackle the question of my own identity before I attempt to unpick the identity of others.

I was born in a mud hut in a village called Bagir Ghat in the district of Sylhet, northeast Bangladesh. The place where I was born means a great deal to me. It is where my roots lie, it is where my ancestors are from. Where I was born is very different to where my childhood memories are. Taking advantage of Britain's liberal immigration policy, my father came to the UK in 1963. Working all the hours possible, he migrated from one industrial city to another in the north of England before he settled down in the East End of London. My mother, my older brother, sister and I came to Britain in 1980. I was only two years of age and my immediate childhood memories revolve around black and white photographs of me as a toddler and stories told to me by my parents and other relatives.

My earliest memories of childhood are bound up with what became known as the 'Whiteside' FA Cup Final of 1985, the magic of Maradonna in Mexico 1986 and the concrete football pitch in a housing estate in Bethnal Green, East London, which essentially became my second home. This is where my friends and I congregated routinely and played endless hours of football. It is within the insularity of the estate and the concrete football pitch that we became aware of ourselves as both an ethnically and racially homogeneous community. My 'identification' with fellow Bangladeshis on the premise of common origin, similar physical characteristics, shared history and 'native country sentiment' was being constructed (Hall, 1996: 2–3; Weber, 1997: 18). All of my immediate friends spoke Bengali, we wore similar clothing from the same market stalls, we looked the same and were bound together by a Bangladeshi moral and ethical code and rituals.

Even at school, this sense of being different from non-Bangladeshis was compounded on a daily basis. But what seemed to be the problem? I, I mean we, were different. We wore grease on our hair, did not eat pork and spoke English with an accent. We experienced much racism and physical violence from what we called the 'white boys' in the school playgrounds, on the local streets and in the concrete football pitches of our council estates. Neither community understood the other's way of life. Chants of 'smelly' and 'Paki' were commonplace.

We were, however, young children just like anybody else and as well as differences we had many similarities. Just like my black and white peers, I too loved playing the game of football and my superheroes were also Superman and Spiderman. I could not understand why I was made to feel different, why I was made to feel like an outsider, somewhat inferior and second class. I just wanted to fit in and be accepted. If, as Woodward (2004: 7) argues, 'identity is marked by similarity, that is of the people like us, and by difference, of those who are not', then my experience of Bethnal Green made a clear racial and cultural distinction between 'us' Bangladeshi 'Pakis' and the 'white boys'.

Everything changed in 1988 when we moved to Forest Gate in the London Borough of Newham. It was in Forest Gate that I was introduced to a more diverse mix of people. My teenage years were very cosmopolitan. Not everyone around me was Bangladeshi. My immediate community and my secondary schooling consisted of people who spoke a variety of languages: Urdu, Gujarati, Hindi, Bengali, Patois and English. My black and white dichotomization of community and society became colourful and varied. My best friend Richard was himself white. Importantly, the warmth I received from Richard and his family made me realize that whiteness and racism did not inevitably go hand in hand.

By storying my lived experience as I have done thus far, I am trying to make sense of my own identity (Sarup, 1996: 15–16). There are other incidents in my life that have contributed to my starting point for writing this book. For example, the racism I encountered as one of the few non-whites in the Sussex County League while captaining the university football team during 1996 and 1998; the feeling of international displacement during my time studying in California (1997) when being dismissed as a 'Mexican'; and the many late-night conversations with my liberal university friends defending the notion of arranged marriage against the supposed cultural backwardness associated with this practice. These encounters compounded a sense of difference and deficiency associated with my Bangladeshi culture.

I want to end this brief account of my background with an experience that has contributed significantly towards the shaping of my complex identity. Perhaps the most significant inroad made in my personal development and my search to the 'who am I?' question has been the relationship I have developed with my father since I broke my leg in a football-related accident in February 2002. While undergoing rehabilitation at home, I had an entirely new experience – spending time with my father. I soon realized that we had a lot in common. This time that we had in abundance soon turned into hours of conversations about Bangladesh, ancestry, heritage and culture. He spoke in depth about his own childhood, family, about how he met my mother and his traumatic migration experience of displacement and rejection. Despite having lived in Britain for nearly 40 years, he consistently referred to Bangladesh as *Desh* (home). His stories filled a void, a gap in my knowledge. I suddenly felt an urge to revisit the motherland. I felt immensely proud that I was a Bangladeshi and I had to return home to explore further. My father's storytelling had whetted my appetite for further personal and academic inquiry into notions of home and identity.

I visited *Desh* during the winter of 2002 when, despite my injury, I was asked by Sporting Bengal FC to accompany them on a footballing tour of Bangladesh. I was too young to have absorbed the atmosphere and experience back in 1992 during my first visit back to Bangladesh. But now I was ready. Equipped with many questions, a hunger for knowledge and a guidebook in hand, I was ready to delve into the 'who am I?' question even further. I felt a special sense of connection and belonging with fellow Bangladeshis and the country as I met my relatives, visited the physical space of my birth and the capital city of Dhaka, and toured the eastern part of Bangladesh. This feeling of belonging was stronger than ever before. I finally felt as if I had found home. I felt comfortable. I felt secure. I was not forced to be conscious of my ethnic or racial identity, although my national identity as British and my obvious social-class differences became a muted talking point among the locals. I was entering a thought process where I was distilling the 'dilemmas of negotiating identities' as I crossed borders 'geographically, politically and psychologically' (Kearney, 2003: 10). The world around me, although different to what I was used to, made sense to me. My complex dynamic and multifaceted identity was taking shape.

These episodes of my life have left me seeking the answers to many complex questions. For example, where is home for me? East London or Sylhet, Bangladesh? What do I understand by 'home'? Why is the concept of home so important to my father's generation? Where do I feel like a foreigner? East London or Sylhet? Where do I find a sense of belonging? Are variables such as language, where I was born, my gender and class background, skin colour and religion important determinants of my identity? Importantly, who and what am I? Am I working class because of where I grew up and because my father was a machinist? Am I middle class because I am educated? Am I a Bangladeshi? Am I English/British? Am I a Muslim? Am I bound by national borders? Am I patriotic towards England or Bangladesh? From a philosophical point, who is the 'other' I constantly define myself against (Hall, 1996)? Why do I need to define myself?

This book is not an attempt to answer all of these questions. Neither is the book about me, although there is an element of self-discovery involved through the process of research and writing. For I, like Kearney (2003: 11), believe that the best learning 'occurs when we have a personal desire or a need to know'. The personal identity question is intersubjective and relational and is entangled with the identity of others. So it is important to understand the many layers of my own identity before I unpick the identity of others.

The purpose of the book

> ... my aim is general and modest: to create a better understanding of the problem by highlighting the historical perspective and providing some previously unknown information and fresh insight. If at the end of [this book] the reader feels that he is able to see the wood instead of the tree, the purpose of [this book] will have been amply served.
>
> (Hiro, 1971: 7–8)

Buoyed by the in-depth conversations with my father about culture, heritage and community, in my MSc dissertation I examined the complex notions and meanings of home and the politics of long-distance nationalism for a group of ten first-generation Bangladeshi settlers in Britain during the 1950s and 1960s (Hoque, 2003; 2005). This, along with many years of voluntary and professional experience of grass-roots community work with Bangladeshi young people from East London aged between 7 and 25, convinced me that there was scope for a longer, more detailed study that examines the experiences of the British-born third-generation Bangladeshis. How did they understand and experience the complexity of culture, nation, community and heritage? What was their story of identity?

Why the British-born third-generation Bangladeshis? Their stories and experiences are somewhat different and more complex than those of their parents and grandparents. These stories are often misunderstood or ignored altogether. The notions of home, identity, culture and heritage hold different meanings for this social group. In general, they dress differently, they speak English, they have a different diet, have a separate network of friends, do not regard Bangladesh as *Desh* and as the eventual place of return, and they engage in a different set of geopolitics that does not focus around Bangladesh. Many ridicule Bangladeshi cultural events such as weddings and weekend get-togethers with the family. Many are active participants of the global techno-generation symbolized by the smartphone and the proliferation of social media. There has been a cultural shift. They have become more overtly 'British' (Ward, 2004; Lewis, 2007) than their ancestors. While the emergence of this gap is interesting in itself, this book concentrates on the lives and multifaceted identities of the British-born third-generation Bangladeshis from East London. Many yearn to be British yet they are excluded from being so. They also want to be Bangladeshi but their actions and lifestyle have contributed to the development of a generational and ideological gap between them and their older family members. This mirrors the experiences of the Muslim 'postmigrant marginal man' who 'finds himself suspended between two cultures, neither of which offers him secure footing' (Leiken, 2012: 265).

British-born third-generation Bangladeshis are part of many overlapping and interwoven discourses and narratives. They are also part of multiple representations and social constructions. They have been constructed as 'Westernized' by their Bangladeshi elders and community, 'un-British' by many sections of the wider British polity, 'British' by fellow kin in Bangladesh, 'radicalized Muslims' by sections of the tabloid press and far-right groups, and have also become intertwined with the political language of welfare, gangsters, hoodies and criminality. Their dynamic identities must be viewed within these competing sets of complex representations.

As a result of this multifaceted process, many exert a 'hyphenated' identity (Zwick, 2002; Newsweek Staff, 2006) where the hyphen acts as a symbol of the inner struggles they face in trying to blend in with the norms of their new culture while maintaining the traditions of their ancestors (Bhabha, 1996: 54). Are they British-Bangladeshi, Bangladeshi-British or British-Muslim? It also denotes a sense of simultaneous belonging to multiple homes, nations and communities (Garbin, 2005; Barrett *et al.*, 2006). The British Islam discussed in this book remains un-hyphenated as it is a fusion identity rather than a hyphenated one.

I have kept in touch with my roots and have found comfort in my Bangladeshi heritage and culture. But this is not the case for many third-generation Bangladeshis. Many have carved out a completely new identity, a 'third space' (Bhabha, 1994: 66–84) and a 'creole world' (Hannerz, 1992: 261) for themselves. This book focuses on the development and construction of this new British-Islamic identity. Importantly, this search for a new sociolinguistic religious identity is a symbol of resistance by many third-generation Bangladeshis against assumed, imposed and non-negotiable identities that position them in undesirable and subordinate ways in wider British society.

This book tackles many issues that are important to wider academic, public and social debate. The key questions guiding it are as follows:

- What does the experience of third-generation Bangladeshis tell us about British multiculturalism?
- Is language a vital component of identity construction?
- Is birthplace a vital component of identity construction?
- Can you be born in Britain and still engage in discourse that refers to the motherland outside of the British Isles?
- Do third-generation Bangladeshis experience issues of racism, displacement, alienation? Is skin colour a major barrier to societal participation? How does the experience of racism help form alternative identities?
- What is the relationship between ethnic and national identity? Are both necessary in the construction of identity? Can you be Bengali (ethnic) and British (national) at the same time?
- How do third-generation Bangladeshis view themselves? Are they British or Bangladeshi?
- Are they constantly forced to re-examine their own identity by 'the other'? Who is the other?
- Where is home for them?
- What is the role of religion (Islam) in this whole debate?
- Is there a specific Bangladeshi female identity?

My aims in writing this book are multiple. I hope to:

- provide a voice to the voiceless, marginalized and powerless
- use the subjective experiences of local third-generation Bangladeshis to determine a way forward in making Britain a more inclusive society

- assist teachers and other social pedagogues in understanding the important role played by religion and home culture in children's education
- assist teachers in understanding the complex notion of identity, and how identity (or the lack of it) can present itself as a major barrier to learning or can open up innovative avenues for new learning experiences
- help people understand the complex nature of ethnicity and how it feels to be a marginalized minority growing up in urban Europe
- help overcome the concern of cultural ignorance by exposing the subjective feelings of Bangladeshis to wider society
- help 'the other' to understand the complex nature of identity, especially the identity of people whose roots lie elsewhere
- help government policymakers and academics to understand minority culture and experience of displacement and exclusion, and introduce a range of policies that will help accommodate different religious minority groups in Britain.

Many anthropological and sociological studies have been conducted on the East London Bangladeshi community in recent years (Eade, 1998; Gardner, 1995a; 2002). However, there is as yet no phenomenological ethnographic study of the Bangladeshi third generation. Much of the literature written on the British-Bangladeshi community has focused its attention on issues such as poverty, immigration, crime, housing, arranged marriages and education, and has predominantly examined the first and second generation of settlers (Adams, 1987; Phillips, 1988; Tomlinson and Hutchinson, 1991; Eade *et al.*, 1996). What makes this book important is that it tackles complex notions of identity and its relationship to language, religion, the concept of multiculturalism, gender, ethnicity and race, and frames it within the context of self-narratives from the third generation. It provides important insight and understanding of the many stories of identity that are important to them.

How I conducted this study

The book is based on the many stories told to me as part of an in-depth ethnographic PhD study that explored the multifaceted identities of six third-generation British-born Bangladeshis from the London Borough of Tower Hamlets, East London (Hoque, 2011). Although a triangulation of methods was used throughout the study (questionnaires, participant observations, focus groups), the predominant research method utilized to gather the data was in-depth one-to-one interviews with each participant.

The overall study was conducted between 2004 and 2010, with the main series of first and repeat one-to-one interviews taking place between 2006 and 2008. The six participants are introduced in Chapter 3. None of the six was known to me prior to the research. They nominated themselves through my youth-work contacts in Tower Hamlets. The locations for the recorded interviews varied between youth-club settings, cafes, college canteens, family homes, community centres, training centres and public parks.

The interviews all followed a semi-structured thematic format and were predominantly conversational in tone (Ellen, 1984). The less rigorous face-to-face interview has become known as a 'soft' approach to research (Davies, 1985; Jayaratne and Stewart, 1995). This soft approach allowed for authentic and honest conversation to take place between the participants and myself. While the central question of identity guided the interviews, the themes covered within the conversations were designed with a life-history narrative of the participants in mind, and with a focus on areas such as childhood memories, family and schooling life. Retelling stories and recalling memory is a difficult skill (Ellen, 1984). These interviews brought out these skills within the participants.

The study underwent three stages of fluid analysis. **Stage 1** involved a questionnaire with 103 pupils from a local secondary school (2004) and a pilot study, which comprised in-depth one-to-one interviews with three additional participants. This enabled me to crystallize and refine the main themes, focus and research questions for the main study.

Stage 2 (2006–08) involved in-depth interviewing, engaged listening and participant observation of six participants as part of the main study. The stories (data) epitomized the complexity of identity – dynamic, messy and contradictory. To begin to make sense of their stories, I colour-coded the key emerging data, looking out for the patterns that connected the participants. I also organized the data into categories of analysis and themes. This stage also involved the transcription of data and many repeat interviews with participants. The follow-up interviews allowed me to take the correspondence from the previous interviews – issues, themes and patterns I had identified as well as any areas of confusion that needed clarification – back to the researched, probe further any areas of confusion and engage in further dialogue (Riessman, 1993).

Stage 3 involved making sense of the many stories of identity that participants told me. The overlapping narratives from the participants were purposefully analysed within the wider theory and literature available on linguistic, racial, religious, national and gender identities.

Self-narratives can be problematic as they are social constructions (Gergen and Gergen, 1984; Gubrium *et al.*, 1994), reliant upon memory, selection, fiction and interpretation of past, present and future events (Olney, 1972; Carr, 1986; Murray, 1989; Miller and Glassner, 2004). However, if the life history of the individual is seen for what it actually is – a subjective personal construction situated in culture, history, time and place (Glassner and Loughlin, 1987; Hatch and Wisniewski, 1995; Goodson and Sikes, 2001) – then it enables the reader to enter the world of the participant. The storytelling narrative approach to research enabled me to capture the complexity, messiness and fluidity of identity. My decision to adopt such an approach has been guided by four important interrelated factors.

First, the narrative life-history approach (Hankiss, 1981) is rooted firmly within a qualitative (Kvale and Brinkman, 2008), interpretivist (Bartlett and Burton, 2012: 41–2) and phenomenological (Francis, 1993; Denscombe, 2010) research paradigm. Essentially, this research philosophy attempts to view the world through the eyes of the participant. It takes into account and provides rich insight into human experiences, opinions, aspirations, feelings and viewpoints. It allows the participants to talk at great length about issues important to them and to tell their own stories in their own ways. The ethnographic focus on issues such as culture, community and identity also provides us with a great deal of in-depth information about life in East London. It is the insights, the details, the 'thick description' of their lives that I, as an ethnographer, am concerned with in this book (Geertz, 2000b[1973]: 9–18; Ryle, 1971).

There is an acknowledgement that there is no such thing as a 'single story' (Adichie, 2009), that our lives are a series of complex and overlapping stories. These multiple realities are socially constructed by human beings who attach their own meanings and construct their own social reality through their life experiences and through interaction with others around them. There is no objective reality beyond these subjective meanings, which are individualized and steeped in local history, context, culture and rituals (Charlesworth, 2000).

From a social-constructionist perspective, knowledge is co-produced and jointly constructed between social actors (Burr, 2003). Identity, therefore, is constructed through dialogue, interaction, discourse and representation. The telling of stories enables the individual to construct their personal and social identities (Murray, 1989) and also make sense of their identity in an era undergoing rapid technological, social, economic and political change (Giddens, 1991; Hall, 1996; Kearney, 2003). The modern world is a place where individuals face so much insecurity, dislocation, confusion, rejection and risk (Gubrium and Holstein, 2000). It is also a world where it is difficult to grasp a sense of self, since we cross so many cultural, racial, ethnic, linguistic and geographical boundaries. Riessman (1993) argues that, amid this uncertainty, narratives can sometimes provide a common platform for people to retell or come to terms with particularly sensitive or traumatic times and events. The storying of the self is a 'reflexive' process that undergoes continuous editing and revision (Giddens, 1991: 5; Davies, 1999; Byrne, 2004). We make sense of our history, our self, our identities through the storying of our experiences, through autobiography (Sarup, 1996: 15–16). Importantly, therefore, through the storying of the self and identity, the ethnographic narrative approach to research seeks understanding and insight into human phenomena and experiences, as opposed to solutions or answers.

Second, the narrative approach puts the emphasis on the researched. This approach has been labelled a 'methodology of listening' as it allows the participants to 'thematise the phenomenon of interest' (Glassner and Loughlin, 1987: 37; Francis, 1993: 70). It also gives them the freedom to tell their side of their story and to voice their version of events. It was important to hear the voices of the participants in this study and let them lead the many conversations that took place throughout the research process. The voice is central to the personal accounts of identity, family, culture, community and so on. These are phenomena that are constantly in motion and difficult to capture, and mean different things to different people.

As part of an emerging new sociology of childhood, children are now seen as active participants in the interpretation and construction of their own cultural knowledge (James, 2007; Gray and Macblain, 2012). Young people have been regarded as the 'best sources of information about themselves' (Docherty and Sandelowski, 1999: 217). This study focuses on young people aged between 15 and 19 who are of ethnic-minority origin. It is important to view the world through their perspective rather than through the lens of the adult. Young people differ from adults in regards to status and power. They also differ in their life experiences and what they consider to be important issues in their lives (Arksey and Knight, 1999: 116). It is important to hear these invisible and ignored voices, especially the voices of people who are marginalized and alienated (Parker and Lynn, 2002). Allen usefully asserts that 'we must learn to listen to the silent, and make the hidden visible' (2005: 64). There is therefore a critical emancipatory element behind this study (Swain *et al.*, 1998).

To this effect, along with many other principles designed to keep the participants engaged and involved, my study adhered to the 'paramountcy principle', as taken from the Children Act 1989, when working with young people (Walsh, 2000). This principle puts young people at the centre of everything. It empowers them by engaging them in the decision-making process, by keeping them involved and informed of developments and by consulting them on important issues. It encourages confidentiality and applies the same standards for engaging with children as expected for work with adults (Hoque, 2004a). This 'two-way process' (Silverman, 2005: 47) and co-authored approach to research generated confidence within the participants and kept them motivated throughout. It also enabled me to negate much of the inbuilt 'asymmetry' and imbalance in power relations that exists between the researcher and researched (Heritage, 1984: 237).

A third factor to consider in the narrative approach to research centres around the concept of 'rapport' (Bogdan and Taylor, 1975: 45–8; Berg, 1989: 29–30). It is the 'truthfulness' and 'trustworthiness' (Riessman, 1993; Alasuutari, 1995: 47) of the stories that the participants told me that are of crucial importance. This truthfulness and authenticity is enhanced by the level of rapport and trust established in the researcher–researched relationship. The building of rapport was vital in this study. Building rapport with the respondents ensured a relationship built on trust (Oakley, 1981) and contributed to more candid, open and honest conversations throughout the research process. The six individuals took me on many journeys and told me many stories about themselves. They introduced me to their friends, invited me into the warmth of their houses to meet their families and walked me through landmarks important to their identities. These included the estates where they grew up, the parks where they had their first fight, the mosques where they go to pray every Friday, the shisha bars where they congregate routinely on a Saturday evening and the battered fence that was climbed to play truant from school.

I attempted to enter their world. I deliberately spent much time getting to know each participant. I wanted them to feel comfortable with me. These initial in-depth informal conversations and multiple journeys to areas of the participants' interest were very important in the research process. Not only did they establish a relationship built upon the tenets of trust and rapport but, crucially, they provided me with much rich context, insight and understanding of the many stories that the participants told me during the subsequent one-to-one interviews. It was important that rapport enabled the participants to feel comfortable enough during the interviews to 'talk back' and provide insight and meanings of their social worlds (Blumer, 1969: 22).

Rapport was established with the participants through a thorough consideration of ethical guidelines. Our relationship was based on the premise of confidentiality, non-judgemental responses, trust, authenticity and honesty (Alasuutari, 1995: 47–62; Miller, 2001). Getting informed consent from the participants, respecting their autonomy as well as ensuring full confidentiality of their identities through anonymizing their names and personal details were also key considerations (Alderson and Morrow, 2011; Hammersley and Traianou, 2012).

Finally, I had to grapple with 'insider/outsider' complexities while engaging in this research. This is an area of ethnography that has grown in significance in recent years among social researchers (Miller and Glassner, 2004; Humphrey, 2007; Keval, 2009; Paechter, 2013). This is a critically reflexive approach to qualitative research that examines the role of the researcher within the research process. There is an admission that the researcher remains at the centre of the research process (Ball, 1990; Dwyer and Buckle, 2009; Taylor, 2011) and an acknowledgement that social researchers are part of the cultural world that they are studying (Hammersley and Atkinson, 2007). The emphasis is on the concept of 'intersubjectivity' and the understanding that the researcher is 'active' during the interview exchange (Becker, 1970; Gubrium and Holstein, 2004) and therefore contributes to the production of knowledge (Shields and Dervin, 1993).

I was positioned as both an insider and an outsider within this research. How accurately and authentically did I represent and understand the participants given that my experiences, worldview and what many feminist philosophers such as Tanesini (1999) and others (Harding, 1986; Stanley and Wise, 1993) have referred to as my 'standpoint epistemology' is significantly different to theirs? For example, I am older than they are, I am from a different generation (second generation), have experienced different sociopolitics, now live in a different part of East London and am steadily aspiring towards middle-class status. I am a different gender to the female participants. In addition, did I really understand the context and coding of modern urban youth language? These factors make me an outsider to the research. How did these differences enable me to see the world from the participants' point of view? How did I make sense of their life stories in light of these differences between us?

While there may be some advantages as an outsider, such as detachment and objectivity (Rabe, 2003), I argue that this study has been enhanced because of my insider knowledge. There are some obvious insider advantages, such as easier access to the field and the willingness of participants to speak to someone who is significantly like them. Many champions of the reflexive ethnographic approach such as Davies (1999) have echoed the benefits of the researcher's familiarity with the participant's world. Along with establishing a rapport with the participants, familiarity with their world enabled me to make sense of many of the context-specific cultural and localized nuances. It is not always possible to be objective in the research process; I was unable to remove myself from the research account.

Despite the social differences discussed above, I shared many ethnic, cultural, religious and territorial commonalities with the participants. I am also a Bangladeshi, have the same skin colour, have experienced life in a Tower Hamlets housing estate and am from a similar cultural background. Like them, I am embroiled in the identity conundrum and also share a history of exclusion and marginalization. We are both trying to get to grips with the complex processes of social and political change that we are living through. It is argued that our shared experience and 'politics of solidarity' (Tanesini, 1999: 153) has instilled a deep sense of connection and thus puts me in a critical position to understand, make social commentary on and deconstruct the many stories that were told to me. As discussed earlier, there is an admission that I have come to the research with my own pre-constructions of the East London Bangladeshi community and what is happening within it. The fact that I knew that I was subjectively engaged with the researched propelled me to try that extra bit harder in my attempt to gauge authentic accounts of third-generation Bangladeshi identity.

Key theoretical framework

There are four interrelated schools of conceptual thinking that underpin this book.

First, the concept of 'the other' was central in the stories of the six participants (Akbar, Azad, Saeed, Sanjida, Taiba and Zeyba). The 'non-Muslim', 'the white man', 'Bangladesh', 'British culture', among many other examples, represented notions of otherness to the participants. Equally, a negative and racialized representation of the immigrant and Muslim 'other' has also revived notions of 'in'-group and 'out'-group status (Said, 1979; Hagendoorm, 1993). This self–'other' relationship, argues Mandair (2006: 93), can be viewed as an automatic process of othering that constitutes a repetition of the colonial experience. The practice of 'othering', therefore, is a complex two-way process. Hall (1996) and others (Foucault, 1980; Butler, 1990) argue that it is only through the relation to the 'other' – the representable, the symbolic and powerful, the relation to what it is not – that identity is constructed.

Second, the six participants of this book were engaged in a continuous process of negotiating and socially constructing (Burr, 2003) their identities of being a British-born Bangladeshi Muslim. The emergence of British Islam, it is argued, is a dynamic postmodern identity that provides a space for the participants to manage their complex and often conflicting identities (Hall, 1991, 1996; Butler, 1993; Kershen, 1998; Kearney, 2003).

Third, due to the disconnection both from a 'backwards' (Azad) Bangladeshi and an exclusive British culture, my participants find a sense of belonging and identity with the global Muslim population. Many have become politically and ideologically entangled in the idea of a global Muslim *umma* (community). The 'imagined community' (Anderson, 1983), therefore, is an important theoretical concept to consider when examining the identities of British-born Bangladeshis.

Finally, the findings of this book must be located within the politics of recognition. In many ways, there is a demand for 'recognition' from minority communities living in contemporary Western liberal multicultural societies (Taylor, 1994). Taylor (1994) argues that non-recognition or misrecognition can inflict harm, can be a form of oppression, imposing on someone a false, distorted and reduced mode of being. Within this context, exerting a British-Islamic identity should be viewed as an 'equality seeking movement' for the participants of this study (Modood, 2005a: x). Public space is essentially created through ongoing discursive contestation and political struggles for recognition from differing groups, especially those groups experiencing multiple levels of deprivation, disadvantage and discrimination, and who are therefore engaged in a struggle for social and economic justice, visibility and representation. Identity, therefore, is a political act: an attempt to readdress the social structure of modern society that positions young Bangladeshis at the periphery in subordinate and undesirable positions (Giddens, 1984). These concepts emerge continually through the book as I seek to understand and analyse the many complex components of third-generation Bangladeshi identity.

Structure of the book

The main argument of this book is that a British-Islamic identity has developed for many third-generation Bangladeshis from East London in the year 2015 that enables them to fuse together the many components of their multifaceted identities. In order to explore this argument, I have divided the text into four interconnected parts.

Part 1 serves as an introduction to the overall study. The present chapter is included within Part 1. It has outlined what the book is about, presented some of the key arguments, research questions and theoretical concepts underpinning it, discussed a reflexive personal and academic rationale behind the research and examined the methodological considerations guiding the study.

Chapter 2 provides important and necessary background, history and context for the whole book. In particular, it outlines a complex sociopolitical history of Islam in Britain and examines the local Bangladeshi community of East London. Who are the Bangladeshis of East London? What is their history? What are some of their struggles? Why has the religion of Islam become problematic in Britain and across the world? These are some of the questions that this chapter examines. It also explores the complex relationship between youth, religion and identity.

Part 2 introduces the participants of this study and outlines some of the key themes and issues emanating from their stories. **Chapter 3** examines the following questions. Who are the participants? What are their stories? What are their experiences? What are the common themes that emerged from the conversations I had with them? What are the patterns that connect these individuals? The chapter outlines and briefly introduces the many components of their complex identities, which are discussed in greater detail in Part 3.

Part 3 examines the five core components of the participants' identity, their stories of what it means to be a British-born Bangladeshi Muslim. These components are organized in light of the following factors:

- linguistics
- race
- religion
- nationality
- gender.

These facets of individual and collective postmodern identity are complex, dynamic, contradictory and overlapping, and Part 3 locates the self-narratives of the six participants within these complexities. The voices, experiences, feelings, stories and opinions of the six participants are interwoven and located within the key theories and literature available in these areas of sociological inquiry and are analysed in the following five chapters.

Chapter 4 examines the complex relationship between the Bengali language and the Bangladeshi culture. It examines the powerful role of the English language as a language of modernity and also of an emerging global Arabic linguistic identity as part of a new British-Islamic culture.

Chapter 5 argues that the 'problem of the colour line' (Du Bois, 1995 [1903]) and the related actions of racism and discrimination remain real issues in the year 2015 for many of the participants. Experience of racism still governs their daily social lives, locates many within a social and political position of inferiority and thus constructs their identities. As well as discussing some of the theories of race and ethnicity, this chapter examines the racialized local history of East London in order to contexualize the stories and experiences of the participants.

Chapter 6 pushes forward the main argument of this book – the development of a British-Islamic identity. It locates the stories of the six participants within the wider debate of what it means to be a British-Bangladeshi Muslim. In deconstructing and defining British Islam, the chapter is both a theoretical analysis of the importance and growth of religion in the modern world and provides much empirical evidence illustrating the existence and components of a vibrant British-Islamic identity in East London.

Chapter 7 analyses the question of a British national identity. It locates British Islam within the complexity of British multiculturalism and argues that space should be afforded for publicly assertive religious identities in secular Britain. As well as debating various theories of Britishness and of British and global multiculturalism, the chapter examines British-Muslim assertiveness in public spaces, which challenges the secular tradition of modern European history. British Islam must be recognized and accepted in secular public spaces. Muslims must not be viewed as 'the other', but rather as part of the plural British us. British Islam is not at odds with the concept of 'Britishness'; rather it is simply a 'different kind of British' (Ward, 2004: 138).

Chapter 8 considers the development of a specific Bangladeshi female identity within British Islam. With a focus on the complexity of patriarchy, the chapter locates the stories of the three female participants within the wider feminist discourse in relation to the Bangladeshi culture and Islamic religion. It discusses the status of women in Islam, making a key distinction between spiritual Islam and various cultural interpretations of Islam. The 'multiple meanings' (Bullock, 2007) and representations of the hijab (the headscarf) are also debated, locating the discourse within an anthropological and sociological framework. The central argument of this chapter is that an unequal gender space has developed in British Islam that does not afford the same rights and liberties to its female members as to its males. Tensions remain between progressive British Islam and traditional conservative Bangladeshi-Muslim patriarchy. However, British Islam is gradually creating a space for its female members to manage their multiple identities of being British-born Bangladeshi-Muslim women. Many have developed strategies of resistance against patriarchal cultural structures and against sections of wider British society that has constructed them within the orientalist framework as oppressed and as victims.

Part 4 outlines the three broad conclusions of this book. First, from a **sociological perspective,** the main argument is that Islam, in its many guises – spiritual, social and ideological – provides a sense of belonging and acceptance to many third-generation Bangladeshis against years of racism, poverty and marginalization. Membership of a fluid and dynamic Islamic identity provokes the desire for 'recognition, visibility, acknowledgement, association' and 'protection' that West (1995: 15–16) refers to in his discussion of identity. Islam also provides a safety net against a Bangladeshi culture and way of life that is increasingly becoming alien and irrelevant to the everyday lives of many young Bangladeshis. Second, from a **policy and community perspective,** the conclusion sketches out a social programme for policymakers, Bangladeshi parents, community leaders and professionals working with Bangladeshi youth as a way forward in their ongoing struggle for 'recognition' (Taylor, 1994) in wider British society.

Finally, from an **educational point of view**, I argue that teachers, educators and policymakers need to become more aware of the sociopolitical climate in which young people in inner-city urban areas such as East London are growing up. People do not live in a vacuum and there should not be a distinction between wider society and the educational world – they are part of interconnected social worlds. There is considerable overlap, and young people do not vacate their cultural worlds once they enter the school gates. The educational world is an important part of the social world. This includes not only valuing their culture and languages (Bengali, Arabic) within the school curriculum, but also constructively tackling local-area issues identified in this book (such as identity, local-area history of immigration, race and racism, Islamophobia, the complexity of Britishness, issues of social and material deprivation, intergenerational conflict, foreign policy, etc.) within the curriculum and teaching pedagogy.

Before we hear the stories of identity from the study's six participants, I provide background information and context about East London, and Tower Hamlets in particular. I also examine the history of Bangladeshi settlement in East London and discuss the diversity and sociopolitical complexity of Islam in Britain. The next chapter provides the historical and sociopolitical context to the complex stories of identity that follow in Parts 2 and 3 of the book.

Chapter 2

The history and settlement of Bangladeshi Muslims in Britain

Introduction

This chapter outlines the history and settlement of Bangladeshi Muslim migrants in Britain. It examines the complex macro-picture of Muslims in Britain and then analyses the micro-picture of the Bangladeshi community of Tower Hamlets. With a Bangladeshi resident population of 32 per cent (Tower Hamlets, n.d.), the London Borough of Tower Hamlets has the highest global concentration of Bangladeshis outside of Bangladesh itself.

The chapter has a dual function. First, it provides a historical and sociological context for the voices, feelings and experiences of the participants in this study. Second, it provides a backdrop to the many complex and contested facets of third-generation Bangladeshi identity: language, race, religion, a multicultural Britishness and gender. Importantly, out of the 513,000 estimated Bangladeshis living in England and Wales in 2011 (up from 283,000 in 2001), 90 per cent identified themselves as Muslims (Sedghi, 2013), so the terms 'Bangladeshi', 'migrant' and 'Muslim' have largely become synonymous and are used interchangeably throughout the book. There are also many overlapping issues such as poverty, racism and discrimination that affect most Bangladeshis and Muslims in Britain.

This background chapter is divided into six interconnected parts that consider the following:

- the process of South-Asian Muslim immigration into Britain
- the depth and diversity of the many faces of Islam in Britain
- some of the sociopolitical factors that have contributed to the increasing popularity of Islam in Britain, especially among the younger generations
- the national and international factors that have transformed British Muslims from a 'passive' to a 'troubled' community (Hai, 2008)
- the local micro-situation, presenting a detailed historical examination of the Bangladeshi community of Tower Hamlets

- the sociopolitical issues affecting the Bangladeshi community of Tower Hamlets.

South-Asian Muslim immigration into Britain

There is evidence of a Muslim presence in Britain as far back as Tudor and Stuart times (Matar, 1998: 45–9). There are many benefits to migration such as higher earnings, better healthcare and education and the opportunity to send remittances back to the land of origin (Dahya, 1974; Bermant, 1975; Islam, 1987; Mahmood, 1991; Gardner and Shukur, 1994; Massey, 1997). However, migration and settlement has been difficult, raising many practical and social challenges over the years. Like many other immigrants, South-Asian Muslim migrants have left families and familiarity behind in order to establish a new life for themselves in Britain. This new life has often involved much transition, pain and upheaval (Hoffman, 1991; Papastergiadis, 2000). In addition, as Geaves (2005: 66–7) points out, British Muslims have had to address and negotiate their citizenship within a 'new' world, with its emphasis on democracy, secularism, individual rights and pluralism, and 'have needed to discover how to participate in a society which has no need for Islam in its public life'. In his anthropological analysis, Lyon (2005: 78) reasserts Iqbal's question and asks how you can promote notions of cultural blending and 'melting' between Islam and white Europe when there are 'fundamental differences' in values between post-Enlightenment Europe and revivalist Islamist populations around the world. And as British broadcaster Jon Snow (quoted in Lewis, 2007: x) reminds us, the majority of Bangladeshi and Pakistani Muslim immigrants are a rural community in urban life and are still adjusting to the demands of urbanization. Importantly, as former subjects of Britain's colonial past, many South-Asian Muslims in Britain have been forced to negotiate their citizenship, social status and identities within the context of the racist, orientalist and suspicious 'gaze' that reinforces essentialist, simplified and stereotypical perspectives of each other (Said, 1979; O'Donnell, 1999; Geaves, 2005: 67). It is this gaze that has been one key determinant in the construction of a bipolar, insular, ignorant and isolationist Muslim and non-Muslim British world.

It has been and continues to be difficult to be a Muslim in Britain. Within the context of third-generation Bangladeshi identity in contemporary society, the construction of the orientalist gaze has intensified with the international war on terror as a backlash to the tragic events in recent times, the 11 September 2001 attack on the New York World Trade Center and the London Underground bombings of 2005. Geopolitics have become entangled with the national identity question, asking British Muslims to choose whether they are British or Muslim. Within a lengthy backdrop of examples, recent controversies such as the 2014 'Trojan Horse' inquiry into the Islamification of Birmingham schools has constructed Islamic and British values/identity as incompatible. I discuss these issues later on within the book, but note here that the majority of the wider British population apparently do not hold prejudicial views against the British Muslim population.

However, the recent English Defence League campaign against Muslims in Britain and the pan-European Stop Islamisation of Europe movement are just two illustrations of anti-Muslim hostility that is growing in prominence among the British and European far right. Some sections of the British media and certain politicians have been criticized for propagating negative stereotypes of Muslims and fuelling anti-Muslim prejudice (see Richardson, 2004; Dodd, 2010). Recently, there have been cases of threats, fatal attacks and more arson attacks on mosques as well as persistent low-level assaults such as spitting and name-calling aimed at Muslims (Githens-Mazer and Lambert, 2010; FOSIS, 2014). The Metropolitan Police recorded 500 anti-Muslim hate crimes in 2013 and a group set up to monitor Islamophobic incidents (Tell Mama) said it had dealt with 840 cases in the aftermath of the murder of soldier Lee Rigby in May 2013 (Press Association, 2013). A British Social Attitudes Survey of 2010 found that the general British public are concerned about the rise of Islam in the UK and many feel that Islam poses a threat to the British national identity. The study, in which 4,486 people were surveyed, found that 55 per cent would be 'bothered' by the construction of a large mosque in their community (Wynne-Jones, 2010).

The majority of British South-Asian Muslims have settled in post-industrial cities such as Bradford, Manchester, Glasgow, Birmingham and London since mass immigration in the 1950s and 1960s. Currently, London has the highest proportion of British Muslims (1,012,823) (ONS, 2012a). Britain needed labour after the Second World War to rebuild the economic infrastructure, and many immigrants from the Commonwealth nations (the Caribbean, East Africa, Indian subcontinent) came over to work in certain industrial sectors that were no longer attractive to the domestic workforce (Jones, 1978). The 20-year period from 1940 witnessed a visibly multi-racial and poly-ethnic society that had a profound and irreversible effect on the whole 'character' of the British social order (Ballard, 1994: 1). British residents might now be of non-European origin and the indigenous British population, especially in the cities, was overtly exposed to new and diverse cultural, religious and linguistic traditions and customs imported by the multitude of immigrant communities (O'Donnell, 1999).

Many of these immigrant workers settled in neighbourhoods with a large white working-class population. Overt racial hostilities towards these immigrant communities is examined in Chapter 5, but a brief discussion of 'host' reaction is needed here (Tinker, 1977: ix), as it explains the process of segregation among the Muslim immigrant communities upon arrival and this is important in the discussion about being young, British, Bangladeshi and Muslim today. As Kershen (1998: 18–19) notes, 'superficial, or surface, physical differences provide the most immediate and obvious means of "identification with" or "difference from" [other people in society] ... [leading to the] processing of group separation'.

Settlement in British society was far from easy for the primary Bangladeshi Muslim migrants of the 1950s and 1960s and, arguably, they encountered many of the problems that migrants into urban cities around the world experienced, such as poor housing, low-paid jobs and second-class citizenship (Tinker, 1977: 20–50). In an account of a range of white-British reactions to the growth of minority presence in Britain over a hundred-year period, Holmes (1988: 275–317) maintains that minority presence in Britain, especially in domains of employment and ethnic and religious expression, has given rise to intense hostility from many sections among the ethnic white-British hosts as it has been deemed to present a challenge to the white status quo. This hostility, according to Marxists such as Miliband (1987), was a desperate attempt by the established white working classes to improve their bargaining power in the competitive climate of a capitalist economy. In addition to competing for scarce local resources – a key factor behind riots in Bradford, Burnley and Oldham in 2001 (Lewis, 2007) – non-European settlers have found themselves subjected to racial 'marginality' (Westwood, 1995: 197–221) that contributes to a sense of separateness. Skin colour, therefore, remains an 'inescapable social marker' for many of the migrant settlers (Ballard, 1994: 2–3). Accordingly, the majority of South Asians have engaged in what Robinson (1986: 32, 67–98) has termed a form of 'social encapsulation' away from a discriminative host society (see also Hiro, 1971; Tinker, 1977).

Although there was much racialized tension, Abbas (2005) argues that limited acceptance of immigrants by some white working-class indigenous communities was based on the belief that South-Asian Muslims and other ethnic minorities would eventually return to their land of origin once their employment period was completed. In fact, many 'primary' settlers themselves also believed that they would return to the motherland as the main aim of migration was to earn enough money very quickly and send it back to Bangladesh for investment in land and property (Gardner and Shukur, 1994: 142–7; Hoque, 2005). However, Anwar (1979) argues that the idea of 'return' to the homeland remained a 'myth' for many South-Asian Muslims, as most settled into the harsh economic, social and housing conditions of urban British life, forming segregated communities. Kershen (2000) notes that demands for remittances and the inability to save as much capital as they would need to settle down to a comfortable life in Bangladesh meant that the temporary migrants soon became permanent settlers. The cost of 'return migration', while ideologically appealing, was too complex and financially risky (Gmelch, 1980). Therefore, while the ideal for many first-generation migrants was to 'return', the economic reality, coupled with settlement of family and better healthcare, led to permanent settlement in Britain (Grillo, 2001: 13).

The depth and diversity of Islam in Britain

There is a common misconception that Islam is a monolith – that there is a singular British-Muslim community as opposed to plural communities. This view is erroneous. British Islam is a complex mosaic of people divided along lines of class, sect, clan, caste, ideology, levels of religiosity and ethno-nationality (Garbin, 2005; Peach, 2005; Lewis, 2007; Modood, 2010). While an 'imagined identity' links global Muslims together in a de-territorialized world (Anderson, 1983; Roy, 2004: 18–19), the reality is that no domestic or global *umma* (single Muslim community) exists.

According to the UK census of 2011, there are 2.7 million Muslims in England and Wales (ONS, 2012c), of which around 1.6 million are from South Asia (Sedghi, 2013). Peach (2005: 18) notes that it has grown to this number from an initial count of around 21,000 in 1951. Furthermore, nearly half of the Muslim population is under the age of 25, and 88 per cent are under the age of 50 (Sedghi, 2013), so it is expected to increase markedly by 2021. At 4.8 per cent of the population, this figure of 2.7 million places Islam as the second-largest organized religion in Britain after Christianity (ONS, 2012c).

Muslims in Britain are the most ethnically diverse religious group. Two-thirds of the current South-Asian Muslim population in Britain originate from Pakistan, a quarter from Bangladesh and the remainder from India (Sedghi, 2013). Muslims from North Africa, the Middle East, Africa, Eastern Europe and Southeast Asia make up the remaining 1.1 million Muslim population, and their characteristics, history and socioeconomic backgrounds are very different to those of the Pakistani and Bangladeshi

Muslims (Halliday, 1992). Peach (2005) notes that, due to the numerical advantage of South-Asian Muslims in Britain, there is a danger in essentializing Islam and viewing South-Asian characteristics as representative of Islam itself. There is also an increasing number of converts to Islam, estimated in 2011 to be around 100,000 (Nye, 2011), which contributes to the number of Muslims (210,000) who identify themselves as 'white' (Sedghi, 2013; see also Ansari, 2004: 14-17; Hoque, 2006). Internationally, the global Muslim population is currently estimated to be 1.6 billion, accounting for nearly a quarter of the world's population (Pew Research, 2011).

British Islam is also divided according to ideology and religiosity (Bowen, 2014). There remains a minority of deeply conservative British Muslims who hold an oppositional and isolationist position against British society, such as the Tablighi Jamaat, the Salaffis or Deobandis (Geaves, 2005), and also groups such as the Hizb ut-Tahrir that propagate the establishment of an Islamic state (*khilafah*) (Akhtar, 2005). There are also countless other fringe organizations that have been caught up in the global rhetoric of terror against the Muslim *umma* and preach violence against the infidel (non-believer). There is not the time, context or space in this book to discuss the growth and impact of radical Islam in Britain. This area of research has been covered by numerous journalists, writers and academics (McRoy, 2006; Abbas, 2007; Husain, 2007; Leiken, 2012). This book focuses on the life stories and identities of the third-generation Bangladeshis from Tower Hamlets that are governed by questions of social and economic justice rather than a preoccupation with violent revolutions and an alternative Islamic state.

The diversity and complexity of the British-Muslim community is best illustrated by Sahin's (2005) typology of Muslims in Britain. Sahin's study of 400 16–20-year-old Muslims in three Birmingham sixth-form colleges found that three main attitudes emerged in regards to personal religiosity. First, there were the 'foreclosed Muslims'. These devout, conservative Muslims held an ahistorical view of sharia (Islamic law), eternally applicable for all times, contexts and places. These Muslims expect situations to adapt to Islam rather than the other way round, because they consider sharia to be a perfect system of law and governance that cannot be expected to adapt to changing circumstances. For them, Islam was the only conceivable organizational principle. There is no such thing as 'modernizing' Islam. Lewis (2007: 44) notes that the respondents of Sahin's study who identified themselves as foreclosed represented an 'unbridgeable gap' between themselves and the rest of society. They viewed themselves as living in a land of non-believers who were morally decadent, contact with whom was to be avoided. They were in, but not part of, multicultural Britain. The foreclosed Muslims, it must be highlighted, were the minority of Sahin's sample.

Second was a group of Muslims categorized by Sahin as 'diffuse'. This group showed little interest in religion. While not practising Muslims, they still subscribed to the main tenets of Islam. Although lacking personal spiritual commitment, they still strove to preserve Islam as an identity marker in their lives, a cultural stronghold from which they could resist assimilation into what they called 'white culture'. They remained committed to the idea of Islam without subscribing to all of its norms. According to Siddiqui (2004: 57), Islam is a private matter for them, determined by their personal experience, interpretation and 'picking' and 'choosing'.

The third group were what Sahin called 'exploratory' Muslims, those searching to make sense of religion. This represented the majority view. Unlike their tradition-bound, culturally enclaved parents, these self-identifying 'British' Muslims sought to make sense of Islam as a living entity relevant to their everyday lives inside and outside the home. Sahin notes that those who were foreclosed tended to be male, while most of the females were in the exploratory category, in part a response to the control to which they were subject at home and within their immediate ethno-religious communities.

As we see in later chapters, the participants of my study corresponded with Sahin's typology of being either 'diffuse' or 'exploratory'. There are some who are culturally Islamic and use it to make an identity distinction between themselves and the 'white' 'other', and there are others who are more theologically oriented and are trying to make sense of what it means to be a British Muslim. None of the participants were in the 'foreclosed' category but this does not mean that this voice does not exist in East London. Sahin's typology reinforces the argument that British Muslims are divided along not only ethnic but also ideological lines.

The increasing popularity of British Islam

Certain sociopolitical factors have contributed to the popularity of Islam in Britain, especially among the younger generations. There has been a shift in the religious practice of British Muslims over the last 25 years. At a time where evidence points to a general decline in the practice, affiliation, belonging and attendance level of believers of other world religions such as Christianity (Voas and Crockett, 2005), British Muslims have become more aware of their Muslim identities. An explicit Muslim identity in a non-Muslim or Western context is being expressed. French academic Olivier Roy (2004: 23) describes this process as the 're-Islamization' of European

Muslims: Islam has become an integral part of their personal identity. This visible 'religiosity' (Akhtar, 2005: 164) has been more evident among the younger generations of British Muslims, many of whom are religiously more devout and assertive of the Muslim faith than their parents.

This is apparent in Tower Hamlets where nearly seven thousand worshippers attend the London Muslim Centre on the 27th night of Ramadan each year, 30 per cent of whom are under the age of 25 (Khan, 2014). Other polls and studies conducted over the past ten years confirm this religiosity among Muslim youth. In a report entitled *Living Apart Together*, the conservative think tank Policy Exchange found that 86 per cent of Muslims aged 16 to 24 believe that Islam is important in their lives (Mirza *et al.*, 2007). A workshop involving 103 young British Muslims, organized by the *Guardian* in 2004, found that 80 per cent of the group prayed at least once a day and 50 per cent prayed five times a day. This level of religious practice, argued *Guardian* columnist Madeline Bunting (2004: 17), was 'higher than any other community in the UK'.

So why is there a spiritual, ideological and practical revival of Islam in the lives of many British Muslims? One key explanation revolves around the idea of victimhood. As a consequence of intense political scrutiny and the public and media reaction to recent domestic and global events such as 9/11 and 7/7, many British Muslims in 2015 have developed a 'victim' mentality (Hoque, 2004b, 2004c; Marranci, 2005). Sarup (1994) and others (Abbas, 2005; Kibria, 2006) argue that when a minority group is faced with hostility, one of its first responses is to become more insulated and display a strong collective and 'reactive' identity to those who oppose it, which can lead some members of the group into deliberate disassociation from the host society. One consequence is the emergence of many who are ideologically and spiritually engaged with a revival of Islam within the sociopolitical arena – in essence Muslims by name and identity although not by practice (Akhtar, 2005) – or Muslims who actively practise their faith through symbolic acts such as the daily prayer, growing a beard or wearing a hijab, observing Ramadan, learning Arabic and making annual pilgrimage (hajj) in Saudi Arabia (see Gottschalk and Greenberg, 2008: 45-60). As Castles and Miller (1993) note, for some minorities living in the West, it is their 'difference' that has become a mechanism of resistance against Western ideology and culture.

Birt (2005) argues that many young Muslims have also developed a more politicized identity and are intent to absolve Islam from the charge of inherent violence and barbaric terror. Alongside them are the growing minority of educated professional Muslims who are engaged in mainstream civic life through democracy, economic advancement, political lobbying and debating important issues such as citizenship, women's rights and foreign policy (Kamrava, 2006). British theologian Philip Lewis (2007: 141–4) has argued that this minority Muslim group has gone 'beyond victimhood' and engaged in what the Swiss Muslim academic Tariq Ramadan (2004: 5–6) has termed 'critical citizenship'. This critical citizenship has become intertwined with the demand for rights, recognition and social justice.

The relationship between the international and the local

Certain international factors have influenced the evolving of the British Muslim from ethno-racial ('Paki') to religious ('Bin-Laden') identifications, from peaceful neighbours to global threat (Marranci, 2005), and from a 'passive' to a 'troubled' community after 9/11 (Hai, 2008). These are now explored, along with the development of a 'new' type of racism (Barker, 1981) that has replaced skin colour and race as markers of separateness with differences in the culture of the 'other', their way of life and values.

Although domestic factors such as inequality, poverty and social cohesion are important in the question of a British-Muslim identity, the international political climate has also pushed many Muslims into siding with an Islamic *umma* against a perceived and antagonistic British state. In the modern global world enhanced by technology and communications, international factors such as interventions or wars against Muslim countries have further heightened a sense of global Islamic awareness and contributed to a brand of political Islam focused around protest and contest. International incidents have direct local ramifications, as local stories of discrimination and injustice are played out in the international arena.

There is strong evidence for this analysis. For example, the first Gulf War (1990–91), American military intervention in Somalia (1992), the genocide in Bosnia-Herzegovina (1993–6), the Taliban in Afghanistan (1997–2002), massacres in Grozny and Kosovo (1999), the continuing plight of Palestinians in Gaza, the struggle for Kashmir, the War on Iraq (2003) and the current violence in Syria have all played a part in creating a transnational Muslim solidarity and a conscious identification with others of the same religion (Abbas, 2005). In its most vibrant democratic example, Muslim solidarity was evident in the 2003 anti-war protest against the government in London, in which many thousands of Muslims and non-Muslims took part. In its most extreme manifestation, the 7/7 bombings in London in July 2005 were supposedly carried out in the name of Islam, in reaction to US and UK military intervention in Iraq. These two examples remind us of the dual function of the politicization of Islam in both its democratic and violent extreme capability. Modood (2005b: 160) notes further that the international wars involving Muslims reinvented the *umma* from global community to global 'victims'.

The international geopolitical climate has fostered Islamophobia in Britain. 'Islamophobia', used as a term and as a form of unconscious – and in some cases conscious (BNP, 2002) – 'fear or dread' of Muslims (Abbas, 2005: 11), has crept into British political and public debate. Runnymede Trust (1997) and recent studies by the European Muslim Research Centre (Githens-Mazer and Lambert, 2010) and others (Boulding and Oborne, 2008; Allen, 2010; Muslim Council of Britain, 2010) all report that a 'fear' and 'dread' of Muslims has become naturalized and normalized in many segments of British society. Fear and dread of Muslims is steeped in history as Western Europe, to prevent conversions to Islam, has for centuries resisted the imperialist virtues of hugely successful Islamic empires (Abbasid, Moghul, Ottoman – see Armstrong (2004) for a detailed discussion of the history of Islamic civilizations). Esposito (1999) argues that despite the many positive contributions made to Western science and culture by the Islamic world, Western European governments have characterized Muslims from the East as barbaric and intolerant religious zealots. Huntington, in his famous article of 1993, took this supposed division between the Islamic East and Christian West even further by claiming that the two civilizations were diametrically opposed and irreconcilable. Although Huntington's theory of a supposed 'clash of civilizations' has been criticized for its oversimplification and generalization (Said, 2001; Berman, 2004; Sen, 2006), the popularity of his article has deepened the ideological divisions between Islam and the Christian West.

Abbas (2005: 11) argues that the 'otherization' of Muslims – the construction and reduction of people to be 'less' than what they are (Holiday *et al.*, 2004; Ameli and Merali, 2006) – is still prevalent today, especially since 9/11. For example, there is much research to suggest that since 9/11 more low-level abuse is aimed at Muslims, such as the negative alteration of the 'gaze' (Geaves, 2005: 67), people staring, bearded men being called 'Osama' (N. Ahmed, 2005: 203), being spat at (Birt, 2005) and being called a terrorist because they wear Muslim clothing (Ansari, 2005). Much of the rhetoric that came from racist groups post 9/11 was highly inflammatory, encouraged insult and provocation and employed language and images designed to foster hatred (e.g. BNP, 2002; see Allen, 2005: 55–60). In extreme cases, individuals have been killed for wearing Muslim dress (FOSIS, 2014). Anti-Muslim culture based on the demarcations of 'difference' and 'subordination' (Allen and Nielsen, 2002) was not limited to Britain; the Turkish community in Germany and the Algerians in France also experienced a political, public and media backlash after 9/11 (Jocelyn, 2006). And violence – often fatal – towards European Muslims has intensified in the aftermath of the *Charlie Hebdo* murders in France in 2015 (Sabin, 2015).

Contemporary Islamophobia is rooted in 'orientalist' philosophy. The image constructed of Muslims is of a distinctive 'other' different to that of the civilized West – a people unable to govern themselves, who lie, are cunning, lack initiative, and who cannot think logically. It is an integral part of the way some Westerners, especially the political elite, understand themselves. The concept of the 'other' is discussed by Said (1979, 1995) in his analysis of 'orientalism'. He identified it as a colonial ideology, a discourse that involves the exercise of power from the benevolent West (occident) towards the uncivilized East (orient). This thinking has helped the West to maintain hegemony over the oriental 'other' and to legitimize existing systems of political domination and subordination (Abbas, 2005). Said (1995) observed that the historical discourse of orientalism can be applied to Islam in the modern context too. This is most evident in the Arab–Israeli conflict, presented as a clash between freedom-loving democratic Israelis versus evil, totalitarian and terroristic Arabs. In his later works, which examined media constructions of Muslims, Said (1997) argued that Muslims were generalized in terms of their violence, primitiveness, atavism and threatening qualities.

It was a report by the Runnymede Trust in 1997, entitled *Islamophobia: A challenge for us all*, which first examined this 'fear' and 'dread' of Muslims. Its findings were controversial in a pre-9/11 world. Islamophobia, it suggested, was akin to xenophobia – a dislike of anything foreign. Despite over fifty years of residence in Britain, Muslims were still viewed as 'foreign'. The Runnymede report highlighted seven other core features of this irrational fear and dread of Muslims (quoted in Abbas, 2005: 12):

- Muslim cultures were seen as monolithic
- Islamic cultures were viewed as substantially different from other cultures
- Islam was perceived as threatening
- followers of Islam used their faith for political or military advantage
- Muslim criticism of Western cultures and societies was rejected and held no weight
- the fear of Islam was mixed with racist hostility to immigration

- most notably, Islamophobia was presented as being natural and unproblematic.

Allen (2005: 49) argues that the findings of the Runnymede report confirmed a shift in the focus of racist attitudes towards people of South-Asian descent from race to religion:

> …while racism on the basis of markers of race obviously continues, a shift is apparent in which some of the more traditional and obvious markers have been displaced by newer and more prevalent ones of a cultural, and socio-religious nature.

The focus of much racist ideology in the present era, argues Allen (2005: 51), is now upon issues of cultural and religious 'difference'. Events such as the reception of Rushdie's *The Satanic Verses* (1989), which many commentators have argued led to the beginning of a problematic and specific 'Muslim identity' in Britain (Ahsan and Kidwai, 1991; Geaves, 2005), 9/11, the 2001 street riots and 7/7 have provided credence to the rhetoric of 'difference'. These events have entangled Muslims across the globe with violence and anti-Westernism and have also put the spotlight on the everyday values and norms of British Muslims (Abbas, 2005). Central to this debate is the question of how Muslims can be allowed to practise their faith, beliefs and cultural lifestyles, and yet co-exist in the very society that their religion is supposedly so critical of – Western Europe.

The British-American historian of Islam Bernard Lewis has stated that, due to high rates of immigration and Europe's low birth rate, Western European countries will have Muslim majorities by the end of the century (quoted in Farouky, 2007). Bruce Bawer (2006), in his book *While Europe Slept*, has suggested that Islamists are determined to colonize Europe. And in 2015, terrorism expert Steven Emerson claimed on US news channel Fox News that parts of London were now patrolled by Muslim religious police who 'beat' up anyone not dressed in Muslim attire, and that the British city of Birmingham had become a 'totally Muslim' city 'where non-Muslims simply don't go in' (Fishwick, 2015). Sensationalist and fictitious claims such as these have heightened the fear and suspicion aimed towards Muslims in Europe. They cite the London and Madrid bombings, the French riots, the Danish cartoon protests, the brutal murder of British soldier Lee Rigby in 2013, the documented involvement of British-born Muslims in the Syrian uprising in 2014 and the shooting of the editorial staff of *Charlie Hebdo* in Paris 2015 as being violent indicators of future events. Bagguley and Hussain's (2005) study in Bradford after the riots of 2001 adds weight to

Allen's assertion that Islam has been presented as incompatible with British norms and values. Bagguley and Hussain (2005: 213) found that two government-funded reports into community cohesion (Cantle Report, 2001; Denham Report, 2002) added to the overall essentialist and stereotypical portrayal of British Muslim 'otherness', which was constructed around themes of 'intergenerational conflict, tolerance of criminality, a failure to integrate with mainstream white society and the oppression of women'. It was their 'difference' that was identified as the cause of the riots (Bagguley and Hussain, 2005: 211).

In recent times, dress choice, language choice, national allegiance and questions of arranged and forced marriage have all become publicly debated media issues and have presented Muslims as being somewhat un-British in their attitudes, norms and values. A new political language, championed by 'new' Labour, emerged across the political spectrum after 9/11 and the 2001 riots, centred around integration, community cohesion and shared British values and identity (Bagguley and Hussain, 2005; Geaves, 2005; Lyon, 2005). Many public figures held Muslims responsible for their own predicament. For example, within a few months of 9/11, Home Secretary David Blunkett quoted a key conclusion of the Cantle Report (2001), openly criticizing the self-styled segregation of South-Asian Muslims living in Britain, arguing for the need for oaths of allegiance and pushing for immigrants to take the English language test (Dodd, 2001; Glover, 2001; Travis, 2001). Peter Hain MP contributed further by suggesting that it was the Muslim community's isolationist behaviour and customs that were responsible for the climate in which the far right was prospering (see Open Society Institute, 2002: 87). MP Norman Lamont (2002) weighed in, criticizing the British-Muslim community for participating in 'forced marriages, polygamy, burning books and supporting fatwas' and fighting against British soldiers.

The debate took on new significance in 2014 with the Trojan Horse inquiry over allegations of a hard-line organized Muslim takeover of Birmingham schools with a view to running them according to Islamic beliefs and values. In the wake of these highly contested findings, then Education Secretary Michael Gove reiterated the need for all schools to promote the 'British values' of tolerance and fairness (Hope, 2014). Although he made a distinction here between Islam and the 'totalitarian ideology' of Islamism, Gove (2006) previously followed the Huntington (1993) school of thought, presenting Islamism as the conflict of our times because it challenges Western values, culture and freedoms in, he claimed, ways akin to threats posed historically by fascism and communism. And in 2015, Communities Secretary Eric Pickles's letter to more than a thousand Muslim leaders in

Britain in which he asked them to 'explain and demonstrate how faith in Islam can be part of British identity' appeared both to single out the British Muslim community for not being British enough and to blame the radicalization of youth on the British Muslim community as opposed to the internet, social media, global geopolitics and wider issues of social injustice (Wintour, 2015). This somewhat hostile attitude towards Islam and Muslims, and its tendency to associate Islam with intolerance and extremism, effectively asks British Muslims, yet again, to decide whether they are Muslim or British by constructing these two facets of identity as oppositional and incompatible. The construction of Muslims as un-British is problematic and oversimplified. Britishness is a highly contested and fluid component of personal, national and political identity, and this complexity is viewed through the eyes of my participants in Chapter 7 of this book.

In some areas of Britain Muslims are densely concentrated. For example, the proportion of Muslims in the London boroughs of Tower Hamlets and Newham is 34.5 per cent and 32 per cent respectively, and in Blackburn it was 27 per cent in 2012 (ONS, 2012c). Ethnically concentrated areas such as these have been described as 'encapsulated communities' (Eade *et al.*, 1996). While the segregation of many Muslims from mainstream society is a statistical reality, it is misleading to suggest that this segregation is by choice or is self-styled, since many sociopolitical complexities are involved. Abbas (2005) and Parekh (2006: 185) remind us that the criticism of Muslim communities by Blunkett and his colleagues is yet another example of how British Muslims are viewed as 'perpetrators of their own misfortunes' as opposed to victims of the 'hostile and racist structures of post-war British society and the institutions that form the very fabric of it' (Abbas, 2005: 4). Important issues of poverty, class inequalities, racism and Islamophobia seemed to be ignored altogether. Abbas (2005: 11, 12–13) argues:

> …the young South Asian Muslim men of Oldham, Bradford and Burnley, who battled with the police in such dramatic scenes during the summer of 2001, do not suffer from 'under-assimilation'. Indeed their predicament is that of a society divided by racism and discrimination … segregation of Muslims [is] seen to be self-imposed and the cause of racism rather than a result of it … It is easy to blame people and their values and to ignore processes and institutions.

Although important positive strides have been made in policy and practice that are slowly recognizing Muslims in Britain as equal and ubiquitous social partners in British society (discussed further in Chapter 7), numerous studies further Abbas's (2005) argument of structural and institutional racism (Macpherson, 1999). For example, Anwar and Bakhsh (2003) found that Muslims continue to experience discrimination in the fields of employment, education and housing (see also Parekh, 2000a; Hepple and Choudhury, 2001; Weller *et al.*, 2001). Employers hold negative views about the hijab, and the lifestyle choice of many Muslims prohibits them from engaging with a working culture that involves drinking after work. Data from the Office for National Statistics' Labour Force Survey (2014) of more than half a million people found that up to 76 per cent of Muslim men and 65 per cent of Muslim women were less likely to have a job of any kind compared to white male and female British Christians of the same age and with the same qualifications. The research concluded that religion is the cause for more prejudice than colour of skin in contemporary society (see Dobson, 2014).

The findings from these studies suggest that Muslims in Britain are segregated because of structural inequalities (Abbas, 2005; Parekh, 2006), institutional racism, social and economic marginalization and ingrained sociocultural reasons such as staying close to family and community rather than out of choice (Ballard, 1990; Ahmad, 1996; Modood *et al.*, 1997; Anwar, 2005; Bagguley and Hussain, 2005; Peach, 2005). As Anwar (2005: 44) notes, 'hostility and discrimination against Muslims forces them to seek support from their own communities'.

The Bangladeshis of Tower Hamlets

Against the wider sociopolitical history of Islam in Britain, this chapter now focuses on Bangladeshi Muslims from Tower Hamlets. Located in the East End of London, the borough has a rich history of immigrants (Bermant, 1975; Thornton, 1983; Bhatia, 2006), from the Irish Catholic settlers (O'Connor, 1974; Lees, 1979) and French Protestant Huguenot refugees (Plummer, 1972) during the late seventeenth and early eighteenth centuries to the influx of Eastern-European Jews (White, 1980; Newman, 1981) during the late nineteenth century and now of Bangladeshis (Adams, 1987). Tower Hamlets also has a rich history of political and social struggles. The Battle of Cable Street in 1936, in which immigrant residents clashed with Oswald Mosley's British Union of Fascists, and the Bangladeshi demonstrations against the National Front in the late 1970s are examples of the tradition of protest and opposition.

Overseas, South-Asian communities have different historical trajectories because they have developed in widely divergent historical contexts in various parts of the world. So there is great diversity – numerically, socially and politically – within the experiences of South-Asian settlement in Britain. The third-largest South-Asian settlement in Britain, after the regions of Punjab and Gujarat, comes from the region of Sylhet in northeast Bangladesh. British Sylhetis represent by far the poorest segment of the South-Asian population in Britain and they have the largest population growth rate. From an estimated 6,000 in 1961 (Eade, 1998: 139), the number of people who identified themselves as ethnically Bangladeshi in England and Wales in 2011 had risen to nearly 513,000 (ONS, 2012b). Historical sources suggest that over 90 per cent of the Bangladeshi immigrants have come from five districts of Sylhet: Biswanath, Maulvi Bazaar, Beani Bazaar, Golapgonj and Nobigonj (Islam, 1987: 360). However, this demographic is likely to change as a result of the volume of Bangladeshi students from urban locations in Bangladesh such as Dhaka and Chittagong who have entered Britain on the student visa scheme.

The story of Sylheti emigration goes as far back as the late seventeenth century when, along with people from the regions of Noahkali, Chittagong and elsewhere, Sylhetis performed menial tasks as seamen (lascars) on British ships (Visram, 1986). By the start of the Second World War, nearly 50,000 out of the 190,000 servicemen in the British Merchant Navy were lascars, largely of South-Asian origin and often working as galley-hands (Lavery, 2006: 62). This highlights the magnitude and importance of the role of lascars not only for Bangladeshi migration patterns but for the region of South Asia as a whole. The lascars tended to slip ashore illegally when docked in either Britain or New York. Most resided in guesthouses such as the aptly named Strangers Home located in Tower Hamlets.

Most Sylheti migration into Britain took place in the 1950s and 1960s through a process of 'chain migration' (Desai, 1963: 1–67; Begum and Eade, 2005: 184) – a complex system where primary settlers brought over other men from their village and provided them with work and accommodation (Adams, 1987). This explains the high concentration of Bangladeshis from one particular region of Bangladesh (Gardner, 1998). Shah (1998: 20) notes that the existence of familiar community, kin and culture in the country of settlement 'humanize[d]' the often traumatic experience of migration. Consequently, the borough became the hub of the Bangladeshi Sylheti settlers in Britain. Latest census figures show that Tower Hamlets is home to over a sixth (81,000) of the total British-Bangladeshi population (ONS, 2012c; Tower Hamlets, n.d.), of which approximately 70 per cent are aged under 34 years (Greater London Authority, 2011).

Migration was initially by men (Davison, 1964), until their families started to come over in the 1970s and 1980s. The tightening up of British immigration laws that restricted travelling back and forth from Bangladesh (Anwar, 1995) convinced many male Sylheti workers to terminate their status as 'inter-continental commuters' (Ballard, 1994: 150) and bring their dependants over to Britain. Family reunification brought up the issue of how family life was going to be pursued in a non-Muslim and secular country.

As a result of second-generation involvement in micropolitics, local government and other influential institutions such as community, health, education, youth and housing organizations (Asghar, 1996), sufficient pressure was exerted to allow a process of 'Islamicization' to occur within the local social system (Begum and Eade, 2005: 184). For example, while mothers primarily took charge of the religious and Bangladeshi language education of the second generation (N. Ahmed, 2005), Islamicization also occurred at a structural level on matters such as halal food and Eid holidays at schools, cultural and religious dress being confidently worn in public places, training health and social workers to be culturally sensitive, supplying multilingual literature informing Bangladeshis of important events and news and, most notably, the expansion of local mosques and prayer halls to facilitate the diversity, growth and expressions of the local Bangladeshi-Muslim community (Marranci, 2005; Lewis, 2007; Islam, 2008).

While a large section of the Bangladeshi community remain politically marginalized from mainstream society, a small minority have recently become part of the decision-making process by actively engaging in civic life, media debates and taking up political office. The election and re-election of Lutfur Rahman as the first-ever executive mayor of Tower Hamlets in 2010 and 2014 illustrates the political maturity of the local Bangladeshi community. The close-knit nature of the large Bangladeshi community in Tower Hamlets has therefore offered individuals a safe environment in which to confidently express and practise their faith and cultural life in public (N. Ahmed, 2005).

However, despite the sense of safety found in Tower Hamlets, there have been many incidents of racial tension that have led many Bangladeshis to re-examine notions of home, personal identity and national belonging (see Chapter 5). The voices of my participants remind us that underachievement, intergenerational conflict, identity and racial alienation remain prime areas of concern for the third-generation Bangladeshis. These voices must also be located within the construction of Islamophobic geopolitics and new racisms discussed in this book.

A history of deprivation, poverty and underachievement

Abbas (2005) notes that the South-Asian Muslim immigrant population during the 1950s and 1960s, like other immigrant communities, filled lower-echelon gaps in British society and were positioned at the bottom of the labour market. They were often recruited into manual non-skilled jobs. According to Abbas (2005: 9), South-Asian Muslims were disdained by the host society and 'systematically ethnicised and racialised'. Abbas even suggests that their economic and social positions were located below their white working-class neighbours, thus forming what sociologists term an 'underclass'. A sociological examination of the complex and heavily critiqued concept of 'the underclass' (Ely and Denney, 1987; Lister, 1990) echoes a strong case for Bangladeshis being members of such a class. Bangladeshis in Tower Hamlets share many of the features of the underclass, such as multiple deprivation, social marginality (Rex and Tomlinson, 1979) and welfare-state dependency (Dahrendorf, 1987; Saunders, 1990). By comparison, as Castles and Kosack (1973) argue, many white working-class indigenous communities in Western Europe were able to attain upward mobility in status and economic prosperity as they were in an advantageous position over the immigrant other.

In many ways, the Bangladeshi immigrant story in Britain is more about poverty and class than race (Rahman, 2007), although all three are inextricably interlinked. The Pakistani and Bangladeshi first-generation settlers in Britain, especially the Pakistanis who originated from the rural areas of Azad Kashmir, Mirpur and Punjab, and the Bangladeshis from Sylhet, were located in some of the most disadvantaged areas in Britain. They were likely to be living in inferior and overcrowded housing conditions, have low literacy and educational achievement and the poorest health, with exceptionally high rates of diabetes and heart disease. They also suffered high unemployment due to deindustrialization and the decline of the manufacturing, textiles and catering sectors (Tinker, 1977).

Nearly sixty years on, British Muslims are still in a position of social and economic deprivation and alienation. Like their pioneer forefathers, British third-generation Muslims still occupy the lower echelons in modern society. Poor social housing, low income (Babb *et al.*, 2006: 80), poor health, high unemployment and underachievement in education are still widespread (Modood *et al.*, 1997; Brown, 2000; Gillborn and Mirza, 2000; Strategy Unit, 2003; Anwar, 2005). In 2009, 70 per cent of Bangladeshis lived in low-income households (The Poverty Site, 2010) and in 2012 13.5 per cent of Bangladeshis aged 16 to 24 were also unemployed (Institute of

Race Relations, 2012). However, poverty is not limited to the Bangladeshi community. A survey by the Prince's Trust found that Tower Hamlets has the highest number of jobless families in the country: 47 per cent of the children had parents on unemployment benefits (Collins, 2010: 1). It is Tower Hamlets itself that has a long relationship with poverty, as opposed to a particular ethnic group, although the Bangladeshis remain over-represented.

Politicians, social commentators and academics have sought to explain the connection between the Bangladeshi community and poverty, exploring a range of factors including self-imposed segregation (Travis, 2001; Abbas, 2005), increasing competition in labour market, lack of ambition (Rahman, 2007), difference between the attitudes and values of immigrants from rural backgrounds as against those from cities and towns (Snow quoted in Lewis, 2007), investing of money in Bangladesh and Pakistan and not in Britain, structural and institutional racism (Macpherson, 1999) and cultural racism (Abbas, 2005), linguistic barriers and deindustrialization.

The historical concern of educational underachievement also merits discussion. The underachievement of Bangladeshis in education cannot be separated from the underachievement of working-class pupils in general as there is a 'crucial relationship' between education and poverty (Joseph Rowntree Foundation, 2007a; Archer *et al.*, 2010). Historically, Bangladeshi pupils have consistently underachieved at GCSE level. However, recent GCSE attainment in 2011 has seen Bangladeshi pupils achieve above the national average, with 59.7 per cent of pupils attaining 5 A*–C grades, including Maths and English (Department for Education, 2012). The improvement at GCSE level has been dramatic for Bangladeshi pupils. In 1996 and 2006, the pass rates were 25 per cent and 48 per cent respectively (Babb *et al.*, 2006). Education attainment has been aided by the proliferation of tuition centres and weekend supplementary schools as well as critical educational involvement by English-speaking parents who 'not only understand the system but are shaping it' (*Economist*, 2013). In addition, there is a correlation between those families and parents who are themselves educated, which means that their children are likely to follow suit (Platt, 2005).

However, despite attainment gaps decreasing among Bangladeshi pupils, they still experience unequal outcomes at university and in employment. In 2009, 44 per cent of all black, Pakistani, Bangladeshi and Indian graduates attended post-1992 universities compared to 34 per cent of other ethnic groups. Bangladeshi students were awarded a higher proportion of lower second-class degrees and 33.3 per cent of young Bangladeshi people looking for work were unemployed (Runnymede, 2012). Thus, despite significant progress at GCSE level, wider systemic and structural issues still exist and contribute to the cycle of poverty and deprivation.

Despite these structural restrictions, and informed by the decline in traditional Bangladeshi employment sectors such as catering and the rag trade, younger third-generation Bangladeshis are gradually entering into more diverse employment fields. They are slowly becoming part of a growing educated and professional class (Bunting, 2004; Kamrava, 2006). This is reflected in the career ambitions of the six participants of this study: Zeyba hopes to go on to university, Taiba wants to go into youth work, Sanjida wishes to become a teacher, Akbar and Saeed want to become entrepreneurs and Azad hopes to go into accounting. There is, therefore, cause for some optimism, although the structural constraints of poverty, Islamophobia, race and class politics still govern their everyday lives.

Conclusion

The main objective of this chapter was to provide a historical and sociopolitical context of Bangladeshi-Muslim settlement in Britain. The remainder of this book is written in the context of the complex issues raised here.

This chapter examined the diversity of the British-Muslim community and argued that there are many faces of Islam in Britain. It outlined some of the sociopolitical reasons for the growth and popularity of Islam, particularly among the third generation. Its popularity must be viewed within the context of the global war on terror that has given impetus to the growth of Islamophobia, constructing the fear of Muslims as natural, normal and unproblematic. Domestic and international events involving Muslims have transformed the Muslim community from 'passive' to 'troubled' (Hai, 2008). However, Muslims have been depicted throughout history as the barbaric other whose values and lifestyle pose a threat to the Western/British way of life. This has to be stressed as it is within this theoretical context of the other – the orientalist gaze – that the fears, stories, concerns and voices of the six participants of my study must be located and that the study has been researched, written and analysed.

Although there is reason for optimism as education pass rates slowly increase and a professional class emerges among the East London Bangladeshi population, the stories of the six participants in Part 3 remind us of the historical and ongoing struggles that affect them. The identity question is important in this discussion. For British-born third-generation Bangladeshis, the complexity of identity and the related questions of belonging and home remain in flux. The remainder of this book tells their stories and seeks to shed light on the question of who the third-generation Bangladeshis from East London are.

Part Two

The participants

Chapter 3

Getting to know the participants

It was a very wet evening in November 2006. I had already met Saeed twice before – once at a local cafe and another time in a snooker club. This time around, he'd invited me to have a game of football with him and his friends at his youth club on the Isle of Dogs. They routinely met every Thursday to play football with the local boys. Apparently it was intense and hugely competitive. Here is an entry from my field notes:

> I arrived 30 minutes before the agreed meeting time of 7pm.
> I knew the area very well but I didn't want to leave anything
> to chance, especially knowing the rush-hour traffic near the
> Blackwall Tunnel area. After parking underneath one of the
> few working streetlights, I made my way to the youth club.
> I knew of this youth club but had never visited it before. I
> also loosely knew the youth worker in charge, who I'd met
> a few times in local area meetings. It was located right next
> to a common green area with a mini adventure playground
> that had seen better days. The youth club itself was typical of
> many other youth clubs in Tower Hamlets – medium-sized,
> tired, under-resourced, under-staffed and in desperate need of
> a lick of paint. The fences around the five-a-side football pitch
> were battered and the nets on the goal frames were missing.
> I introduced myself to the youth worker, who remembered
> me. She offered me a cup of tea. I politely declined as I had
> already had a cuppa before leaving home. Justin Timberlake
> was playing loudly in the background. There were about thirty
> kids there already. They were of all ages ranging from 12 to 25,
> representing different ethnicities – African Caribbean, Somali,
> white and Bangladeshi. The handful of girls present were mainly
> congregated around the one working computer – desperate to
> get on the internet. The boys were hanging around the pool
> table and others were intensely engaged in a PlayStation game.
> A girl and a boy sat together on a red sofa at the corner of the

main room, obviously besotted with each other. Some of the
older boys were smoking outside.

I was not noticed. Everyone was busy doing their own things.
Saeed was not here yet. I was already dressed in my shorts,
t-shirt, knee-high socks, shinpads and hoody. I wore a hoody
not because I wanted to fit in with the local youth but because
that's what I normally wear. It was cold. I went outside onto
the pitch. I was warming myself up doing short sprints, jumpy-
uppies and stretching my hamstrings and calves. I needed to
warm up, especially as I had still not fully recovered physically
and mentally from my injury of 2002. I was lost in my own
world of fitness training when I heard a familiar voice, 'Aminul
bhai, wagwan? You made it. I was sure you weren't gonna
come.' 'I'm always up for a game of footie,' I replied. He
came and embraced me and introduced me to his friends …
By 7.20pm, the football pitch had become alive. It was noisy,
there was excitement and arguments. There were twenty-five-
odd players. Somali boys, white boys, Bengali boys. Some were
wearing jeans and shoes, others were dressed in their *thobes* and
skullcaps (coming straight from after-school madrasa) and only
two other players apart from me were wearing proper AstroTurf
boots and shorts. Saeed was wearing an overgrown tracksuit
bottom and a huge navy duffle coat with what looked like very
expensive trainers. I came across as keen. Perhaps too keen and
also oddly overdressed for a game of football with Saeed and
his mates. I noticed very quickly that I was the only one who
was wearing shinpads. This had to be rectified. I quietly took
them off and rolled down my socks. I didn't want to be the
odd one out…

…the teams were already picked. It was the same team every
week – the Somali team, the white team, the Bengali team.
No youth worker in sight. The boys were left to sort things
out on their own. This felt normal – I never felt threatened or
scared, just slightly nervous. This was almost like an initiation
test. 'Come on, let's see what you got old man,' Saeed said
[laughing]. I was obviously picked for the Bengali team. I was
normally hugely competitive in football. I didn't want that to
come across tonight, so I volunteered to go in goal … it was a
feisty affair and there was no referee. Still no youth worker in

sight. The game was self-refereed. Every tackle, save and shot was contested. It was winner-stays-on rules and nobody wanted to lose. Surprisingly, some of the players were very skilful, with good first-touch and passing ability, despite wearing footwear unsuitable for AstroTurf. But most of them didn't have a clue about football and saw it more as an excuse to hang out with their mates.

We lose a game and have to sit out the next. Saeed approaches me. 'What you doing after, Aminul *bhai*?' 'Nothing,' I replied. 'OK, cool. Do you wanna go for some chicken and chips with us?' Before I could answer, a fight breaks out on the pitch over a very nasty tackle. Finally, the youth worker emerges. In an instant, Saeed and his mates run onto the pitch eager to throw a punch or two. In motion, he looks back at me and shouts, 'Welcome to my world, Aminul *bhai*.'

Introducing the participants

The decision to focus only on the life stories of six individuals was deliberate. Governed by an ethnographic inquisitive desire and a phenomenological philosophy, the benefit of having such a small sample size was that I was able to spend much in-depth time with the participants, which allowed me to gain a deeper insight into and understanding of their lives, feelings, experiences and aspirations. By no means am I suggesting that the experiences of the six participants of this study represent the experiences of all third-generation Bangladeshis in East London. I am aware that there is much diversity and complexity involved.

The six participants were unknown to me prior to the research, and none of them knew each other. They all nominated themselves through my youth-work contacts in Tower Hamlets. The in-depth interviews were held in various settings – youth clubs, cafes, college canteens, family homes, community centres, training centres and public parks. All followed a semi structured format and were usually conversational in tone. The interviews were focused around the life stories of the participants and their experiences and were guided by the central question of identity. The participants had to meet certain criteria. So all six:

- were ethnically Bangladeshi
- were born in Britain
- lived in East London (mainly in Tower Hamlets)
- had a grandparent who had emigrated to Britain

- were secondary-school or college age (15 to 19)
- were willing to partake in in-depth repeated interviews over a long period of time
- were eager to share their stories and memories.

There was an equal gender split among the participants. Their names and area of residence have been anonymized to protect their identities.

Saeed Rahman, male aged 19

Saeed is a third-generation Bangladeshi from Poplar. Saeed has two brothers and one sister and lives with his mother and father in a council estate. They are a very tight-knit family. His father is unemployed and his mother is a full-time housewife. His father was brought over to the UK from Sylhet (Bangladesh) at the age of 14 by his grandfather in the late 1970s. Saeed enjoys 'cotching (socializing) with his boys ... smoking shisha (flavoured tobacco) ... and eating biryani (flavoured rice) and chops' and playing football.

Saeed has had a troubled education. Constantly 'kicked out' of the classroom during his secondary education, he was eventually sent to a Pupil Referral Unit (PRU) at the age of 14. He did not get along with his teachers and was 'bored' with school. So he does not have a positive view of education although he is proud of his older sister, who is studying law at university. 'She is the clever one in the family [pause] she is the one who will bring us a good reputation,' he says. This confirms the dual importance of education and reputation within many Bangladeshi families. Saeed has been in constant trouble with the police, having being cautioned and also imprisoned for what he refers to as 'stupid trouble'. Saeed's early memories of childhood revolve around the estate-bound football pitch and gang fights. He remembers vividly the 'older boys' fighting nearly every week with knives and machetes. He has a very negative view of the police: 'I am always stopped and searched by the police. It's mainly because of the way I look and dress.'

His distrust of authority (teachers, police, politicians) is evident throughout our conversations. Although very resentful, angry and frustrated, he is remarkably mature for his age. This he attributes to his street education, having to 'do things on my own' and also having always 'hung around the older boys in my area'. Saeed has ambitions of one day owning his own business and he hopes volunteering in business industries will give him the knowledge and insight to realize his ambition.

Akbar Khan, male aged 19

Akbar is a third-generation Bangladeshi from Globe Town. He has recently moved with his family to the neighbouring London borough of Newham. At the time of interviewing, he was studying for his A Levels at college and hoped to go on to university to pursue a career in business. His father died when Akbar was only 5 and he now lives with his mother and three brothers. He is extremely close to his mother, and his life experiences and values have been heavily shaped by her. He plays a 'lot of football' and likes watching television. He also likes to 'hang out' with his friends and reads tabloid newspapers (*Metro*). He is a West Ham fan and works part-time at West Ham Football Club's hospitality kiosk.

Azad Miah, male aged 18

Azad is a third-generation Bangladeshi from Bow, the eldest of two siblings. He lives in a three-generational family household with his grandparents. Azad is the only participant who has never visited Bangladesh. This perhaps explains his pessimism towards the Bengali language and culture. At the time of interviewing, Azad was studying for his A Levels at college and hoped to go on to university to study accounts and finance. He would like to leave Bow and live in an area where there is 'more interaction with people from other cultures and communities'. Azad is a keen sportsperson and likes to read fictional crime novels during his spare time. His favourite author is John Grisham. He also likes 'hanging around with his mates'. Azad went to a madrasa (Islamic school) as part of his secondary education.

Sanjida Begum, female aged 16

Sanjida is a third-generation Bangladeshi from Bethnal Green. She was born in Whitechapel, also in Tower Hamlets, but the expanding family moved to Leytonstone and then to Bethnal Green in 2000. She attended a culturally diverse secondary school, although the predominant ethnicity was white/ British – 'white people' as Sanjida refers to them. Sanjida's grandfather came to Britain in 1960 and she now lives with her mother and father, her two sisters and twin brother in a four-bedroom council flat. The twins are the eldest children. Her father is a machinist and her mother teaches Bengali part-time at an after-school club. Sanjida has been to Bangladesh twice in her lifetime (1999, 2003) and has a close connection with what she calls her 'motherland'.

Sanjida likes 'hanging out with her friends', watching documentaries on the Discovery Channel, going to the cinema and eating out at Nando's restaurant. At the time of interviewing, she was about to go to college and hoped to go on to university and study for a PGCE to become a teacher.

Zeyba Hussain, female aged 15

Zeyba is a third-generation Bangladeshi from Mile End. She is the youngest of all the participants. She has five sisters and lives with her mother and father in a freehold house. Her father works in a bank and her older sisters are all university graduates whose professions are doctor, journalist and banker. Her mother is a full-time housewife. There is a huge emphasis on education within Zeyba's family and she is given the support, resources, space and tuition to succeed in her education. Zeyba is expected to follow in her sisters' footsteps and pursue an equally good profession. According to Bourdieu (1994), Zeyba has the 'habitus' (lifestyle and values) to succeed in the education system. Through education, Zeyba's family have undergone a dual process of upward social mobility (Giddens, 1973) as well as 'intergenerational' mobility (Roberts, 2001), as her father's non-manual profession is different to her grandfather's working as an unskilled manual worker (Goldthorpe, 1987).

In contrast to the other five participants, Zeyba's family are firmly rooted within the middle class in terms of values, assets, income and profession (Giddens, 1973; Savage *et al.*, 1992; Bourdieu, 1994; Wynne, 1998). However, despite a high level of education and a liberal upbringing, Zeyba's family are, paradoxically, still firmly rooted within Bangladeshi culture and are guided by Islamic principles. For example, two of her elder sisters had arranged marriages and both wear the headscarf. Zeyba also wears the hijab and attends an after-school Islamic class.

Socially, Zeyba enjoys travelling, reading books, going to 'women-only' karate classes and spending time with her family.

Taiba Khatun, female aged 17

Taiba is a third-generation Bangladeshi from Poplar. She is the eldest sibling of four. Her father was brought over to the UK by her late grandfather in the 1970s. Taiba has lived a traumatic life. Her mother suffered domestic violence at the hands of her gambling and alcoholic father. During one incident when her father put a knife to her mother's throat, Taiba called the police and a legal investigation followed. Despite this incident, Taiba's mother did not press charges and blamed Taiba for getting outside authorities involved. In Taiba's words, she became the 'black sheep of the family'. She was ostracized by the rest of her family and soon became a persistent runaway. She also started to self-harm and overdose and started to socialize with the 'wrong crowd'. She has now left home, lives in a women's refuge and has lost all contact with her family. At the time of interviewing, Taiba was pregnant and her boyfriend was in prison for attempted robbery. Her parents are unaware of her pregnancy and Taiba has asked the local imam (a Muslim priest) to act as a mediator and break the news to her parents. Despite her history, her 'family' and her 'religion' remain important to Taiba.

Like all the participants, Taiba spoke to me candidly about her family history, childhood memories, her views of Bangladeshi culture and her aspirations.

Themes, sub-themes and patterns that connect the participants

Before the interviews began, I spent much time with the participants, seeking to build a relationship based around the tenets of trust, rapport and respect. I adhered to key methodological principles and practices throughout so as to ensure that each participant's autonomy and confidentiality were protected and that they were comfortable and willing to share their stories with me. For example, I never lost sight of the fact that their participation was entirely voluntary and worked around their timetable as much as possible when organizing interviews. It was important that I presented myself as someone who was trustworthy, willing to listen and genuinely interested in their stories. And it was essential that the conversations were collaborative. In this way, the participants provided authentic, truthful and genuine accounts of their multifaceted identities.

The semi-structured interviews followed a flexible chronological thematic order:

1. a little about themselves – their background, likes, dislikes, hobbies
2. childhood memories
3. neighbourhood
4. family life
5. schooling
6. social life/peer groups
7. culture and community
8. the 'who am I' identity question
9. birthplace and homeland
10. aspirations for the future.

These themes were explored in the in-depth conversations. They were informed by both the study's research focus and the findings from the pilot. Within these broader themes, however, many interwoven stories of identity emerged that connected the participants in terms of history, experience and aspirations, along with stories of divergence and contradiction. The narratives were complex, often contradictory and continually overlapping. This was in keeping with the fluidity and messy nature of identity that I was trying to capture through the interviews. Searching for the patterns that connected the participants, I realized that many sub-themes emerging from the in-depth narratives reoccurred. I decided to colour code the themes and the most consistent sub-themes (see Table 1) in an attempt to organize the stories. The laborious task of manually transcribing and replaying the interview recordings was in itself a crucial part of the research process. It enabled me to capture the complexity of identity. It was important to view the identity-riddle from the participants' perspective. I wanted to capture their emotions, feelings, behaviours and attitudes from a phenomenological viewpoint and felt that using computer-assisted software programs designed to analyse and code qualitative data was inappropriate.

However, I acknowledge that by imposing my own conceptual thinking and categories on the interviews, I may have deflected attention from other categories that might have been important to the participants' identities (Atkinson, 1992). To avoid this, the questions were open-ended, allowing the participants to speak freely about issues important to them. I am also aware that the coding, categorizing and typologizing of narratives can result in subjects telling parts of stories, rather than presenting them in their 'wholeness' (Miller and Glassner, 2004: 127). Nonetheless, the coding and categorizing of the sizeable interview data became useful when trying to make sense of the complex and overlapping stories. I did not make a distinction between the first interviews with participants and the later ones. I viewed all the interviews and observations as part of one overall fluid process.

I neglected some themes that emerged from the interviews, such as the role of modern technology in shaping the identities of some of the participants, the mixing of languages in creating new ones and the emergence of traditional patriarchy among some younger Bangladeshi men. Although these are important components of their stories and hence their identities, these themes were more individualized and therefore relevant and specific to only a few of the participants; they remain elements of identity that present opportunities for future ethnographic research. One of the key objectives guiding the interviews was to illuminate the common themes and patterns that connected the participants. Therefore, the stories discussed and analysed in Part 3 of this book were selected for their consistency and commonality to all six participants.

Five broad components of identity (key themes) emerged from the in-depth conversations:

- language
- race
- religion
- nationality
- gender (in the case of the females).

The sub-themes that emerged from the broader themes were coded and categorized as shown in Table 1.

Table 1: Participant identity sub-themes, categorized and coded

LANGUAGE (L)	
Abbreviated code	**Sub-theme**
L – BLPC	Bengali as a language of practical communication
L – ECL	English as a commercial language important for progress and modernity
L – BLCI	Bengali as a language of history, heritage, culture and identity
L – CA	Emergence of new colloquial Arabic in everyday language

RACE (R)	
Abbreviated code	**Sub-theme**
R – CR	Experience of early childhood racism
R – WM	A stereotypical view of the 'white man'
R – RS	A racially segregated East London leading to lack of interaction with other communities
R – SC	Skin colour presented as a barrier to societal participation, marking them as 'different'
R – OTH	Bengali and Islamic culture presented as 'the other'

RELIGION (RL)	
Abbreviated code	**Sub-theme**
RL – ISS	Islam as a social and spiritual force
RL – IPI	Islam as a political identity leading to victim mentality

RL – ICI	Islam as a cultural identity
RL – IHI	Islam as a hyphenated identity
RL – II	Islam as a core identity
RL – UvsT	Muslim 'us' vs non-Muslim 'them' polarization of society
RL – ID	Islamic identity through dress
RL – IGL	Islam as a global identity
RL – BrI	Islam as a modern, trendy and Westernized identity (British Islam)
RL – IBC	Islam becoming more important than Bangladeshi culture
RL – NR	Experience of new racisms (Islamophobia)

NATIONALITY (N)

Abbreviated code	Sub-theme
N – BB	British by virtue of birthright
N – LB	Legal right to be British
N – BBI	A multifaceted British/Bangladeshi identity
N – BrC	A fluid and contested Britishness
N – GENB	A generalization of Britishness
N – EW	Englishness as associated with whiteness
N – CH	A fuzzy and complex notion of home: Britain is home but also a sense of displacement due to different culture and skin colour; Bangladesh is 'hot' and full of 'mosquitoes'; no fixed sense of home
N – HBR	Home as equated with family, familiarity and place of birth
N – CCBEL	Sense of community and connection with fellow Bangladeshis in East London
N – DBC	Disconnection from Bangladeshi culture and Bangladesh as a country; Bangladesh viewed as a place of 'holiday' and Bangladeshis viewing the respondents as 'tourists'
N – HCM	Home having a close relationship with childhood memories
N – BM	Deep connection with Bangladesh (the 'motherland')

GENDER (Bangladeshi female) (GBF)	
Abbreviated code	Sub-theme
GBF – GBG	Notion of the 'good Bangladeshi girl' still wielding importance (somebody who is quiet, religious, domesticated, studious, respects her parents and is concerned about family name and reputation)
GBF – CGBG	Challenging and resisting the notion of the 'good Bangladeshi girl'
GBF – I+	Impact of Islam as a force for change
GBF – MMH	Multiple meanings of hijab/covering
GBF – HP	Hijab as a symbol of politicization
GBF – HS	Hijab as a symbol of spirituality
GBF – HB	Hijab as a symbol of trendiness/modernity/fashion ('hijabi barbie')
GBF – EC	The importance of education and career

The five key components of identity and the many sub-themes that emerge within them highlight the multifaceted, contradictory and competing identities of the participants. The complexity is captured in much of the narrative presented in the remainder of the book. Although I present the participants' stories under five separate components of identity, it is impossible to capture the dynamism of identity and life stories under a single heading. Because the components of human identity overlap, there is some fluidity and repetition between the five components of identity analysed in Part 3.

Conclusion

This chapter has two purposes – first, to introduce the six participants and provide some background information about them, and second, to outline the key themes and sub-themes, issues and components of third-generation Bangladeshi identity that emerged from the in-depth interviews that I co-authored with Akbar, Azad and Saeed, Sanjida, Taiba and Zeyba. The sub-themes set out in Table 1 indicate the multiple and complex issues these young Bangladeshis are grappling with. The key issues and stories that connect the experience of being a third-generation Bangladeshi from East London are:

- the disconnection from Bengali culture and the evolving role of language in the lives of many of the participants
- experiences of early childhood racism leading to feelings of rejection and displacement and, for many, a 'them vs us' mindset
- the development of a new and vibrant British-Islamic culture that imbues its members with identity, acceptance, belonging, recognition and visibility
- a confusing, problematic and evolving discussion of Britishness, national identity and the location of home; despite being born in Britain, the concept of home was not clear cut for the participants and many felt disassociated from the country of their birth
- the establishment of a gendered British Islam for many young Bangladeshi women, which remains governed by Bangladeshi culture, patriarchy and tradition.

The multiplicity and complexity of these five components of identity informs Part 3 of the book. Chapters 4 to 8 unpick and analyse the findings in depth. All evidence from the narratives points towards the construction of a modern and vibrant British-Islamic identity among the participants, which is enabling them to negotiate their identity-riddle of being British-born Bangladeshi Muslims. There are many sociocultural factors to consider in this complex construction of a British-Islamic identity, informed by a history of alienation, deprivation, disaffection, displacement and marginalization. British Islam also needs to be located within a contemporary geopolitics of Islamophobia that depicts Islam as backward, barbaric, anti-Western and inherently violent (see Figure 1, p. 111). It is appropriate to talk about 'identities' rather than 'identity', as the young people are members of many different communities. Their identities are not fixed, but are complex, multiple and fluid.

The narratives that follow are interwoven with wider theoretical discourse so as to provide context and to locate the voices and stories within a historical and contemporary theoretical framework. There is a reciprocal relationship between theory and data (Coffey and Atkinson, 1996). I use many short and lengthy quotations from the participants to reveal the complexity of the patterns that connect them and to illustrate the development of a dynamic British-Islamic identity. In doing so, I hope that I have faithfully represented the stories and the views of Sanjida, Zeyba, Taiba, Saeed, Akbar and Azad.

Part Three

Multiple stories

Chapter 4

Bengali language and culture: Implications for identity

Introduction

> The Bengali people are so backwards and the Bengali language
> is useless. What is the point of speaking it? My first words were
> 'mum' and 'dad' not '*amma* and *abba*'. I prefer English.
>
> (Taiba)

> If we don't know how to speak Bengali, it's going to be stupid
> in a way. We are Bengali and we must be able to speak our own
> language.
>
> (Saeed)

It is telling that all of the participants spoke to me in English throughout our conversations and not in their mother tongue of Bengali. Unlike their grandparents and many of their parents, they were not part of a Bengali-speaking linguistic community. By choosing to speak English over Bengali, they are essentially exerting an identity preference. There is a direct relationship between language, culture and identity, which suggests that by rejecting a language you are also essentially rejecting the history and culture associated with the language, and that by assuming a language you are at the same time forging new cultural identities for yourself. This chapter examines the complex role of languages within the lives of the six participants and whether there is a relationship between their linguistic and their cultural identity.

So, if the Bengali language is central to Bangladeshi national and cultural identity, what role, if any, does it play in the lives of third-generation Bangladeshis from East London? Clearly, it provokes ambivalence and confusion, as is apparent from Taiba's and Saeed's words. Identifying with being 'Bengali' or 'Bangladeshi' is steeped in Bangladeshi nationalism. The Bangladesh War of Independence from West Pakistan in 1971 was fought over race, geopolitics, economic disparity between East and West Pakistan and, most importantly, over culture and language. The Bengalis from East Pakistan wanted to protect their own distinct culture and language from the dominant Urdu-speaking West Pakistanis. So while the emergence of Bangladesh as a nation resulted from a number of sociopolitical factors, the protection and preservation of the 'Bangla' language became embedded in the struggle for independence (Choudhury, 1974: 10–12). While Bangladesh as a nation is still a relatively new concept, there is a complicated yet crucial relationship between being Bangladeshi as an identity marker and being able to speak the Bengali language.

The role of language has an important bearing on how the participants identify themselves. As for all of us, language plays both a practical and personal role in their lives. Some use the language purely for functional communication, some see it as having no relevance whatsoever to their lives and future aspirations and reject it, whereas others view it as central to their heritage and cultural identity. We do not become part of a linguistic community in a practical, psychological and ideological sense just by speaking a certain language. There are complexities such as race, class, ethnicity and nation that determine membership of a linguistic and cultural community. A complicated picture emerges in which some of the participants are consciously resisting both their mother tongue and their cultural heritage, replacing the Bengali language with other languages of communication. Many are engaging in political acts by rejecting Bengali and its associated Asian national 'backwards' character (Fryer, 1985; Banton, 1997) and assuming others – English and conversational colloquial Arabic – that provide practical and ideological meaning to their lives. By speaking English, they are trying to become accepted, modern, liberal and forward-thinking.

The recent development of an Islamic and Arabic sociolinguistic identity is a double rejection: of a British social system that has systematically excluded working-class immigrants from its benefits (Shain, 2003); and of an alien and, for many, a somewhat irrelevant Bangladeshi culture. It is the central argument of this chapter that my participants are assuming positions of power, representation and rejection by the language they choose to communicate in.

The chapter is divided into five sections, dealing with:

- key distinctions between the Sylheti and Bengali language
- the complex relationship between language and cultural identity
- the role of English as an international language of power (Pennycook, 1994)
- the emergence of Arabic as a language of power, acceptance and belonging
- a concluding summary of the key arguments.

Distinctions between Sylheti and Bengali

Although there are some phonetic commonalities and overlaps in terminology, there remains much difference and also tension between the official language of Bangladesh (Bengali, sometimes referred to as Bangla) and the language of Sylhet, which all six participants speak at home. The first difference is numbers. With approximately 181 million speakers worldwide, the Bengali language is ranked as the sixth most spoken language in the world, covering Bangladesh and the Indian state of West Bengal (Ethnologue, n.d.). The Sylheti language, in comparison, is spoken by approximately nine million people and is mainly confined to Sylhet and the Cachar district of Assam, India (STAR, n.d.). The country in which Sylheti is spoken most widely outside Bangladesh and India is the United Kingdom. Gardner (1995b) estimates that approximately 95 per cent of the British-Bangladeshi community speak Sylheti.

The second issue is the status of Sylheti. Regarded for decades as a dialect of Bengali, Sylheti is now seen as a language in its own right. Extremely poetic and influenced by Persian and Arabic, the Sylheti language has its own distinct grammar and a rich heritage of literature written in the Sylheti Nagri script, which dates back at least two hundred years (STAR, n.d.). But Sylheti became a casualty of the 1971 War of Independence when the newly formed government discouraged its use in favour of Bengali (Kershen, 2007). Historically situated within a backdrop of strong linguistic consciousness (which led to the Bengali Language Movement in 1952) and bound up within the politics of Bangladeshi nationalism, the 'unofficial' Sylheti language underwent a process of 'symbolic violence' (Bourdieu, 1991) as the political elite sought to unite the nation against West Pakistan under a single, powerful, 'official' language (Bengali) in 1971.

Third, many other sociopolitical and historic binaries emerge from the analysis of the distinctions between Sylheti and Bengali. It is often argued that Sylheti is spoken by poor, illiterate, unskilled, rural peasants whereas Bengali has become associated with the urban educated economic and political elite; that, somehow, language choice is linked to social and cultural mobility and economic opportunities. Such a binary is problematic, as many urban Bengali-speaking people are living in abject poverty and many educated Sylheti speakers can communicate well in Bengali when they choose to (STAR, n.d.).

Although it is important to draw out these distinctions between the two languages, I use the terms 'Bengali', 'Bangla', 'Syhleti' and 'Bangladeshi' interchangeably throughout the book. My decision to use these terms generically has been influenced by the fluidity with which they are used within the British-Bangladeshi community. The participants, like a large proportion of the British-Bangladeshi community, make no distinction between these terms. For many, the term Bengali has a dual meaning: the language spoken by Bangladeshis, and a term to describe the national cultural identity of Bangladeshis. As Sanjida states, 'We speak Bengali because we are Bengali.' And, as will become apparent through the personal narratives in this chapter, while all six participants speak and understand Sylheti, they themselves call it 'Bengali' or 'Bangla'. Their linguistic identities have become entangled within a national as opposed to a regional discourse. Sanjida and Akbar say they are 'Bengali' and their mother tongue is also 'Bengali'. I use their terminology when trying to retell their stories. And, as the majority of British Bangladeshis originate from Sylhet and all my participants are Sylheti, all reference to Bangladeshi culture or Bengali language relates to one particular Sylheti rural Bangladeshi culture and language.

Language and cultural identity

As Lyon and Ellis (1991) point out, the relationship between language and cultural identity is no better highlighted than in Wales, where speaking Welsh is required in certain political and media offices. The Welsh language has become entwined with maintaining Welsh nationality and a distinctive cultural identity. There is a complex relationship between language, culture and identity (see Cummins and Skutnabb-Kangas, 1988). But does language play a role in determining the identities of my study's participants?

> The Bengali language is central to who I am. I am Bengali.
>
> (Sanjida)

> Bengali is our mother tongue … We are Bengali and we must be able to speak our own language.
>
> (Saeed)

> My mum only understands Bengali. I need to speak Bengali to communicate with her.
>
> (Taiba)

> My parents only speak bits and bobs of English. I know my children will speak mainly English in the future. Therefore my parents will need to learn English in order to communicate with them.
>
> (Azad)

> English is important as it allows me to express myself and also socially interact with my friends. It also allows me to access the internet and will help me secure a good future. I find it difficult to understand and speak Bengali ... Bengali holds no relevance in my life.
>
> (Zeyba)

> We are Muslims and it is important to learn Arabic so that we can understand the meaning of the Qu'ran. English is also important for future job prospects.
>
> (Akbar)

Many questions need to be considered when examining bilingual identities, especially in a country like the UK, with a dominant and official language – English – that is the language of communication, commerce and power (Bourdieu, 1991). So do people adopt 'multiple' linguistic identities depending on context and social environment? Do we become Bangladeshi only when we speak Bengali or are spoken to in Bengali? Or can we remain British and still speak Bengali with our friends? Is our culture being transformed when we start to exert our bilingualism and does this also mean that we are bicultural? Just as we can speak both English and Bengali, can we also be culturally Bangladeshi and British/English? Can a Bangladeshi enter into English cultural life just because they speak fluent English? Similarly, can a white Anglo-Saxon person access Bangladeshi life and understand the experiences of Bangladeshi people just because they speak Bengali fluently? These are important questions to consider.

Bilingualism can determine identities. All six participants grew up in an environment of a bilingual family and community where a combination of languages were spoken. They all alternate naturally between Sylheti-Bangla and English, using both within familial and community contexts. The languages are often combined in everyday speech. For example, 'There was so much *maya* (love) between everyone' (Sanjida); '*Khano* (where) shall we meet?' (Saeed); 'I have to call home every day at 6 p.m. *Amma sinta koron* (my mother worries)' (Taiba). The use of language by the participants during the conversations all had an element of code switching. They adapted to certain contexts through their choice of language. This level of code switching within a sentence or a conversation indicates their awareness of me, the researcher, as a Bangladeshi who understands Bengali – which, in linguistic terms, enables them to make an adjustment to 'insider' and 'outsider' status (Baker, 1993). I have coined the term 'Banglish' to describe this free alternating between English and Bengali to communicate with people. Building on Harding and Riley's (1986) classification of bilingual family types, the language usage by the participants could be described as fitting into Romaine's (1995: 183–5) 'type six' family as there is a mixing of languages. Indeed, Akbar himself suggests that he would like to 'mix' the languages of Bengali and English when communicating with his own children in the future.

It is well documented that 'unnatural' patterns of speech tend to break down and have a short shelf life (Grosjean, 1982: 174). A context where a mix of languages is used freely by the third generation seems natural, as they are living in a multicultural country with exposure to mainstream and community languages. Free alternation of languages is natural but there is also a danger associated with this pattern: as Mills (2001: 387) points out, 'the majority language may slowly become dominant when a child reaches school age and is affected by school interactions and friendship patterns'. However, the majority language in many schools in Tower Hamlets is not English. For example, 95 per cent of the pupils from Smithy Street Primary School are of Bangladeshi origin, of whom 99 per cent speak Sylheti as a primary language (Primary Languages, n.d.). However, English remains the 'dominant' (Bourdieu, 1991) language in East London. This is an important point, especially in regards to my participants who, although they understand Bengali, still choose to speak English as their main form of communication. This preference for English over Bengali is emphasized by Zeyba: 'Bengali holds no relevance in my life.'

Also important is whether people choose or are coerced into speaking the dominant language. Although recent studies have examined the role of bilingualism in the lives of children from ethnic-minority communities (Ghuman, 1995; Conteh, 2003; Kenner, 2004; Issa, 2005; Hatt and Issa, 2012; Kenner and Ruby, 2012), the field of childhood bilingualism has nonetheless been dominated by accounts of the experiences of middle-class children from European or North American backgrounds. Crucially, argues Mills (2001: 387), this 'brings to the fore issues of choice and representation'. And it highlights the argument that 'many children have had no choice in becoming bilingual' (Romaine, 1998: 61). The notion of choice is important for the participants. They have been coerced into speaking and learning English. Most books, the internet, mass media, the schooling system and the system of governance and commerce all demand that they learn English. Furthermore, as Zeyba says, English for many 'secure[s] a good future'.

The 'choice' factor was a key determinant in Mills's (2001) study of ten third-generation Pakistanis from the Midlands who spoke Urdu,

Mirphuri, Punjabi and English. Building on Romaine's (1998) work, Mills makes a distinction between 'elite' and 'folk' bilingualism. Elite bilingualism is the domain of the middle class and privileged members of any societies and cultures who choose to learn a language. Folk bilingualism, on the other hand, is a domain participated in by ethnic-minority groups who become 'bilingual involuntarily in order to work and take part in the educational and welfare social structure' (Mills, 2001: 387). They are bilingual by necessity and not through choice. The participants in my study are firmly established within the folk parameters of bilingualism. They are making a conscious choice to learn English in order to benefit from and become members of the society that they are living in. In Taiba's words: 'English is not only natural for me, it is also a must in order to live in this country.'

Bilingualism cannot be isolated from its political context. Phillipson (1988) describes the notion of a process of 'linguicism' in which the ideologies and structures that are used to legitimate, effect and reproduce an unequal division of power and resources between groups – both material and non-material – are defined on the basis of language. Linguicism is thus similar in its workings and effects to racism, sexism, classism, ageism and other structures and ideologies that serve to maintain inequality in society. In this instance, and as Azad, Zeyba, Akbar and Taiba observe, the language of English reinforces old orientalist demarcations. It takes on a role of power, progress and modernity, whereas Bengali and, to a lesser extent, Arabic (as community languages) are viewed as archaic and backward.

Such tensions, according to Cummins and Skutnabb-Kangas (1988), are rooted in the power relations between dominant and subordinate groups in wider society. Educational establishments have typically reflected and reinforced such power relations through actions such as punishing a child for speaking their mother tongue at school and through the centrally developed, nationalistic, Eurocentric and imposed curriculum, which pushes on the learners a particular brand of knowledge and power determined by the political elite (Apple, 1982, 1993; Ross, 2000). As Conteh (2003: 18) argues, the pressure in school is to learn English as quickly as possible in order to progress economically and socially.

Minority languages are largely ignored within the school environment and young learners speaking in their mother tongue are viewed as problematic (Kenner and Hickey, 2008: 2). This, argues Cummins (1996, 2000), often results in a 'subtractive bilingualism' – and this has negative cognitive effects. 'Subtractive bilingualism' leads to the child not valuing and developing confidence in their own cultural identity and linguistic heritage, causing them to question their academic abilities. The phenomenon of bilingualism, therefore, has become entangled with questions of social class, power relations and national identity; it is not the language itself that is the issue, but rather the attitude towards minority community languages that reflects and reinforces power relations in society (Miller, 1983; Conteh, 2003).

To what extent are bilingual people also bicultural? Mills suggests that 'biculturalism, in the sense of two distinct cultures co-existing or combining, in some way, in one individual, is related to that individual's sense of identity' (2001: 389). Mills concluded that language was a 'crucial' component for maintaining the children's sense of identity of being both British and Pakistani. Although they spoke English fluently, their less-proficient mother tongue allowed them to maintain their important bond with their families, religion and communities. The English language and the mother tongue allowed them to enter two different worlds, bilingual and bicultural, and thus created multiple identities. Mills found that the children accepted the identities of both British and Pakistani with 'equanimity' (2001: 383). Language played a significant part in 'managing [their] identities'.

Some of my participants were embroiled in the tension between language, culture and identity. For Sanjida, the Bengali language is an important part of the Bangladeshi culture and is intrinsically linked to the question of identity. Both she and her parents recognize the importance of the preservation and maintenance of the Bengali language:

> I must get into the habit of speaking Bengali especially at home. If me, my brothers, sisters, cousins and Bengali friends stop speaking Bengali then the language will die. Our children will not speak Bengali and our language is important for preserving our culture.

This narrative must be viewed within the context that Sanjida's mother is a Bengali teacher at an after-school club and her father has close connections to Bangladesh. What Sanjida said is relevant to the debate about the relationship between language and identity. She is making a direct link between the Bengali language and her personal and cultural identity. She feels that her language is under threat because it is not being spoken enough, so she feels the need to maintain the language and 'pass it down into the future'. Crucially, she has a clear understanding of the relationship between language and identity, and for her, language, culture, identity and heritage are mutually interdependent. Although Sanjida was born in Britain, she saw her language affiliation in terms of belonging to her country of origin, to Bangladesh.

Sanjida was also influenced by her prescribed Bangladeshi gender role that emphasizes marriage, family and the preservation of culture (Aston *et al.*, 2007). Accordingly, she felt the need to maintain and 'pass down' her cultural language. And although she speaks both English and Bengali at home, her language choice is guided and influenced by her parents' policy of 'speak Bangla only' at home. This form of 'linguistic parenting' (Mills, 2001: 386) is a deliberate strategy adopted by many second-generation immigrant parents around the world who try desperately to preserve the mother tongue and to mould the personal identities of their children (Dosanjh and Ghuman, 1996; De Houwer, 1998). Because her parents constantly say to Sanjida and her siblings, 'You're Bengali, why are you talking to us in English?', Sanjida is essentially being asked to make a language choice and therefore a choice of identity. She is being reminded that she is not English but a Bangladeshi and that her mother tongue is important in preserving her sense of identity. While Akbar put more emphasis on English and his Arabic Islamic identity as a marker for 'progress' and 'spirituality', he echoes Sanjida's thoughts when he suggests that the Bengali language is a 'part of our heritage ... it's a part of who we are'.

Biculturalism is a complicated concept. Having access to two different languages, whether by choice or social coercion, does not mean that you have access to two different worlds. The experiences of all my participants, and of myself, add to the argument that being bilingual does not mean that we are bicultural. These complex entities are not 'necessarily coextensive' (Grosjean, 1982: 157). While the third-generation Pakistanis in Mills's (2001) study accepted both English and the mother tongue with equanimity, this is not to suggest that the two languages can merge to forge a single multicultural identity. Crucially, you are either Pakistani or British. When you are presented with language choices, argues Mills, you are also choosing an identity. In contemporary multicultural society, people are judged, defined, included and excluded by a multitude of factors. Despite linguistic commonalities, class status, skin colour, language, gender, religious affiliation and sexuality remain barriers that prohibit full societal participation and set Bangladeshi people apart from others.

What our bilingualism allows us to do is to 'have access to experiences in different communities and also acquire features of different cultures in various combinations' (Mills, 2001: 389). This leaves our sense of identity in a state of flux. Bilingualism allows us a window into another world and culture. Whether you understand that culture or are accepted or invited into it remains a complex journey. Understanding another language and being able to speak it enables you to communicate and maybe understand some of the nuances. But our self-identity is based more on heritage, experience, memory and what others define us by. We socially construct ourselves and become self-aware through dialogue, discourse and representation (Bakhtin, 1981; Burr, 2003).

English as a language of power

The importance of using English as a language within home, schooling, community and social environment was a recurring theme for the participants. Mills (2001) argues that language choice informs choices of identity and, as Grosjean (1982: 127) suggests, 'in the end, language attitude is always one of the major factors in accounting for which languages are learned, which are used, and which are preferred by bilinguals'. Most of the participants held very positive attitudes towards English. Zeyba told me:

> I speak English all the time. I was born here, my friends speak English, my sisters all speak to me in English. Even my dad speaks to me in English. I find Bengali difficult to understand and speak. English is natural for me.

Akbar says, 'If I can explain something better in Bengali, then I will speak Bengali. If I can explain something better in English, then I will speak English.' Although English has practical communication implications for him, it becomes apparent in the conversations that he equates English with 'modernity', 'progress' and also as 'helpful' towards his ambition of becoming a successful businessman. Akbar is driven and ambitious and equates materialism with success. He views Bangladesh as a place to go on 'holiday' and would only contemplate living there if the country 'develops'. Akbar chooses to speak English at home with his family and adopts a form of Banglish with his friends. As it is for Zeyba, the English language is 'natural' for Akbar.

Similarly, Azad puts higher value on English than Bengali and equates it with a successful career in education and accounting. Confirming what many language theorists (e.g. Skutnabb-Kangas *et al.*, 2006: 4) have termed the 'economic, social and political returns [of English] that are at present stacked against most mother tongues in the world', Azad ridicules the backward and impractical nature of the Bengali language, saying, 'You tell me, what relevance will Bengali have for my career?' Taiba also equates English with progress and modernity: 'We need to speak English as we are modernizing and want to fit in.'

Central to my understanding of the theoretical reasons as to why the English language is held in such high esteem by so many people from all over the world is my interpretation of Alastair Pennycook's (1994, 1998) examination of the role of English as a international language, and Pierre Bourdieu's (1991) analysis of symbolic power associated with certain languages.

English as an international language gives access to many privileges – a better education, better job prospects, better life opportunities, more opportunity to travel, a universal medium for communicating with others, to engage in debate, listen to and interact with print and digital media, access to the internet … the list goes on. English is the main language of international newspapers, airports, international business, science and medicine, academic conferences, sports, advertising, and popular culture (music and media), and the use of the language by number of people and in prominence is growing. English as a global language is likely to reach a peak of around two billion in the next ten to fifteen years (Graddol, 2006: 14). Symbolically, English promises access to an ideal life for those wanting material success based on modernity and progress, as highlighted in some of the narratives above.

Pennycook's (1994) examination of the complex interplay between English as a 'gatekeeper' to higher social and economic positions (Tollefson, 1989; 1995) and as an international language of media and commerce reveals a convincing argument that English as an international language is neither neutral, natural nor beneficial. Taking a critical look at the spread of the English language across the globe, Pennycook (1994) argues that placards written in 'English' to support a televised demonstration by 'Chinese' students in China over political change is more potent because it has mass universal appeal. So English is a political language as well as a language of power and commerce. This is why the new states emerging from Eastern Europe and Central Asia during the 1990s adopted English as their second official language and modelled themselves on their European and North American counterparts in terms of tourism, banking, commerce, industry and English-language teaching. It was their attempt at modernizing and connecting with the outside world.

Pennycook (1994) argues that English is widespread across the globe because it enables people to access positions of material and social success. This is a view that Azad, Zeyba, Taiba and Akbar buy into. The theory of language as a form of symbolic power was developed by the French political scientist, Pierre Bourdieu (1991), in response to the ideas of one of the forefathers of sociological thought, August Comte. Comte suggested that language was an entity for all to use. Bourdieu disagreed, arguing that two types of languages exist in most societies: the 'official' ('legitimate') language, speakers of which include the privileged elite, and the 'unofficial' language. He said that the legitimate language is usually the official language of a society (e.g. English in the UK) and is seen as a symbol of national unity giving people the 'linguistic capital' to progress and survive in the employment and educational market. This linguistic capital became part of what Bourdieu called the 'cultural and social capital' that helped define membership of, or exclusion from, certain sections of society. Bourdieu argued that all other linguistic practices and dialects were measured against the mainstream official language, with the result that other languages were defined negatively. This 'symbolic violence' towards other languages led to a form of intimidation that caused people in possession of a community or other language to devalue that language because of the symbolic responses they received from others when they spoke it. This pattern of viewing English as the official language within the UK, the symbolic power associated with it and the subsequent devaluation of Bengali as a result of the symbolic violence perpetrated on it mirrors the linguistic journeys of some of my participants, especially Akbar, Taiba, Zeyba and Azad.

The spread of English as a global language of power and prestige also has practical implications. Human interaction and communication has expanded as a result of globalization (Baylis and Smith, 2001), rising global tourism, the internet revolution (Aronson, 2001), growth of world political organizations and geographical unions between countries, increased influence of non-government organizations and the explosion of social networking sites such as Facebook, Twitter and WhatsApp – all making a universal language of communication more necessary. The English language is everywhere. As Pennycook (1994: 5) observes, 'English and English language teaching seem ubiquitous in the world, playing a role everywhere from large scale global politics to the intricacies of people's lives.'

Pennycook contests that the proliferation of the English language across the globe is bound up with notions of strategy, profit, exploitation and power. Phillipson (1992) has called this a form of 'linguistic imperialism'. Pennycook further argues that there is a cynicism behind the growth of English as an international language. Adopting a critical view towards the characterization of English by Platt *et al.* (1983) and Kachru (1992) as a neutral, natural and beneficial language, Pennycook (1994: 13) highlights some obvious problems with English as an international language:

> ...there are [detrimental] cultural and political effects of the
> spread of English: its widespread use threatens other languages;
> it has become the language of power and prestige in many
> countries, thus acting as a crucial gatekeeper to social and
> economic progress; its use in particular domains, especially
> professional, may exacerbate different power relationships and
> may render these domains more inaccessible to many people;
> its position in the world gives it a role also as an international
> gatekeeper, regulating the international flow of people; it is
> closely linked to national and increasingly non-national forms of
> culture and knowledge that are dominant in the world; and it is
> also bound up with aspects of global relations, such as the spread
> of capitalism, development aid and the dominance particularly of
> North American media.

Embedded within a historical context of British colonialism and American imperialist penetration, there is no denying that English as a language wields international economic, social, cultural and symbolic power. The findings of Graddol's (2006) study, however, highlight some of the limitations of Pennycook's argument. In his illuminating study of the decline of English as an international language, Graddol argues that there are signs that the global predominance of the language may fade within the foreseeable future. Complex international economic, technological and cultural changes, he argues, have started to diminish the leading position of English as the language of the world market and weaken British interests that enjoy advantage from the breadth of English usage. One of Graddol's conclusions is that, in the modern globalized world, monoglot English graduates face a bleak economic future when qualified multilingual young people from other countries are proving to have a competitive advantage over them in global companies and organizations that increasingly cater for a new market.

Yet, while many countries are introducing English into their primary education curriculum, British students do not appear to be gaining greater fluency in other languages. This does not necessarily affect the symbolic power of the English language but it does highlight Britain's disadvantage when fluency in a range of languages – notably Spanish, Arabic, Mandarin, Japanese and German – is required in order to compete in a global economy. Hindi will also become important as India undergoes rapid economic expansion and the status of English declines there. These are not minority languages but reflect actual and symbolic power status, especially in the commercial world. For example, the rise of oil prices and the ongoing political instability in the Middle East has made Arabic an important economic and political language.

Clearly, level of skill with the standard form of English language makes you part of a prestigious club or excludes you from it. That skill level opens up or excludes you from further education, the decision-making and power/political process, employment prospects, better life chances and social and political positions. This is the line of thinking of Akbar and Azad as they seek to do well in the British education system and become successful. They feel that Bengali education has held them back. Azad's constant mocking of the Bengali alphabet ('*ko, kho, go, gho…*') and his disdain for Bengali culture typify the orientalist construction of Bengali as backward: 'Bengali people are so backwards and stagnant. I really do not like the Bengali culture and the language. Tell me why do I need to speak Bengali? What relevance does it hold?'

Although Akbar is proud of his Islamic background, he still values a conventional English education over his Arabic and Bengali education, as a marker for 'progress' and essential if he is to 'live in this society'. It reveals the psychological legacy left by British colonialism (Pennycook, 1998). Furthermore, Akbar wants to run his own business in the future and move to central London. He is aspiring to become part of the educated and economic elite and sees his English education as vital.

A complicated thought process is evident. Both Akbar and, to a lesser extent, Azad understand the importance of the Bengali language as a marker of their identity. As Akbar states, 'Being Bangladeshi is important to me as it shapes my identity and how I am, my attitude and everything.' Yet they question the practical relevance of this language in their everyday lives. They favour English education and the English language as a 'symbol' of power, modernity and progress (Bourdieu, 1991). They and Taiba are conforming to Pennycook's claim that the prominence of English as a 'gatekeeper' is both giving such aspiring youths access to certain positions of social and economic esteem while at the same time threatening their heritage languages. Akbar's question, 'Why do they [his future children] need to learn the language of Bengali?' illustrates such a threat.

Language cannot be 'divorce[d]' from its 'ideological impletion' (Volosinov, 1973: 71). The negative values attached to Bengali as opposed to Arabic and English are a significant reason why many of my participants chose to speak certain languages over others. Languages are generally arranged in a hierarchy, one carrying prestige and power over another that is considered peripheral and inferior. The role of Arabic and Islam as new forms of linguistic and political identity is discussed below. Everyday conversational Arabic has become entwined with a language of resistance and 'recognition' (Taylor, 1994).

An alternative source of power, identity and meaning

The remainder of this chapter discusses the growth of Arabic as an alternative language of power and meaning in the eyes of some participants. Whereas English was practically and commercially relevant to Taiba and Zeyba, a tool for them to 'moderniz[e]', 'fit in' and 'secure a good future', Arabic is steeped in ideology. It provides linguistic membership to a global 'imagined' (Anderson, 1983) Islamic community that has a rich history of 1,400 years (Saeed *et al.*, 1999).

Importantly, the Arabic that is widely used and learned is not the ancient classical Qu'ranic Arabic. Qu'ranic Arabic is poetic and rhythmic and differs from the everyday modern standard Arabic spoken by millions of people from the Middle East and beyond. Qu'ranic Arabic is still taught to many young Bangladeshis in madrasas and in after-school classes in Tower Hamlets, and thus has a theological purpose. Young people mainly memorize verses of the Qu'ran without understanding their meaning. Many experts on Islam, however, have suggested that in order to understand and appreciate the true meaning of the Qu'ran, one must be able to read and understand the text and the many books written about the meaning of the Qu'ran in Arabic (Huda, 2015; Khan, n.d.). People who learn modern Arabic are more likely to be able to interpret and understand the ancient scripture of the Qu'ran. This is one of the key reasons for the growth in Arabic language learning (Khan, 2010).

Although there is a growing trend among many young Bangladeshis to learn modern standard Arabic (Khan, 2008), in practice they rarely use it as a form of in-depth communication. English or 'Banglish' are still the languages generally used. Arabic is thus an 'imagined' (Anderson, 1983) rather than an actual linguistic community. Colloquial and everyday conversational Arabic, however, is commonly used in East London. Many young people are increasingly using ad hoc colloquial Arabic phrases to refer to and greet each other, such as *salaam alaikum* (hello, peace be upon you), *kyaf a haal* (how are you?), *aaki* (brother), *ukthi* (sister), *walahi* (I swear) and *jazakallah* (thank you). I see this as reflecting the growing importance of Islam in their lives. Furthermore, four out of the six participants (Sanjida, Akbar, Taiba and Zeyba) greeted and said farewell to me in Arabic, and Saeed used Arabic phrases throughout our conversations. Many do not even understand the meaning of some phrases but use them nonetheless because people around them do. They are caught up in a youth 'street' subculture of

'Arabic slang which is slowly replacing other terms of endearment such as "alright mate", "geeza" and "dude"' (Khan, 2010). It appears that the wide usage of English mixed with conversational slang Arabic in Tower Hamlets performs a dual function. It symbolizes a resistance towards a 'backward', distant and 'traditional' Bengali language and culture (Kibria, 2006), and it provides a linguistic base for the development of British Islam.

Evidence points to the growth of modern Arabic. Graddol (2006) notes that the fastest-growing global languages are Arabic and Chinese and that both languages have a particularly youthful demographic. Also, Arabic as a GCSE and A Level subject is increasing in the UK and the Islamic studies degree is becoming more prominent. Data from the National Centre for Languages (CILT) indicates that, between 2000 and 2009, the national entries for the JCQ (Joint Council for Qualifications) GCSE in Arabic rose from 1,318 to 3,130 (+137 per cent). During the same period, however, there was a decrease in entries for the JCQ GCSE in Bengali. from 2,124 to 1,407 (–37 per cent) (CILT, 2010). These statistics support my view that the relevance and general use of Bengali is diminishing.

Local anecdotal evidence confirms my observation of an emerging linguistic British Islam. The deputy director of the London Muslim Centre, Shaynul Khan (2014), who has an expert overview of the growth of Islam in East London, notes the following:

- There are increasing numbers of young Bangladeshis who are deviating from using Bangladeshi names and changing their own or their children's names into more Arabized Islamic names such as Hamza, Usama, Mohammed, Mariam.
- Islamic bookshops, such as the Blackstone bookstore outside the East London Mosque in Whitechapel Road, have become ubiquitous in the streets of East London.
- More young women are wearing the hijab and jilbab, both as a symbol of spirituality and a fashion movement, and for social acceptance (BBC News, 2008; Lewis, 2013).
- After-school madrasas, Islamic schools and Saturday Arabic classes have become oversubscribed, to the detriment of the Bengali language. For example, the waiting list for enrolment at the East London Academy is approximately one year.
- Increasing numbers of professional people are enrolling in Arabic evening classes at London universities such as Birkbeck and SOAS. The language centre at SOAS has more than a thousand registrations on its various Arabic language courses each year (SOAS, n.d.).

- There is an increasing trend for young married couples to spend one or two years in countries such as Syria (pre-2011) and Egypt to study Arabic and the Qu'ran.
- Broadly speaking, mosque attendance during Friday prayers and Ramadan observance has increased in recent years.

Thus we see a growing local, national and international trend for Islam as a 'new' source of sociopolitical identity for many people (Kibria, 2006). This chimes with globalization trends (Henzell-Thomas, 2002).

Although my analysis of Arabic as a new language of protest, power and meaning has been fuelled by my conversations with the participants, it stems from a heated discussion with one of my cousins in 2004 over the role of the Bengali language for our sense of identity. He suggested that:

> Islam teaches us to read the words of God as revealed to us by the Prophet Mohammed, peace be upon him. It then tells us to learn the language of the country that we are living in (English) and then if the child has time and energy during the week, he/she should learn his/her mother tongue. We are Muslims first, British second, and Bengali third.

Clearly, he had a hierarchy (Alladina and Edwards, 1991) in terms of the importance of language to him. And he has tried to fuse his religious obligations to the divine with his sense of British citizenship. His Bangladeshi ethnic identity was non-existent. When I asked him how his children were going to communicate with their grandparents, who only spoke Bengali, he was hesitant and unclear. His views were echoed by some of the participants whose sense of identity was rooted within a religious arena:

> *Inshallah* (God willing), I would like to go to Egypt to study Arabic after university.
>
> (Akbar)

> I would love to go to Arabic classes and learn the language but I hate classrooms.
>
> (Saeed)

> I go to Arabic classes four times per week. The classes are boring and the *mudarris* (teacher) is very strict but I understand the importance behind the Arabic language.
>
> (Zeyba)

> Islam and Arabic education is more important to me than Bengali.
> I don't know why.
>
> (Azad)

Taiba reiterated the importance of Islam in her life:

> ...my religion [Islam] is very important to me. It guides me and
> is a vital part of my identity as a Muslim. It makes a distinction
> between me and others. I would like to practise my faith better
> ... For example, wear the headscarf all the time, pray and learn
> Arabic. *Inshallah*, in time, I will.

These comments highlight three interrelated modes of thinking. Firstly, some, like my cousin, are adopting a hierarchical thought process, placing their Islamic identity above their cultural background and language. By placing more emphasis on their global religious affiliations, they are at the same time involving themselves in a process of resisting their Bangladeshi cultural identities. In his study of young Bangladeshis in the UK and USA, Kibria (2006) argues that the 'weak' Bangladeshi public identity resisted by many younger generation Bangladeshi Muslim youth stands as a point of contradistinction for their own modern 'new' Islamic identity. Second, the combining of English with Arabic colloquialisms was evident, and arguably this is like 'Banglish', a form of 'Arabinglish'. Third, for some, such as Sanjida, while Islam remained an important identity marker, the Bengali language was 'central' to her sense of Bangladeshi identity. Like the third-generation Pakistanis in Mills's study (2001: 400), being Bangladeshi and speaking Bengali was an 'emotive and emotional tie' for some of the participants in my study, and operates more symbolically than practically, helping to maintain a sense of their origins, their heritage, their affiliation with and belonging to a country they might never even have visited.

The notion of language choice is confusing, complex and often contradictory. Some of the participants are engaged in an internal struggle in that being Bangladeshi is 'important' to them yet, at the same time, they don't quite understand or fit into the cultural mosaic of what it means to be Bangladeshi. This was illustrated in Saeed's dilemma in reconciling his Bangladeshi heritage with his British-born Westernized cultural lifestyle:

> I know that the Bengali language is important for my culture,
> but [pause], but I just don't know how and why. I mean, I am
> Bangladeshi and I am not at the same time, if you know what I
> mean? [pause] It's really confusing.

Saeed is involved in what Bhabha (1994) describes as 'past–present' thought process: trying to give meaning to his present by examining his past. This process of syncretism is not without pain and trauma, especially when the values of home and family life have to be reconciled with those of society (Watson, 1977). It seems that some remain on the 'margin of two cultures and two societies which never completely interpenetrat[e]' (Park, 1928: 892; Stonequist, 1935). Consequently, they have developed 'bicultural identities', which perform 'functional response(s)' to their identity predicament – being Bengali at home, Muslim on the streets and local community, and English at school and in the workplace (Dosanjh and Ghuman, 1996: 24).

Furthermore, the emerging British-Islamic identity, which has a linguistic base and a religious infrastructure, is an identity of rebellion and rejection. A rejection of authority, of their parents' backward beliefs and a rejection of mainstream Western values. It is their 'difference' – in dress code, language, skin colour, culture, rituals – that resists the mainstream and challenges the status quo (Castles and Miller, 1993; Gupta, 2009). Their usage of Arabic slang, the prominence of the hijab, the growth of the beard are among the examples of differences that are 'embedded in social, economic and political struggles' (Pennycook, 1994: 15; Kamrava, 2006). There is also the issue of poverty. A report by the Joseph Rowntree Foundation (2007b) found that 70 per cent of Bangladeshi children were growing up in poverty in Britain and Bangladeshis are ranked high in terms of poor housing, low income and unemployment (Babb *et al.*, 2006: 80). All this indicates that a British-Islamic linguistic identity is a form of political opposition to their voiceless and powerless position in society. Embracing Islam and the Arabic language are also status symbols and therefore many are trying to achieve a prestigious Islamic social class (Mills, 2001).

Conclusion

Language played an important role in the complex and multifaceted identities of my participants. All six lived in 'simultaneous' (Kenner, 2004) English, Bengali and Arabic linguistic worlds. Some undertook painful linguistic journeys that led to much confusion and contradiction. All except Azad understood the importance of Bengali as a source of cultural identity. However, the practicality and necessity to learn and maintain Bengali for future generations in an English-speaking British world caused some confusion. Akbar, Azad, Zeyba and Taiba saw their mother tongue as impractical and English as the language of progress, commerce and modernity. Sanjida was the one most deeply troubled by the inability of third-generation Bangladeshis to understand the importance of mother-tongue maintenance as a source of Bangladeshi cultural identity. Akbar made a similar correlation. Saeed viewed Bengali from a practical point of view and spoke it with his parents because they could not speak English.

All six participants, however, were united in subscribing to the emerging British-Islamic identity, which placed importance on the languages of English and Arabic. While English provided a gateway to commerce and a 'good future' (Zeyba) for some, others were committed to learning Arabic in pursuit of ideological meaning and belonging. The language of Bengali will become a victim of symbolic violence (Bourdieu, 1991) as it becomes devalued and redundant in the modern British-Islamic world where English twinned with Arabic will wield the symbolic and linguistic power.

Before I move on to examine the components of this British-Islamic culture and identity, I set out to explain why Bangladeshis in East London continue to be excluded, alienated and marginalized from the wider political process. Their powerlessness and marginalization has caused third-generation Bangladeshis to join a new and vibrant British Islam. They are responding to the dilemma of not belonging fully to either a culturally rooted Bangladeshi community or an ethnically white mainstream British nation and society. It is my contention that racism in its many guises – overt, subtle, institutional, symbolic, cultural – lies at the core of the feelings of alienation, second-class citizenship and exclusion from mainstream society uncovered in my study. The following chapter examines the important role of race and racism in contributing to a multifaceted and complex new British-Islamic identity.

Chapter 5

A question of race: Exclusion and 'second-class citizenship'[1]

Introduction

> THE problem of the twentieth century is the problem of the color-line, – the relation of the darker to the lighter races of men in Asia and Africa, in America and the islands of the sea.
>
> (Du Bois, 1995 [1903]: 54)

> …the capacity to live with difference is, in my view, the coming question of the twenty-first century.
>
> (Hall, 1993b: 361)

> Britain is now two entirely different worlds, and the world you inherit is determined by the colour of your skin.
>
> (Rushdie, 1982: 418)

W.E.B. Du Bois's depressing prophecy about the racial antagonism in the twentieth century was prescient. The Holocaust in Nazi Germany, racial segregation in the southern states of the US and the Apartheid system in South Africa were examples of state-controlled systems of governance based on racial discrimination against people of colour or ethnic-minority origin. Stuart Hall's constructive contribution to Du Bois's prophecy nearly a hundred years later makes the question of 'difference' a twenty-first-century issue too. Although both Du Bois and Hall are writing about discrimination based upon race, Hall departs from the 'colour-line' debate and edges towards the discourse of difference and culture.

The experiences of my participants suggest that the problem of the 'colour line' – or as Sanjida calls it, 'the skin-colour issue' – and 'socially structured racial inequality and disadvantage [still] persist' in the twenty-first century (Bulmer and Solomos, 1999: 3). The 'colour of your skin' (Rushdie, 1982: 418) remains an 'inescapable social marker' (Ballard, 1994: 2–3) and sets Bangladeshi people apart from non-Bangladeshis:

A question of race: Exclusion and 'second-class citizenship'

> Never in a million years will we be ever accepted as British,
> English, European or whatever else … it is because we are
> different, because we are brown, because we are Muslims,
> because we are Bangladeshi, because we are not white.
>
> (Taiba)

Questions of race, racism and ethnicity have dominated social and political debates to such an extent that it has challenged class (Lee and Turner, 1996; Pakulsi and Waters, 1996) and other forms of social inequality such as language, gender, religion, sexuality, age and disability as being the main barrier to societal participation (Goldberg, 1990), although there is an acknowledged relationship between the components of social inequality.

Like their parents and grandparents, my participants have not benefited from full citizenship in the British society into which they were born and resent their position of exclusion and alienation, as illustrated in Taiba's bleak analysis above. Arguably, they are halfway through Gordon's (1964) 'seven stages of assimilation': prejudice, discrimination and power struggles still exist. It is noted, however, that skin colour and difference does not exclude all people of minority origin from mainstream societal participation. There are numerous examples of successful people from the Chinese, Indian and Arabic communities in Britain among the super rich (Luard, 2005; Sonalwar, 2014).

Racism in whatever guise, coupled with poverty and low levels of education, governs the daily social lives of many Bangladeshis and locates them within the politics of 'difference' (Castles and Miller, 1993; Gupta, 2009). This determines their marginalization, powerlessness and second-class citizenship, and thus directs their identities. My participants regularly made a distinction between themselves and a stereotypical view of the 'white man' – a person who was hostile towards non-white people and who 'drinks alcohol, eats pork and does not like Muslims' (Saeed). They were aware of themselves as a separate racial and ethnic community. Their experiences of racism have reinforced the socially constructed notions of difference and otherness and pushed them to manage their identities within the contours of ethnic, linguistic and religious affiliations.

This chapter is divided into four sections, dealing with:

- a theoretical discussion about the complexities of race and racism
- a discussion of 'new' racisms (see Barker, 1981), in particular the concept of cultural racism
- an examination of the racialized local history of East London

- a concluding discussion of the strategies of resistance against racism and an attempt to outline a future beyond racism.

Theories of race

> We became part of England and yet proudly stood outside it. But to be truly free we had to free ourselves of all bitterness and resentment, too. How was this possible when bitterness and resentment were generated afresh every day?
>
> (Kureishi, 1990)

The Jim Crow laws passed in the 1880s in the United States, which, like the apartheid era in South Africa, mandated racial segregation in all public facilities, presented visible images of racial domination and the huge social, political and economic distance that can separate black people from white. As Bulmer and Solomos (1999: 3) observe, '[in nearly all societies] almost always the white person or white group has been in a position of superiority, and the black person or group a situation of inferiority, lesser power or influence, and having to justify themselves'. W.E.B. Du Bois (1995 [1903]: 45) highlights what he calls the 'double consciousness' of black people in the US that results from this social difference between black and white people:

> Why did God make me an outcast and a stranger in mine own house? ... It is a peculiar sensation, this double-consciousness, this sense of always looking at one's self through the eyes of others, of measuring one's soul by the tape of a world that looks on in amused contempt and pity. One ever feels his twoness, – An American, a Negro; two souls, two thoughts, two un-reconciled strivings; two warring ideals in one dark body, whose dogged strength alone keeps it from being torn asunder.

Du Bois's account of double consciousness can be applied to the social position of my participants. They too feel like 'outcast[s]' and 'stranger[s]' in their 'own house'. They too measure and see themselves through the eyes of others. As Kureishi observes above, Bangladeshis are 'part of England' yet they stand 'outside' it. They are 'warring' against the tension of being Bangladeshi, Muslim and British, three 'un-reconciled strivings'. These words of Du Bois illustrate the complexity of race and racism and how the sense of duality and double consciousness are factors that also affect these Bangladeshis. This notion of feeling like 'outcast[s]' and 'stranger[s]' in Britain is real for them and is reflected in their words below.

Akbar's memories of clashes between followers of the British National Party (BNP) and Bangladeshi people in the 1990s, and his upbringing in a predominantly Bangladeshi neighbourhood, have made him separate 'white people' from 'us' (British-Muslim Bangladeshis). This is the twoness of Akbar's identity. Sanjida has experienced direct racism from 'white people' within the school playground and on the streets: 'I have had many scuffles with white girls in school and in my estate simply because they have called me a "paki".' Sanjida routinely experiences direct racism. She recalls an incident when her father was spat at by some white youths in her council estate in Bethnal Green. Her experience exemplifies the feeling of being an outcast, a stranger in her own house. Similarly, Taiba's experience is typical of growing up in a culturally diverse working-class estate in East London. She recalls being called a 'paki' on numerous occasions and replying: 'We are not pakis, we are Bengalis.' This experience of displacement and rejection was complex and painful:

> We would constantly hear things such as 'Go back to your own country, you don't belong here'. I thought [pause] Are we different to other people? Why did we come here in the first place? Where do we actually belong if we don't belong here? ... We used to be scared to come out of our own house even to go to the local shops ... 'Why can't I be white?' I used to ask my mum. I used to scrub myself hard. I used to ask my mum to bleach me. 'Why can't we be English, Mum?'

Echoing Taiba and Sanjida, Zeyba asks rhetorically, 'Where is it exactly that I am supposed to go back to?'

Saeed's opinion of the 'white man' is mainly informed through his interaction with people in authority such as teachers and policemen. He recalls overhearing one of the 'white' activity instructors call Saeed and his friends a 'bunch of monkeys' when he attended a residential in Norfolk with his youth club. It must be noted that Saeed, mainly because of his life experiences, is full of youth bravado. But he is also a victim because he grew up in an ethnically segregated estate and so holds inaccurate opinions of the British white community. He fails to distinguish between racists and the British 'white' majority who probably do not hold negative views specifically towards Bangladeshis.

Racism clearly had a role in directing the identities of the participants. Rejection and displacement have pushed them to re-evaluate their sense of belonging as their differences in clothing, skin colour, way of life – their 'ethnies' (Smith, 1986: 41) – crystallized as they became more self-aware when exposed to the durability and the ubiquitous presence of the 'white man'. In terms of population statistics, being of white Anglo-Saxon origin still constitutes the majority in Tower Hamlets (45.2 per cent) and throughout England and Wales it is 86 per cent (ONS, 2012b).

The theory of race is constantly evolving. Historical discussions of race as a concept are steeped in a colonial and imperial history that maintains that differences based on biology, language, culture, place of origin, membership of an ethnic group and physicality determine a person's morality, intellect and pure culture. Contemporary forms of racism cannot be divorced from this historical concept of racism. There can be no doubt that the enslavement of millions of people of African origin and the subsequent transatlantic slave trade have left a huge social and psychological imprint that still strongly affects black–white relations in today's racialized world. The system of bondage, servitude and subordination of black slaves by white masters did not affect only people from Africa. Tinker (1974) has highlighted the negative impact of indentured servitude on the Indians from South Asia who were exported to countries such as Fiji, Mauritius and Trinidad.

Power relations of domination by the white Europeans in colonial and imperial settings in Asia and Africa during the nineteenth and twentieth centuries have also left their mark (Fredrickson, 1981). Within the British context, many South Asians were brought over to the UK and employed as servants and *ayahs* (nannies) by rich aristocrats during the eighteenth century. These historical movements affirmed the racist ideology of the supremacy of whites. Africans and Asians were somewhat inferior and subordinate – an accessory, a 'status symbol' for the rich and powerful (Visram, 1993: 169). Although strongly discredited by modern genetic research (Fryer, 1988: 61), eighteenth-century European scientific notions of race essentialized 'races' as each embodying a 'package of fixed physical and mental traits whose permanence could only be eroded by mixture with other stocks' (Biddiss, 1979: 11). The whiter you were, the purer you were. Skin colour and biology determined the socially ranked positions of superiority and inferiority (Horsman, 1981).

Racist ideas can be used as powerful ideological tools to promote the economic and political interests of particular social groups. For example, the apparent benevolence of the notion of the 'white man's burden' (Jordan, 1974; MacKenzie, 1984, 1986; Easterly, 2007) in civilizing the world disguised the grasping of material and financial gain for the British Empire, especially for its rich and powerful (Lorimer, 1978). The process of economic expansion and capitalist development went hand in hand with the development of racist ideology (Williams, 1944; Jordan, 1968). The racialization of people around the world was intertwined with Europe's economic and social exploitation of Asia and Africa.

European colonialism, in particular, contributed to the development of European images of Africans and 'other' people within an inferior and subordinate framework (Jordan, 1968; Cox, 1970 [1948]; Lorimer, 1978; Said, 1979; Wolf, 1982). It is noteworthy that not all Europeans who established direct contact with the people from Africa, the Americas, Asia and Oceania viewed them as inferior and barbaric. For example, one of the most influential writers of the French Renaissance, Michel de Montaigne ([1580] quoted in Payne and Hunter, 2003: 473–80) began a long tradition of using what he called the 'natural' and humane habits and lifestyles of non-European people to critique his own culture, romanticizing in the process the oxymoronic concept of the 'noble savage'.

However, most contacts between non-Europeans and Europeans were based on unequal systems of relations, trade and power. By coming into contact with people who ate, dressed and lived differently, the colonial powers helped shape notions of the 'other' (Said, 1979). The complex political, psychological and historical concept of 'othering' has been analysed by prominent theorists, among them Mannoni (1964), Fanon (1967) and Said (1979). It entails a process whereby a body of people are constructed and reduced to be 'less than what they are' (Holiday *et al.*, 2004; Ameli and Merali, 2006: 33).

The othering of people of Africa and Asia in particular played a central role in constructing the colonial discourse that prevailed in British society (Pratt, 1992; Parry, 1998). Gilman (1991: 20) notes how the words 'black people' and 'primitive' became synonymous (Parker *et al.*, 1992). The rhetoric of colonizer vs colonized, powerful vs powerless, civilized vs uncivilized, modern vs backwards, educator vs educated, among other polarizations, helped reshape, redefine and institutionalize class, gender and race relations between the white colonial people and the people from the 'dark continents' of Africa and Asia (Mudimbe, 1994). Subsequently, racist ideas became grounded in dominant and hegemonic ideology (Gramsci, 1973), normalizing a paternal and racialized attitude towards non-Europeans. The discourse of otherness still persists in today's world, constructing British-born third-generation Bangladeshis as 'different' and un-British.

The legacy of colonialism, decolonization and the immigration patterns that followed has generated visible multiracial and polyethnic communities across Europe (Ballard, 1994). The resulting antagonism and conflict between indigenous and newly arrived immigrant communities has given rise to a body of scholarly thought that seeks to understand why racism permeates contemporary society. American sociologist Robert Park takes a social-psychological approach, arguing that the development of racial categories is related to individual needs, such as the need for recognition, esteem and identity. 'Race consciousness' enforces 'social distances' and contributes to an us/them construction (Park, 1950: 81). The 'race relations problematic' was discussed further by Michael Banton in his book *Race Relations* in 1967. John Rex (1983 [1970]) took a structuralist perspective, arguing that race relations are essentially 'social relations' that are encouraged by the structural conditions existing in predominantly urban centres: conflict over scarce resources, harsh class exploitation, inter-group distinctions and rivalry, differential access to power and prestige, cultural diversity and lack of group interaction and the position of migrant labour as an underclass fulfilling stigmatized roles in urban centres. It is these structural conditions in modern society that help 'produce a racially structured social reality' (Back and Solomos, 2000: 5).

Miles's (1984; 1989) Marxist approach diverges from Banton and Rex. Although criticized for its class determinism, Miles argues that it is not the structural conditions of modern society that provoke racist ideology; human beings who are in positions of power have constructed a theory of race that ultimately benefits them. Race is thus a human and political construct that contributes to the reproduction of class relations based on capital accumulation and class exploitation. Race is an ideology that feeds regulatory power within society – it is an ideological effect, a mask that conceals the reality of economic relationships (Miles, 1984). Capitalism in itself is colourless and may just be incidental to racial dominance. It is not always the case that the bourgeoisie will be white and powerful and the proletariat will be powerless and black, as the current emergence of India and China as global economic powers presages. Miles concludes that the real issues of class consciousness shaped by economic relations are hidden within the racialization/race-relations discourse. And he argues that 'the facts of biological differentiation are secondary to the meanings that are attributed to them' (Miles, 1989: 70). This argument is significant for the present book. Certain social meanings are attributed to certain groups on the basis of biology and visible difference.

A cultural racism

Physical or biological differences are irrelevant to social scientists. Race relations are shaped by social factors and social scientists are interested in the social meanings of race (Banton, 1979). Both Banton (1979) and Miles (1982) use the term 'racialization' to describe the way people frame the social world in racial terms. People construct racial categories that they then impose on themselves and other groups, thus feeding racial stereotypes. They use physical appearance and cultural practices to mark out social boundaries between groups. Racism emerges from racialization: it is an ideology of racial domination of one group over another, rooted in the belief that a designated racial group is biologically or culturally inferior. This rationalizes the treatment of the other group as inferior and affects their social position in society (Wilson, 1973). The politics of this racism is at the heart of the third-generation Bangladeshis' experience of displacement, rejection and 'outgroup' status (Hagendoorm, 1993).

The Centre for Contemporary Cultural Studies (CCCS) has enhanced our understanding of race and racialization. Concerned with the important sociological questions of power and inequality in society, the CCCS contested that race as a concept was not static. It can be a vehicle for social and political action and it can contribute to a sense of community and solidarity. The meaning of race is contested and the political meaning of 'black' differs among people. One key thinker associated with the CCCS, Paul Gilroy (1987), suggested that the politics of race can be used as a vehicle for social action, as a political colour of opposition. In this respect, Gilroy is critical of Miles's (1989) class reductionism on grounds that racial identities and movements are social, political and powerful and should remain relatively independent from class relations, although he does acknowledge that there is a 'separate yet connected' logic between class and race (see also Hall, 1980: 34).

If race is a contested arena for people of minority backgrounds and means different things to different people, if race mobilizes people and denotes a sense of community and solidarity and if race can be a vehicle for social and political action and opposition, then the same principles can be applied to the religion of Islam for third-generation Bangladeshis. Like race, British Islam too is an evolving set of ideas and affords power, identity and meaning to the participants, as I discuss in the next chapter.

Here, I discuss the cultural form of racism. The question of cultural production and its relationship with race, and how this in turn informs the politics of identity, is once again under debate. Cultural difference was an important identity marker for some of the participants, setting them apart from others:

> We are different to other local Chinese and white families ... er, we look different, smell different, eat different foods, have different values and habits ... It doesn't really affect us ... When you like grow up with your own culture and with so many of your own ... and then you suddenly go to a different place, its kinda weird.
>
> (Sanjida)

> We eat with our hands, watch Bollywood movies, don't drink alcohol, eat halal food ... we are different to other people.
>
> (Zeyba)

Both Sanjida and Zeyba are engaging in the politics of 'them' vs 'us' based on cultural differences (Hoque, 2004b). Taking Raymond Williams's (1961: 43) 'social' definition of culture as a starting point – 'culture is a description of a particular way of life, which expresses certain meanings and values not only in art and learning but also in institutions and ordinary behaviour' – the Bangladeshi 'way of life' is different from that of the mainstream British. The Bangladeshi way of life as a threat to the mythic British 'way of life' (Barker, 1981) is discussed further in Chapter 7. Akbar defines his cultural way of life:

> There are lots of things we do differently to white British people. Like, arranged marriages, our cultural dress, my mum eating beetlenuts ... I spoke to this American guy the other day on instant messenger and he just could not understand why I am happy for my mum to arrange my marriage. To me, it's normal.

Claiming culture as a marker of difference and as a separate way of life connects closely with how racism is conceptualized, resulting in an explanatory tool of 'cultural racism' (Fanon, 1967; Goldberg, 1993). Cultural racism – the cultural attitudes, beliefs and ideologies that are based on often mistaken notions about 'racial' groups (Richardson and Lambert, 1985) – is arguably the most common form of racism today. It is a cultural form of prejudice, and prejudice relies heavily on stereotypical thinking: making sweeping generalizations that are highly selective, over-simplified and based on historical and contemporary media constructions. Such stereotypes are usually factually incorrect, exaggerated or distorted. So prejudice is problematic; it not only misinforms the prejudiced but it also misjudges those who are stereotyped.

Whiteness as a theoretical concept is intertwined with notions of 'power' and 'race privilege' (Dyer, 1993; Hill, 1997; Wiegman, 1999; Back,

2010). However, it is reductive to suggest that all white people are racist towards people of minority-ethnic origin. The equation of whiteness and racism is not coexistive. The East End of London, for example, has a rich history of white resistance to racism, and famously so with the Battle of Cable Street (1936) where white working-class people stood against Oswald Mosley's anti-Semitic fascists. The Anti Nazi League during the 1970s resisted the National Front and consisted mainly of white youth (Renton, 2006). And, conversely, some of the research participants – particularly Zeyba, Saeed, Akbar and Sanjida – are culturally racist towards the 'white man'; their opinions, too, are based on their experiences, prejudices, stereotypes and sweeping generalizations. For example, not all white people 'drink alcohol' and not all white women are sexually promiscuous, as Zeyba implies, and not all white people 'eat pork' and have a dislike for Muslims, as Saeed asserts. Similarly, not all Bangladeshis eat with their 'hands' and not all white people eat with 'knives and forks', as Sanjida suggests. I probed further:

> **AH:** You seem very angry and bitter towards what you call the 'white man'.
>
> **Saeed:** That's because they are racist. They don't like us.
>
> **AH:** What do you mean by 'us'?
>
> **Saeed:** You know, 'us' [pause] you, me, my breadwins [friends] in the next room [of the youth club]. [pause] You know, us, Bangladeshis, Muslims [pause] basically anyone who is not white.
>
> **AH:** That's a very broad statement to make. Not all 'white people' are racist. Some of my closest friends are 'white' and they are not racist. Er, they are always around my house, eating my food, respecting my culture and my parents. Not all 'white people' are racist. That's a very generalized statement to make.
>
> [pause]
>
> **Saeed:** You've obviously lived a different life to me. In my world and from my experience, the white people I know are racist.

We can see the importance of history and life experiences and that they are highly individualized, subjective and context-specific. Such experiences also shape our ideology as we react to our own histories. Note that Saeed has presented me as both an insider and an outsider. One moment I am part of the Bangladeshi, Muslim 'us' but when I questioned Saeed's claim that 'white people' are 'racist', I was distanced as somebody who has lived a 'different life' to him, as not part of his 'world'.

Racial prejudices are part of the cultural heritage of society and are transmitted across generations. People are exposed to attitudes and beliefs from an early age and the danger is then that prejudiced beliefs become part of society's norms. As Goldberg (1993: 1) argues, 'racial thinking and racist articulation have become increasingly normalised and naturalised throughout modernity' and what is considered normal is entwined with notions of whiteness. In his discussion of whiteness in film and other cultural representations, Dyer (1993) notes how whiteness is equated with normality. Hill (1997: 3) argues that whiteness should also be viewed within the context of the 'power and banality of race privilege'. Furthermore, whiteness should be contextualized within the colonial ideology of white supremacy, discussed earlier. If we accept that normalization, power and privilege is associated with whiteness, this means that the opposite is true for people who are black. Not only do people of minority background suffer from discrimination, alienation and marginalization, but in some extreme cases they can become 'invisible' (Ellison, 1965 [1952]). And the ideals associated with whiteness reinforce the superiority/inferiority dichotomy.

My participants are not biologically inferior to mainstream society; they are culturally different. Their way of life revolves around religion, dress, diet, values, rituals and symbols that are different from mainstream society and that often carry prejudices rooted in orientalist ideology. Their way of life marks them out as different and as outsiders. A cultural pathology is also involved – something inherently inferior is implied to exist in the cultural and familial background of people from minority groups. Minority groups are problematized and positioned in an unequal relationship of inferiority to the white population (Shain, 2003).

Academics today do not view racism as a monolith based on biological inferiority, but recognize that race and racism have many components and are entwined with notions of class, gender, nationhood, nationality, culture and ethnicity (hooks, 1981; Goldberg, 1993: 69–80). So we should be talking not about 'racism' but 'racisms' (Goldberg, 1993: 97–111). Despite the shift in discourse, the concept of 'difference' persists. Shain (2003) argues that often such difference is based on misconceptions that obscure the role of racism and representation in the lives of South-Asian girls and diverts attention from wider questions of social justice and equality. South-Asian men have been characterized in the media and literature as dominant, violent and controlling and South-Asian women as passive, timid, obedient and shy. Shain's study of 44 Asian girls at a Manchester school challenged the popular images of Asian women. She found that they resisted the various types of cultural stereotypes aimed towards them at school and were anything but shy and passive. Sanjida captures the post-structuralist feminist approach to race and gender:[2]

> My art teacher once asked me if my father allowed my mother to 'go out'. I laughed and replied, 'She has a job and earns more money than my dad.' You should have seen my teacher's face [laughing].

The politics of difference, accelerated by their overtly Islamic identity (discussed in the next chapter), is pushing many third-generation Bangladeshis to adopt the 'us vs them' political discourse. Central to this discourse is the idea that they are not part of the British nation; they are part of a 'different' race culturally and now members of a supposedly 'different' Islamic religion, which poses a threat to the mythic British way of life.

We are 'here to stay': Revolt and resistance – a short history of race and racism in East London

Without understanding the historical context of East London we cannot fully appreciate the importance of race and racism in the lives of Bangladeshis in East London today.

Mumford and Power (2003) examined the roles of community and family life in an in-depth study of a hundred families from the East End of London. A major part of their research examined the notion of race within multi-ethnic neighbourhoods. Some of the stories from their participants highlight the culture and attitude of racism that persisted among many East Enders, in particular the white community:

> Vast change. It's more of a multi-cultural area now. Whereas at first it was white dominated. You've got all kinds round here now.
>
> (Louise, quoted in Mumford and Power, 2003: 57)

> I don't like it. It should be mixed. When someone moves, you never see a white family come in. It's all changing to black.
>
> (Naomi, 67)

> I've got nothing against them being with coloured [friends], as long as they keep to their own with partners – blacks with blacks, whites with whites.
>
> (Sonia, 69)

> Racism is everywhere because no one wants different people to come and live in their country. They think we are a problem.
>
> (Kerim, 73)

The last quotation from Turkish immigrant Kerim echoes the experiences of my participants. Racism, feeling 'different' and being on the receiving end of the 'critical gaze' (Morrison, 1992: 90) are experienced daily:

> ...many of my teachers have labelled me as not able because they have certain expectations from people of colour.
>
> (Akbar)

> ...white people think that all Asian people are either pakis or terrorists. [pause] When an Asian man is getting battered or is dying – we don't make the news. When a white man gets battered – it makes the news. They [white people] don't give a fuck about us. We have to lie to police and say that a white boy is getting beaten up because if we say Asian they take their time in coming over.
>
> (Saeed)

> It's just the way they look at you. I cannot explain it or describe it. But it makes you feel like scum ... worthless ... different. It is horrible. I have cried many times.
>
> (Zeyba)

These feelings and attitudes are surprising in an area with such an ethnically diverse population. It is 'normal' (Panayi, 2003: 67–71) to see non-white people in London, and as the 2011 census highlighted, 54.8 per cent of the Tower Hamlets population belonged to an ethnic group other than 'white' (ONS, 2012b). However, the examples of racism from the study by Mumford and Power (2003), like the personal stories of the participants, are rooted in local history. In places like Tower Hamlets, immigrant settlers have experienced occasional hostility from the extreme elements of the established white communities, mainly because of a conflict over scarce public resources, particularly housing, education and jobs (Phillips, 1988; Bhatia, 2006).

But despite sporadic periods of fascist activity and violent resistance in the East End, Tower Hamlets is, on the whole, a good example of a multi-ethnic neighbourhood where diversity, difference and inter-group conflict and rivalry over limited resources have not resulted in far-reaching social unrest in recent history (Begum and Eade, 2005).

Two local case studies illustrate how racism experienced by the Bangladeshi community has reminded them of their difference as a separate and distinct ethnic and racial group. These examples have also galvanized them to unite and exert their Bangladeshi identity. But this is slowly being challenged by the rise of Islam as a force for social mobilization. My first case study concerns the murder of Altab Ali in 1978.

Altab Ali (1978)

Altab Ali was found murdered on the streets of Whitechapel on 4 May 1978 (Bethnal Green and Stepney Trades Council, 1978: 56; Jorda, 1978). His murder was symptomatic of the racial antagonism stirred up in the 1970s by extreme white supremacist groups such as the British National Party (BNP) and the National Front (NF). Both engaged in systematic patterns of violence against the Bangladeshis, using slogans such as 'Blacks Out' and 'White is Right' (Power, 1979). Not only were the Bangladeshis physically fighting against overt racists from the BNP and NF, but they encountered institutionalized and subtle variations of racism from the local police (Murphy, 1978; see also Bowling, 1996: 207). The Bangladeshi community's response was strong and organized. Rex (1979) called this organized resistance the 'politics of defensive confrontation'. In what became known as 'Black Monday' (Duke and Brett, 1978) the Bangladeshis teamed up with the Socialist Party and the Trade Unions and engaged in mass demonstrations and strikes (Fernandes, 1978; Sivanandan, 1981). Activist Jalal Uddin (quoted in Tower Hamlets Trade Council, 1979) from the Bangladeshi Youth Movement for Equal Rights summed up the mood of revolt and discontent in the late 1970s:

> In 1978 we found that the only way we could be effective against racial attacks and intimidation was to organise ourselves. Since the murder of Altab Ali we have taken up wider issues that affect our lives. We have now become more aware of institutionalised racism. As citizens of Tower Hamlets we see the need to be constructively involved in every aspect of the community. Increasingly we are fighting institutionalised racism in order to achieve equality, as part of our human rights in this country. We are here to stay.

Uddin's words 'We are here to stay' were not only in defiance of the extreme elements of white society but also announced to wider British society that the Bangladeshis had arrived and were a physical and also a political community that wanted a place, position and voice in society. To slogans such as 'Blacks Out', Bangladeshis would shout back, 'Come what may, we're here to stay'. Phrases such as these symbolized the shift from a passive to an active community and their assertion of a new determination to fight for their rights.

Quddus Ali (1993)

The 'new racisms' (Barker, 1981), be they classical, symbolic, aversive (Hagendoorm, 1993) or institutional, continued against the Bangladeshis in the 1980s, mobilizing the community and constantly reinforcing the notion of them vs us. Tensions between the white and Bangladeshi communities in the East End, described by the Revd Kenneth Leech (1993) from Aldgate as a 'Civil War', were heightened by the vicious attack by eight white youths on 17-year-old Bangladeshi student Quddus Ali in Stepney in 1993 (*East London Advertiser*, 1993). He was left fighting for his life. The incident again reminded the now-established Bangladeshi community of their racial difference. A friend of Quddus captured the feelings of displacement and non-belonging when he said, '[Quddus's] only mistake was that he was black' (quoted in Mackinnon, 1993: 8).

The culture of fear at the time is apparent. Studies have repeatedly shown that Bangladeshis and Somalis were the most likely victims of estate-based racially motivated violent crimes in the 1990s. Some people of minority backgrounds became 'prisoners in their own homes' (Sampson and Phillips, 1992: 9) and this was a fact of life for many Bangladeshis. Growing up in Tower Hamlets in the mid-1980s, I still remember being chased by the pit bull terrier that white boys set on us and of having to run home to escape the local white boys who ganged up on me.

Fusing the local history of racism with my own experience of feeling like a second-class citizen is useful to this study. Racism in 2015 is not the same as the physical and violent clashes of the 1970s, 1980s and 1990s, but the experience of feeling different, displaced and alienated is still a reality for third-generation Bangladeshis. As Kimber and Cooper (1991) argue, it is the continual 'threat' of harassment and violence that imbues a sense of fear even in the absence of direct racial attacks. The complex racial and ethnic identity of this community should therefore be situated within the local history of struggle. As Azad states, 'My father used to always tell me about the racism he experienced when he first came here. He was genuinely frightened for his own life and for the safety of his family. [pause] He seriously considered going back.'

Because of these historical racialized struggles, race and the politics of difference are important components in the identity of my participants. The context may have changed, but new racisms are still encountered by the third generation, mainly provoked by their religiously visible and ideological Islamic differences. Racism is still widely prevalent in British society, echoing old colonial attitudes. We see it time and time again – the Big Brother race row in 2007 involving Bollywood superstar Shilpa Shetty, Prince Harry describing an Asian member of his platoon as 'our little paki friend' or the Strictly Come Dancing 'paki' joke in 2009. Racisms, in their multiplicity of guises, are still an embedded fact of social life.

Many second- and third-generation Bangladeshis refuse to accept the sort of treatment meted out to their parents and have actively resisted, through riots and demonstrations or by seeking alternative identities – such as British Islam. If power cannot be accessed within a linguistic, ethno-racial or cultural arena, then the quest for visibility, recognition and voice is sought in religion.

Conclusion: A world beyond racism?

This chapter has located the research participants' experiences of racism within a historical, theoretical and localized framework. History – global and local – has played a major role in the racialization of the world in terms of binaries: black vs white, outsider vs insider, Bangladeshi vs British and us vs them. Central within this discourse is the notion of power, which throughout history has been with the colonial merchants, the slave owners, the violent white extremist groups of the 1970s or within the confines of institutional policing and politics. The Bangladeshis struggled to redress this imbalance of power through demonstrations in the 1970s, and now they do this through their Islamic sense of belonging based on a global sense of brotherhood and sisterhood.

Albeit in a different context, the personal stories of the participants show that the 'colour line' persists in contemporary society nearly a hundred years after Du Bois (1995 [1903]) made his prediction. The discourse, as Hall (1993a) observed, has changed from direct racism to the hostility of 'difference' of culture, religion, language and ethnicity. Feelings of alienation, rejection and second-class citizenship have characterized the sixty-year history of Bangladeshi immigration into Britain. Bangladeshis continue to struggle with regards to employment, health, income and housing, so the bleak prospect facing the Bangladeshi community appears to be of poverty and sociopolitical marginalization for the foreseeable future.

However, the new resolve found in the religion of Islam by many third-generation Bangladeshis, and the construction of hybrid identities that seek to accommodate notions of what it means to be 'British, Bangladeshi and Muslim' (Zeyba), is offering them a more positive prospect. Although the politics of difference will be bolstered by the intensification of the global war on terror, we see the third generation finding a sense of power, belonging and acceptance in the religion of Islam as they resist racism and reject mainstream white and alien Bangladeshi cultural values. The role of religion in the development of a British-Islamic identity is the subject of the next chapter.

Notes

[1] The term 'second-class citizenship' is borrowed from an interview I had with a third-generation Bangladeshi as part of the research for a BBC radio documentary in 2004.

[2] For a more comprehensive discussion on the limitations of mainstream feminism in relation to the question of race, see hooks (1981).

Chapter 6

The construction of a British-Islamic identity

Introduction

> I am proud to be a Muslim. Let them call me a terrorist. I don't care.
>
> (Saeed)

This chapter examines the importance of Islam in the life of each participant and situates their stories within the broader national and international geopolitics. The sociopolitical context in which this book is written was described in Chapter 2. With increased hostility towards them since 9/11 and 7/7, British Muslims:

- are one of the most socially and economically marginalized groups in Britain
- are no longer depicted as hard-working, respectful and law-abiding but rather viewed as a 'problem group' (Alexander, 2006: 258) and have become constructed as active participants in street rioting (Amin, 2003)
- have become the target of negative media, state and societal responses.

The exclusion of Muslims from British society along a racialized discourse (see Chapter 5), especially those of Pakistani and Bangladeshi origin, has a long history. Exclusion was initially based around issues of skin colour. Now a seemingly backward, oppositional, anti-modern, un-British and culturally different Islamic culture has been constructed.

The international context is of increasing tensions around the globe involving Muslim countries such as Iraq, Afghanistan, Pakistan and Syria. British-born third-generation Bangladeshis are negotiating their national, ethnic and religious identities in a world post 9/11 and 7/7. Most importantly, it is a national and international context in which religion, as well as race, gender, nationality and ethnicity, has become an important component of an individual's identity (Lewis, 2002). The multiple identities of my study's participants are disseminated and analysed within the broader academic debate of what it means to be a 'British Muslim' (Bunting, 2004; Lewis, 2007; Omaar, 2007).

Islam, for many, helps negate the complexities of identity: being British (birth/citizenship), Bangladeshi (ethno-racial) and Muslim (religious). The notion of this all-encompassing European-Islamic identity is forwarded by Swiss academic Tariq Ramadan (quoted in Lewis, 2007: 143), who asserts that he is 'Muslim by religion, Swiss by nationality, European by culture, Egyptian by memory and universalist by principle'.

I maintain that a new positive British-Bangladeshi Muslim identity has emerged within East London. British Islam is by definition a dynamic culture, which enables third-generation Bangladeshis to comfortably identify with and fuse the many segments of their multifaceted identities: national, linguistic, ethnic, racial, cultural, religious and gendered.

This chapter is not intended as a primer on Islam and some issues have been ignored altogether. It has six interconnected sections that, in order:

- locate the personal voices and struggles of the six participants within the wider debate of what it means to be a British-Bangladeshi Muslim
- examine the complexity of identity
- outline some of the sociopolitical explanations for why Islam has increased in national and global popularity
- analyse the question of what the religion of Islam provides for its members
- examine the emergence and components of a British-Islamic identity and culture, and offer empirical evidence suggesting that there is sufficient institutional and ideological support available for this culture to prosper, develop and be sustained
- summarize some of the key findings.

What does it mean to be a British-Bangladeshi Muslim?

Islam was clearly a sociopolitical, cultural and spiritual force in the lives of all the participants. All were born into the religion of Islam so they were Muslims by cultural habit and birth rather than by choice. The British-Bangladeshi population is a religiously homogeneous community. Approximately 90 per cent of the total number of Bangladeshis in England and Wales (513,000) in 2011 define themselves as Muslims (Sedghi, 2013). Categorization does not allow for overlap (Kamrava, 2006: 13–16), but the participants interpreted Islam as either cultural or politicized. There are other key manifestations of British Islam around Tower Hamlets and the rest of the country, such as devout conservative religious Islam, spiritual

Islam (Vertovec, 1998), radical Islam (Abbas, 2007; McRoy, 2006) and the reformist/modern Islam (Kamrava, 2006) that is mainly the province of the educated and professional class (see Chapter 2).

The ideological and practical outlook for the participants was governed by a cultural Islam – a way of life – that they were born into, and a politicized Islam exerted as a response to social marginalization post 9/11 and 7/7. It is important to make a distinction between the *political* Islam that has risen within the Muslim world and the *politicized* Bangladeshi from Tower Hamlets. Underpinned by the radical philosophies of Islamic thinkers such as Qutb, Mawdudi and Khomeini (Kepel, 2003: 30–42), political Islam has developed largely as a response to despotic regimes and an American-backed imperialism in the Islamic world and is governed by terrorist violence, military coups and revolutions (Anderson, 1997; Ali, 2003; Kepel, 2003). The politicized third-generation Bangladeshi from Tower Hamlets, on the other hand, is frustrated and angry about local and global issues of marginalization and has a sense of injustice. Zeyba echoes this frustration:

> *Zeyba:* In the airport, they took you aside and they had to call the manager just so that you could come through. It just made you feel like, I don't know, a different species or something.
>
> *AH:* Do you think this was because you and your family were religiously dressed?
>
> *Zeyba:* Well, they didn't stop anyone else.

They are less governed by a call to violent action, it seems, and more by membership of a symbolic Islam that affords them a sense of acceptance, belonging and recognition and makes them visible in wider society. This visibility has been accelerated by the involvement of many British Muslims in the anti-war movement, which has brought younger Muslims into local and national politics.

The politicized Muslim is the outcome of local and global events perceived as injustices against Muslims. Many have 'suffered the sentence of history – subjugation, domination, diaspora and displacement' (Bhabha, 1995: 48). Religion often means more to people in diasporic communities away from home as an exertion of identity in an alien environment (Warner, 1998). It is an assertion of individual and personal identity as well as a public show to others of a chosen religious identity. This public show, argues Nilufer Ahmed (2005: 194), provides 'insulation' against the 'isolation' of being a migrant and the hostilities experienced in the host society. Islam, therefore, fills an identity void for third-generation Bangladeshis and allows them to fight for social and economic justice.

Modood (2005: x) argues that the revival of Islam for many British Muslims is a direct result of years of misrecognition of their identity. Becoming a British Muslim, or presenting Islam as an important part of your identity, is both a politicized act and also part of an 'equality seeking movement', and should be viewed within the politics of 'recognition' (Taylor, 1994). For a minority, however, Islamic identity goes beyond an equality-seeking movement and represents a superiority-seeking movement against non-Muslims.

Whether cultural or politicized, Islam for all six participants has involved both defence and reaffirmation of it. The words 'Islam' and 'Muslim' were mentioned 726 times during the interviews, highlighting the importance of Islam in their lives:

> Along with my Bangladeshi heritage, my religion, Islam, is also important to me. These are two important parts of my identity. These are parts of who I am.
>
> (Sanjida)

> We are Muslims. That is our main identity. Everything else does not matter as much … I have made a lot of mistakes in the past … taken drugs, run away from home and upset my parents. I have found out more about my religion just by reading lots of books and speaking to my friends. I want to, *inshallah*, become a better Muslim and a better human being.
>
> (Taiba)

> I am a Muslim. That is the way I view myself and the way I want others to view me as.
>
> (Saeed)

> I wear the hijab to school, when I go round my cousins and when I am out with my friends. It was weird wearing it at first. Now, it feels normal and I would feel weird if I don't have the hijab on.
>
> (Zeyba)

> I do not have any connection with my Bangladeshi roots. I prefer to be known as a Muslim than a Bengali.
>
> (Azad)

> It's in my culture to be a Muslim … I am a Muslim-Bengali boy
> – that's it.
>
> (Akbar)

Storry and Childs (2002) note that the practice of Islam and the heritage of Asian culture have become inextricably intertwined, especially for the first generation. While culture as a concept remains ambiguous (Wallerstein, 1991), complex (Tylor, 1930 [1881]; Kroeber and Kluckhohn, 1963), fluid and multiple (Clifford, 1988), I subscribe to Williams (1980) and Inglis's (2005) definition of culture as a 'whole way of life', so I view it as 'all ways of thinking, understanding, feeling, believing and acting "characteristic" of a particular group' (Williams, 1980: 6–7).

As for the first generation of settlers described by Storry and Childs (2002), Islam and Bangladeshi culture have become so intertwined for these third-generation Bangladeshis that it is difficult to separate Islamic from Bangladeshi cultural traditions. They have fused into one cultural way of life for those who think, understand, feel, believe and act in a particular way. The main difference between the generations is that there are more variables and complexities for the third generation to consider in exerting this whole culture. Along with Bangladeshi culture, they have had to fuse elements of their British-born identity with a politicized Islam post 9/11 and 7/7.

It is natural for Akbar and Sanjida to be both Bangladeshi and Islamic, because being a Muslim is an important part of everyday Bangladeshi culture. Islam and the many symbolisms associated with the religion, such as the hijab, was 'normal' and 'important' to Zeyba, Sanjida, Saeed and Azad. For Taiba, Islam was her 'main identity'. As the majority of third-generation Bangladeshis are born into the religion of Islam, being spirituality devoted to the religion is fairly normal and natural. They are culturally Muslim.

Being a Muslim is a vital component of being a Bangladeshi from Sylhet, where everyday life revolves around Islamic rituals and traditions. Ninety per cent of the approximately 145 million Bangladeshis from Bangladesh are Muslims (Pew Forum on Religion and Public Life, 2009). This religious and cultural homogeneity reinforces a sense of oneness and community in Bangladesh that is also evident in Tower Hamlets. The similarity in ideology, physical attributes of skin colour and dress, and habits of prayer and diet among the third-generation Bangladeshis has contributed to the establishment of a British-Islamic identity. We construct our identity through a complex prism of 'sameness' and 'difference' (Lawler, 2013). As Woodward (2004: 39) observes, 'We present ourselves to others through everyday interactions, through the way we speak and dress, marking ourselves as the same as those with whom we share an identity and different from those with whom we do not.' It is the similarities that mark out differences between *us* and *them*. This 'social' identity (Jenkins, 1996) unites Bangladeshi Muslims under a broad Bangladeshi-Muslim culture.

A multifaceted British-Islamic identity

Religious identities, like concepts of community and culture, are complex and not fixed; they are fluid, multiple, hybrid, syncretic and often contradictory. Cultural theorists such as Stuart Hall (1991) refute the biological determinism of identity as being static and fixed, as asserted by behavioural psychologists such as Phinney and Rotheram (1987), and argue that social environment, historical change and the complexity of modernity and globalization affect individual and group identities. The social environment of my participants centres around issues of deprivation and sociopolitical marginalization, and the popularity of Islam as a local and global badge of identity post 9/11 and 7/7 illustrates a period of historic change.

These changes, along with socially constructed identities (Burr, 2003; Kearney, 2003) that take into account issues of 'representation' and 'power' and the role of 'others' on our own sense of identity (Hall, 1996: 4), have contributed to a multifaceted and fluid British-Islamic identity. In modern complex British society, questions of identity have become less concerned with *who we are* and more with *how have we been represented*. As Laclau (1990: 33) notes, certain identities hold more power than others, notably white vs black, man vs woman. One identity is viewed as a 'mark', for example, being black and being a woman, whereas the other – being a man and being white – is viewed as normal and 'unmarked'. My study indicates that being a Muslim in modern British society constitutes a 'mark' and that the non-Muslim majority are viewed as normal and 'unmarked'. Identities emerge within the play of specific modalities of power and are more the product of the marking of difference and exclusion, actual and symbolic, 'from' a group than membership 'to' a group (Butler, 1993; Hall, 1993a; Bhabha, 1994). Bhabha (1995: 47) also suggests that the ideological discourses in the West have 'attempted to give a hegemonic "normality" to the uneven development and differential, often disadvantaged, histories of nations, races, communities and peoples'. Hall (1996: 4) and others (Foucault, 1980; Butler, 1990) argue that it is only through the relation to the 'other', the representable, the symbolic, the relation to what it is not, that identity is constructed. Identities are consequently 'constructed through, not outside, difference' (Hall, 1996: 4).

Identification with British Islam for many third-generation Bangladeshis is a social construction lodged in contingency and conditional on certain structural and symbolic resources. Among others, these include a seemingly antagonistic foreign policy towards Muslim countries, poverty, the ideal of a global *umma*, a sense of victimhood in an Islamophobic society, shared customs, styles of clothing, diet and social habits. Importantly, once British-Islamic identification is secured, it does not obliterate 'difference' among its members (Hall, 1996: 3). There are still ideological, cultural, gender and class differences despite a common commitment to the idea of British Islam. As the social environment, the conditions of existence and the history change, so will their identities. Identity is always in 'process' and never completed (Hall, 1996: 2–3).

British Islam is a postmodern identity – dynamic, fluid, diverse, open to change and often contested by its members. While preoccupied with personal ethnic, national and religious badges of identity, most participants were at the same time politicized, especially Zeyba and Saeed, and cultural Islam overlapped with politicized Islam (Kamrava, 2006). Kershen (1998: 2, 19) argues that identity, including religious identity, is 'multifaceted and variable and is in a constant state of flux and can never be static … the boundaries of identity cannot be simply and clearly drawn … [it is] fuzzy and complex'.

Religious identity, unlike one's ethnic and racial origin, is a matter of 'choice'. In this sense, 'a Muslim or any other religious identity is dictated by one's conscious acceptance of a way of life' (Bari, 2002: 175). Therefore, Muslim identity in Tower Hamlets is not 'only the way they identified themselves, but also the way that they wanted others to identify them' (N. Ahmed, 2005: 200). The notion that a Muslim identity is a conscious acceptance of a way of life is problematic – most Bangladeshis have not chosen to be Muslim but were born into the religion and it is a normalized part of their culture. Taiba reminds us that it was her father who 'forced' her to wear the headscarf in public and this contradicts the notion of free choice. Rather, it appears to be a form of social control.

British Islam is not like a Saudi-inspired conservative Islam. It is a forward-thinking, progressive and reformist Islam that allows its members to take elements from their Bangladeshi, Muslim and British-born identities and fuse them with everyday urban traits of being an East Londoner. This entails a skilful and complex process of what American-Islamic scholar Hamza Yusuf (quoted in Lewis, 2007: 36–9) terms 'discernment'. Yusuf presents an unproblematic notion of Britishness, arguing that Islam allows for the expressions of local customs, so a Scottish Muslim can still enjoy haggis, albeit from halal ingredients. The purpose of Islam is not to obliterate local customs. Many Muslims, he argues, may be ethnically Punjabi, but they are culturally British. Parents need to allow their children to take the best from both cultures and engage in what he calls 'discernment'. And Bhabha (1996: 54) argues that many postcolonial migrants have developed a culture that is 'in-between' cultures. It appears that British Islam is 'in-between' Bangladeshi, British and Muslim cultures as it takes the best from all its cultural influences and fuses them together (Basit, 1997).

There are clear examples of discernment by the participants of my study. Akbar tells me how his family celebrates Christmas every year with a halal turkey, Sanjida tells me her family celebrates the New Year by going to the fireworks display at Tower Bridge each year and Azad admits to going to the pub to watch football on a large-screen television and feeling comfortable drinking 'Coca-Cola'.

Many have found a space for religious expression within their everyday lives. For example, when I watched Saeed play for his local football team and the game coincided with the mid-afternoon daily prayers, I saw Saeed and some of his team pray publicly in the park during half time. These examples of discernment illustrate the participants' construction of a dynamic and fluid postmodern British-Islamic identity.

Why Islam has become more popular

The theoretical explanations as to why Islam has increased in national and global popularity transcends disciplines. The global Muslim population is currently estimated to be 1.6 billion (Pew Research, 2011) – with 2.7 million in Britain (ONS, 2012c). The large youth population of the British Muslim community means that it is expected to keep growing.

An anthropological analysis of the growth of religion across the globe explains the attraction of religion, especially Islam, to individuals and communities in the millennium. Geertz (2000a) argues that religious identities have become more central to people's lives and have a political role in the developing world, especially since decolonization and the end of the Cold War in 1989. Increased global movement between people means that religious differences in rituals, ideology and customs are immediate and obvious. People have become more aware of and open to religious influences. Social systems such as socialism and nationalism have failed against the power of capitalism, leaving religion as an alternative social system. Geertz (2000a: 176–8) observes that people are frustrated with the materialism, media and consumerism of the modern world and are searching for something more moral and more 'deeply rooted, closer to home ideas and values'. Religion, is therefore, an expression of 'meaning, identity and power'.

Along with Geertz's anthropological analysis, Akhtar (2005: 164) offers a socio-political explanation of the current popularity of Islam. What she terms 'religiosity' (the visibility of Islam) has developed around the world due to two main factors. First, the economic and social exclusion of the majority of Muslims in the West has increased the visible manifestations of Islam. Muslims in Britain live in relative poverty and within economically stagnant areas (see Chapter 2). It is common for individuals living in materially and socially poor conditions to look for a collective identity that enables them to negotiate and improve their social position and status (Kepel, 1997). A recent research project carried out in two deprived areas in Manchester and Glasgow adds weight to Kepel's argument. Findings from the Youth and Religion Project (Religion and Society, 2013) suggests a strong relationship between social deprivation, religious identities and spiritualities of young people.

Munoz (1999) argues that Islam provides a vehicle for protest against people's social conditions, offering alternative programmes of social and political action. Poston (1991) and others (Bari, 2002; Werbner, 2004; Begum and Eade, 2005: 187) concur. They find that Islam is appealing to young Muslims as it offers structure, hope, order, stability and confidence to individuals at a time when they feel powerless because their life chances are largely determined by external structures over which they have no control. The Youth and Religion Project (Religion and Society, 2013) also found that religion and spirituality gives voice to young people who are socially alienated, empowering them to become more active citizens. Muslim identity is, therefore, expressed more visibly because of a sociopolitical climate in which they feel victimized and excluded from mainstream society and the political process. The expression of a more vociferous and visible Muslim identity is an expression of frustration and anger.

Second, Akhtar suggests that in the Middle East, Africa and the Far East, the visibility of political Islam is seen as a response to oppressive regimes (Kepel, 1997). Esposito (1997) argues that many participants of Islamic revolts in the East since the 1970s believe that Islam offers a genuine alternative to corrupt regimes – for example, the Iranian Islamic revolution in 1979 was a reaction to years of oppression under the American-backed Shah. In this and other instances, the return to Islam is a 'response to certain structural constrictions' (Akhtar, 2005: 165). She maintains that the return to Islam for many young Muslims around the world is complicated but it 'offers individuals who feel in some way constrained by their circumstances an alternative ideology, a sense of belonging, solidarity, and a means of political mobilisation' (Akhtar, 2005: 165).

The return to religion does not necessarily mean an increased adherence to spiritual Islam focused around prayer, piety and dress. Instead, what attracts marginalized Muslims in Britain to Islam is the 'idea' of resisting the dominant, negative hegemony (Akhtar, 2005: 165–9). The return to religion according to Akhtar (2005: 168) is also psychological:

> There is a genuine sense of persecution: that the enemies of Islam will victimise Muslims whatever they do, and that it is therefore important to rally around Islam. In this sense, the return to religion is more psychological, built upon resistance to a perceived scapegoating of Muslims. The demonisation of the Muslim image, presenting it as backward and anti-modern, symbolically sets Muslims apart from all that is progressive and 'Western'. This results in the symbolic exclusion of minority Muslims in the West. The turn to religion, in this sense, could be seen as active resistance to symbolic exclusion.

Saeed and Zeyba see things in a similar way:

> This is a testing time for Muslims. Everybody is against us. But we will pass this test and *inshallah* everybody will realize one day that Islam is the only truth … Islam is very important for me.
>
> (Saeed)

> I don't just have three sisters. Even though they are strangers, I feel connected to the many millions of Muslims around the world. Sometimes I feel as if I have millions of brothers and sisters … like one big family.
>
> (Zeyba)

Although situated in class relations, the theory of relative deprivation adds weight to these arguments. The concept of relative deprivation derives from Walter Runciman (1966), who argued that political revolutions only occurred when the oppressed and poor became aware of the differences between them and the wealthy classes. Without this knowledge, they generally accepted their powerlessness. So it is not poverty per se but the awareness of their relative poverty that leads to change and revolutions. Where people feel unfairly excluded and relatively deprived, they may turn to religion both to explain their position and also to gain solace and prestige. Religion offers its members psychological confidence against social alienation and deprivation. The growth of the Pentecostal churches in Britain, attended largely by people of African and Caribbean descent, is one example. Third-generation Bangladeshis from Tower Hamlets are also reminded of their relative deprivation as they are situated in the middle of some of the wealthiest areas of Europe – the City of London and the Docklands Canary Wharf business development – so this may further fuel their heightened interest in Islam.

What Islam offers

Islam helped my participants manage two interconnected troubling issues: the years of systemic alienation and marginalization and their own personal and 'ambiguous' identities (Wallerstein, 1991) of being a generation not fully belonging to either a British nation or a Bangladeshi community. They find themselves on the periphery of two cultures and two societies but, arguably, a member of neither. They have 'marginal' identities as they have two or more conflicting social identities (Park, 1928; Stonequist, 1935; T. Ahmed, 2005).

Islam offers this generation two solutions. The first is empowerment. Islam affords them a neutral space where race, social alienation and poverty become less significant, allowing them to engage in a journey from the 'periphery' to the 'centre' of British society (Saeed *et al.*, 1999; Malik, 2004) via a system of what Geaves (2005: 70) calls 'contest' and 'protest'. While there is validity in Gramscian Marxist claims that religion serves to legitimize power and hegemony exercised by the ruling elite of societies, such as the church's characteristic subservience to the state and ruling-class interests and its hegemonic control over its masses (Jones, 2006), a closer examination of the narratives of my participants counters classical Marxist notions of religion as an 'opiate of the poor' (Marx quoted in Bottomore and Rubel, 1963).

A key theological factor of the Muslim faith is the concept of an afterlife that is in contrast to the difficulties of the present life (Maqsood, 2003: 43). Akbar confirms such thinking by suggesting that 'this life is a test for Muslims in all areas – but we must have a strong sense of faith throughout these difficulties and we know that the end reward will be amazing'. Akbar's belief in the 'amazing' afterlife adds weight to classical Marxist theory that religion legitimizes unequal power relations in society and helps maintain the dominant hegemony, so diluting the demands for change. Equally, however, the call to Islam for some was a platform for their social, personal, political and spiritual advancement and not a form of indoctrination that dampens revolutionary power:

> Once my baby is of nursery age I would like to start a Youth Work Diploma and fulfil my dream of becoming a youth worker. I want to make a difference to the local community and help tackle issues of drugs, crime and low motivation. Not only is this a personal ambition of mine, but our religion teaches us to better ourselves through inner peace, humanity and education.
>
> (Taiba)

> I don't take shit from no one. I respect my parents and some of the older boys from my area. But Islam has given me the confidence to fight against injustice … if something is wrong then I must speak out … I know that no one will employ me because of my history. That is why I want to be my own boss. I want to earn loads of money and do charitable work in the future. This is both my religious and personal belief.
>
> (Saeed)

For those such as Taiba and Saeed, religious faith acts as a source of empowerment (Sanghera and Thapur-Björkert, 2007). Smith (1999) concurs. In his study of the East-London religious community, Smith argued that while faith has been a recruiting tool for international terrorists of different religious persuasions, it has equally been a catalyst for cross-cultural community and social cohesion and advancement, and for social justice in the local domestic arena. Islam within the lives of many third-generation Bangladeshis has a social and political character, rather than being steeped in theology. Religion has, like ethnicity, become a political symbol that not only excludes groups and individuals from mainstream society but also serves as a mode of identity, a symbol of affiliation and political mobilization (Song, 2003; Marranci, 2005).

From a Weberian point of view (Weber, 2001 [1930]), Islam and ideas coming from Islam can be a cause of social change as well as a form of social control and stability. Religion is not wholly about manipulating and exploiting people. Like Weber, Gramsci accepted the possibility that religious beliefs and practices could develop and be popularized, particularly by working-class intellectuals, in an attempt to challenge the dominant hegemony and support the growth of working-class consciousness (Jones, 2006). The idea that religion may play a progressive role in the political struggles of oppressed people has also been proposed by neo-Marxists such as Maduro (1982), who suggested that the religious clergy in many Latin American societies and South Africa has assumed the role of Gramsci's working-class intellectuals, voicing the discontent of the oppressed masses. The clergy have been involved in shaping consciousness and devising strategies of social and political action.

The second solution offered by Islam is belonging. Islam affords my participants membership of the 'imagined' (Anderson, 1983) Islamic global community – the *umma* – where race, nationality, citizenship and the colour of passport is insignificant compared to global brotherhood and sisterhood. Zeyba believes in this imagined community – what she refers to as her 'one big family'. This imagined community, however, remains an ideal. In practice, as we have seen, ethnic, class and national affiliations remain a barrier against the utopian ideal of *umma*. However, it is not the reality but rather the metaphor of the *umma* that is attractive to its members (Malik, 2004). The ideology of *umma* is immensely powerful and provides not only membership of a movement that is the second-largest in the world and the fastest growing, but also membership to 1,400 years of history and a mystical and romantic past (Saeed *et al.*, 1999; Ansari, 2004: 19). As the writer Hai (2008) reminds us, British Muslims may be outcasts in British society, but they were 'secure' and 'confident as part of a greater – Muslim – whole'. The political ideal of the Muslim *umma* is therefore a search for identity, meaning, dignity and power.

As well as the positive impact of Islam in the lives of the participants, there are also the criticisms of the role of religion in contemporary society. Religion and religious nationalism can be a cause for conflict and social division as is the case in Northern Ireland, Palestine, Kashmir and Iraq. And religion can act as a form of social control and serve the interests of those in power. Millet (1970) argues from a feminist viewpoint that religious rituals and myths are used as a way of legitimizing patriarchy. In these ways religion helps maintain the status quo in society, legitimizes economic and gender exploitation and justifies poverty and inequality. From this viewpoint, religion is oppressive and constraining for its followers. And while adherence to a religious belief in a mono-religious society is one thing, in modern, complex multi-religious countries such as Britain it can magnify social oppositions and polarize communities on moral and ethical grounds and heighten a sense of otherness. Note how Saeed and Zeyba engage in stereotypical and religiously based moral judgements against non-Muslims:

> They have no shame ... all they do is drink alcohol, wear tarty clothes and go clubbing. They have no barriers.
>
> (Zeyba)

> Non-Muslims will not go to heaven. You have to be a Muslim to
> go to heaven.
>
> (Saeed)

These views can be considered a form of 'fabulation' (Werbner, 1994) – a process of generalization and essentialism of cultures, nations, genders and ethnic groups.

A new Islam for a new generation

> The challenge [for the younger generation of Muslims] is to find ways to integrate the religious traditions of Islam into contemporary British life and to create a new British Islamic identity. It is a process which involves some difficulty.
>
> (Storry and Childs, 2002: 251–2)

Third-generation Bangladeshis in East London have met the challenge identified by Storry and Childs. They have fused elements of Islam into contemporary British life and this has generated a vibrant British-Islamic culture.

A sense of perspective is needed in this debate. Despite physical and ideological differences, Muslim youth are representative of the general youth of Britain – they face uncertainty, difficulties and a precarious future. Although there is much overlap, most Muslims in Britain fit into Sahin's (2005) 'diffuse' and 'exploratory' category (see Chapter 2). Muslims consider themselves as Muslims chiefly because they were born into the religion – their Muslim identity is as much cultural as it is religious. For example, the vast majority of Muslim males across Britain confine their religious devotions to the weekly Friday prayer and occasional daily prayer 'as and when they can' (Lewis, 2007: 3). Although many are frustrated and angry, they are not radical Islamists espousing change and violent revolutions. They are just meshed into the everyday fabric of life, worrying about routine issues affecting everybody such as rents or mortgage payments and childcare provision. Shareefa Fulat (2005: 69) of the Muslim Youth Helpline argues that 'the problems faced by Muslim youth are similar to their non-Muslim peers: drugs, mental health, relationships, careers, jobs training and sexuality'. Because some of these issues are taboo in Muslim communities, they are often ignored altogether. Far from offering support, the family and the community are often the source of the problem. Thus, although his voice is steeped in religious rhetoric and he is angered by the plight of Muslims across the globe, the life story of Saeed mirrors the characteristics of the diffuse group of Muslims. He does not practise the faith in terms of prayer and dress but is committed ideologically.

In contrast to the 'diffuse' group, the 'exploratory' group – those searching to make sense of Islam as a living and spiritual entity relevant to their everyday lives – are predominantly an educated and professional group of Muslims who are mainly concerned with the revival of an internationally oriented modern version of Islam (Glynn, 2002). The culture and characteristics of this post-Islamist generation are summarized by *Guardian* journalist Madeleine Bunting (2004: 17) who was involved in a workshop involving 103 British Muslims:

> The 103 British Muslims who joined us last week could be described as amongst the success stories of two decades of integration: from mostly humble backgrounds, they have got to university, or are working in jobs as diverse as accountants, pharmacists, social workers, journalists, civil servants, lawyers, nurses and entrepreneurs. Alongside their academic and career achievements, they have drawn from their faith a powerful social conscience; the majority of our participants devote a considerable amount of their time to volunteering in community organisations and political campaigns.
>
> This is a pivotal generation; they have the skills and education which many of their parents lacked to make their experience heard. And that experience will increasingly be one which will have international resonance: the two civilisations of Islam and the west are not abstract concepts to them, but the influences they daily negotiate in their own lives. How they vote, how they dress, how they pray, whom they befriend and whom they marry; all are influenced by the accommodation they find between the two, at a time when internationally, the two are being set in violent opposition.

The emergence of the City Circle in 1999 is a good example of the 'pivotal generation' Bunting describes. The City Circle was established by a group of graduate friends who wanted to create a space in London where professionals could meet and socialize and discuss issues affecting young British Muslims. Lewis (2007: 61) refers to it as the 'halal' alternative to the Friday night pub culture. With its emphasis on professional advancement, education, engagement with civil society, human rights, women's rights including leadership roles, 'critical' citizenry (Ramadan, 2004) and democracy, this group of Muslims is contributing to the modernist and reformist agenda in Islam that Kamrava (2006) and his colleagues have alluded to. With their strong emphasis on education and career aspirations, Zeyba, Taiba, Sanjida, Akbar and Azad will probably become part of this educated professional class. However, the City Circle represents an elitist minority as most Muslims in Britain continue to suffer material and social deprivation.

Both groups (the diffuse and the exploratory) are active agents of the new British-Islamic culture and are part of a British-born modern, literate, trendy, Islamically conscious and technological – MTV, iPhone and Facebook – generation. British Islam acts as a bridge between tradition and modernity. It has theoretical, political and theological credence, thanks to a new body of leaders such as Hamza Yusuf, Usama Canon, Salma Yaqoob and Tariq Ramadan, whose messages of equality, discernment, human rights, democracy and the exertion of civil responsibility is assisting young British Muslims to come to terms with their national (British), ethnic (Bangladeshi) and religious (Islamic) identities.

Through internal debate, self-criticism and articulate advocacy, Muslims are translating anger into argument and shaping the future of British Islam alongside a model compatible with a Western-British culture, albeit within a 'halal' context (Le Quesne, 2001). A brief survey of this new British-Islamic culture suggests the 'complementarity' (Malik, 2004: 1) of Islam with Western concepts and lifestyle, as opposed to stark opposition. With its emphasis on banking, education, entertainment, smaller families, individualism, women's rights, engagement with media and civil society, professionalism and dining out, British-Islamic culture looks like halal capitalism. As Table 2 illustrates, a whole new syncretic infrastructure has emerged catering for the personal, cultural, social and economic needs of third- and fourth-generation British-born Bangladeshi Muslims.

Observing Muslim youth cultures across Europe, Herding (2014) notes the emergence of a 'Muslim cool' subculture focused around religious rap and streetwear featuring Islamic slogans. This has contributed to a global movement involving Muslim hipsters known as 'mipsterz'. Alongside this, journalist Omar Shahid (2014) points to the development of an Islamic entertainment industry dubbed 'Halalywood'. A new generation of young modern Muslims are establishing new ways to entertain themselves while remaining loyal to their faith. American actor and comedian Omar Regan (quoted in Shahid, 2014) notes that Halalywood is committed to provide halal entertainment that Muslims can relate to, a platform for young Muslim artists to tell 'their stories' and a vehicle to re-educate the masses about Muslims and Islam.

Table 2: Social infrastructure accessed by third-generation British-born Bangladeshi Muslims

Facility	Example
Halal banking compliant with Islamic sharia rules on finance	Islamic Bank of Britain (www.islamic-bank.com)
Halal insurance	Salaam insurance (www.salaaminsurance.com)
Muslim media (T.S. Ahmed, 2005)	*Q News*, *emel* magazine, *Asian Woman*, Al-Jazeera, Islam Channel
Gender-segregated eating-out culture	Maedah Grill and the Barakah restaurants centred around the East London Mosque
Halal vacation packages with Islamic values (Suleaman, 2010; Khalil, 2010)	http://islamictravels.com
Islamic social entertainment scene	Music artists (such as Native Deen, Sami Yusuf, Mecca 2 Medina, Maher Zain and Mos Def), Muslim comedians such as Azhar Usman, Muslim speed dating and annual Islamic conferences such as Islam Expo
'Modest' fashion scene for Muslim women (Tarlo, 2009; Lewis, 2013)	http://www.hijabfashionshop.com/; www.yazthespaz.com; http://islamfashionandidentity.blogspot.com/
	Retail outlets such as Inayah in Shadwell and Arabian Nights in Whitechapel
Islamic bookshop culture	Al-Furqan, East London Bookstore, Blackstone – all adjacent to the East London Mosque
Islamic youth support services	www.muslimyouth.net
Women-only swimming and gym sessions	http://www.better.org.uk/leisure (search for 'women only'); Hayaa Fitness

The emergence of this culture could be viewed as separatist and isolationist, conducive to strengthening an us-vs-them mentality and potentially limiting cross-cultural/cross-religious contacts. Nonetheless, these developments provide a practical and theoretical infrastructure for this British-Islamic culture to develop and prosper. It also enhances a positive sense of community, self-esteem and identity. British Islam is more than just a social or religious movement; it denotes a whole new 'modern' British way of life (Kibria, 2006; Al Yafai and Hakim, 2010).

A major element of this culture is the fashion scene for a young and trendy generation. Take the self-labelled 'Hijabi Barbie' (Fanshawe, 2006). A distinctive new Islamic fashion industry underpins the social and political ethos of British-Islamic culture, imbuing it with a positive sense of community and sisterhood. The hijab has become mainstream – a cool, fashionable 'accessory' (Iqbal, 2010). There are catwalk models wearing the hijab (Ahmed, 2004), there are websites and blogs dedicated to the hijab, and many retail outlets cater for the new Muslim woman looking for colourful and trendy clothes in a female-only environment (Scott, 2004).

Generally we see a fusion of Western dress, technology and concepts with Muslim attire and etiquette. Here are the Hijabi Barbies – young women wearing headscarves with jeans, expensive trainers/heels and listening to their iPods, while eating out in restaurants that have segregated gendered seating and do not serve alcohol. Dressed in brightly coloured hijab, flowing skirt and jewelled shoes, the Hijabi Barbies, argues Fanshawe (2006), do not claim to be 'perfect Muslims' and are much like other girls and women. They are fed up with being tarnished with the brush of fanaticism, extremism and oppression and are increasingly choosing to express their identities and faith through their dress. These 'visibly Muslim' (Tarlo, 2009) women are engaged in internal self-criticism and have combined elements of religion with fashion. Modern, trendy, religiously conscious, they are negotiating their femininities within patriarchal practices (Sanghera and Thapur-Björkert, 2007: 187).

The Hijabi Barbie exemplifies the constant negotiation between the different layers of British, Bangladeshi and Muslim identities in 2015. A particularistic Islamic fashion scene constructs a space where women are encouraged to express the complexity of identity in a democratic way and become part of civil society. As Zeyba says, 'I don't like the disgusting clothes my mum wears. I like wearing baggy jeans and baggy tops. I mainly shop in H&M. I have many coloured hijabs to match the colour of my clothes.' Sanjida enjoys occasions: 'Sometimes I look forward to weddings. It's an excuse to dress up … I don't mind wearing the headscarf. Actually, I have some really bright funky ones that match my sarees.'

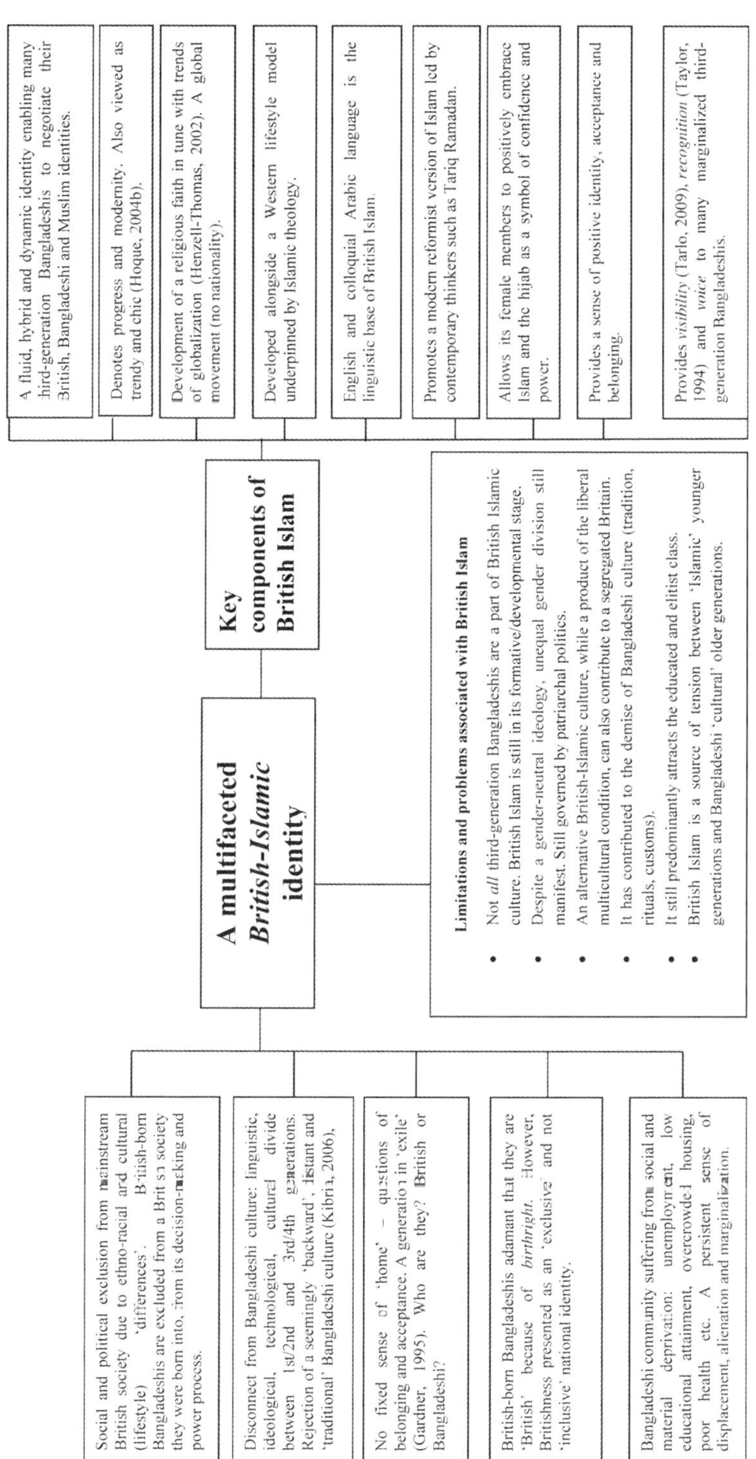

Figure 1: The complex development of a multifaceted British-Islamic identity

Conclusion

This progressive British-Islamic culture, with its emphasis on modernity and reform, mainly recruits members from college, university and professional circles. Since most British Muslims still experience social and material deprivation, it is arguably an option only for the elite (Murad, 2003: 5–6). Do materially poor Bangladeshis have access to computers and the internet? Can they afford travel and entry fees to annual conferences or eating in restaurants? But the stories, aspirations and politicization of my participants reflect the rising popularity of the British-Islamic culture among materially poor third-generation Bangladeshis in Tower Hamlets. Where, then, does Islam fit into the overall complex identity of this community? Figure 1 indicates both the position and the significance of British Islam in shaping who they believe they are.

British Islam is still in its early stages but is developing rapidly. Akbar, Azad, Zeyba and Sanjida have high academic and professional aspirations and will contribute to the modernist agenda. Saeed and Taiba have allowed personal space in their lives for Islam. All six are ideologically connected to the notion of Islam as a progressive modern movement. British Islam provides a space for them to negotiate the many complex, overlapping and dynamic identities they are a part of. The emergence of numerous halal restaurants, Islamic banks, Muslim fashion outlets and an Islamic entertainment scene in Tower Hamlets suggests that there is a target population for such services and the participants are part of it. Taiba regularly goes to shisha bars with her girlfriends and Akbar enjoys eating out in halal restaurants. We are witnessing the emergence of a new and vibrant British-Islamic culture in Tower Hamlets; this is a symbolic victory for multicultural Britain and should be viewed positively. Whether British Islam can prosper and sit alongside and within multicultural Britain is explored next.

Life in East London today

Figure 2: One of the many segregated halal hair and beauty services for women on the high streets

Figure 3: Boys playing football dressed in *thobes*

Figure 4: 'Hijabi Barbies'

Figure 5: Schoolgirls wearing the headscarf although it's not part of the school uniform

Figure 6: T-Shirt identity: illustrating a political identity among Bangladeshi youth

Chapter 7

British-Islamic identity in public spaces

Introduction

> How can I be anything else apart from being British? I was born here ... in the Royal London Hospital ... I have a right to be British.
>
> (Saeed)

> I hate going to Bangladesh. London is my home.
>
> (Zeyba)

The concept of Britishness is complex, problematic and ambiguous (Cohen, 1994). It is the very essence of multiculturalism and British*ness* that promotes and encourages an alternative Muslim identity to prosper and sit comfortably within a multicultural space. British Islam, as discussed in depth in the last chapter, is a positive manifestation of British multiculturalism and although there are a tiny minority who propagate segregation, British Islam is essentially modern in its outlook and integrationist in ideology. All six participants viewed themselves as 'British' by birthright, suggesting that a national civic British identity is an important layer of identity for third-generation Bangladeshis. This chapter is divided into six sections:

- the first and second sections locate the voices of the participants within the Britishness debate and explore the complexity of 'home'
- the third section discusses theories of multiculturalism
- the fourth section is a critical analysis of John Rex's (2005) public/ private precondition of a multicultural society – in which immigrant communities have the right to practise their faith and customs but only within the private domain
- the fifth section examines British-Muslim assertiveness in public spaces
- I conclude that British Islam must be recognized and accepted in secular public spaces; Muslims must be viewed not as the other, as 'them', but as part of the plural British 'us'.

I am British, not Bengali

Unlike the first- and second-generation Bangladeshis who have an emotional and ideological bond with the motherland (Gardner, 1993, 2002; Hoque, 2005), all six participants viewed Britain, and in particular the local community of Tower Hamlets, as their home. Their neighbourhood afforded them a sense of community, comfort and familiarity:

> Although I see my future outside of Tower Hamlets, I do feel a sense of community and comfort living in an area where most people think, behave and look the same.
>
> (Azad)

> Newham does not have the same sort of community feeling that Tower Hamlets does. There is a sense of safety and comfort when you are with your own.
>
> (Akbar)

Despite their experiences of racism in childhood and their feelings of displacement, their place of birth was a determining factor in how they identified themselves. Taiba states that East London 'is my home. It's where I grew up. It's a place where I find comfortable.' Saeed echoes Taiba's equation of home with family, familiarity, place of birth and comfort: 'Home is here, where I am living, where my family are. It's not Bangladesh as I was not born there.' Zeyba asserts that 'I have a British passport therefore I am British.' These views are in keeping with numerous research findings suggesting that people of ethnic-minority origin feel British even if they were born elsewhere (Frith, 2004; Manning and Roy, 2010).

Bangladesh as their 'ancestral home' (Garbin, 2005) still gives some participants a sense of 'deep connection' (Akbar). Akbar recalls his three-month visit to Bangladesh at the age of 12: 'Bangladesh was amazing. I remember going fishing with my cousin and playing football with my bare feet ... I met all my real family ... my blood relatives.' Similarly, despite the 'hot sticky weather' and the 'mosquitoes', Sanjida also feels a connection with what she calls the 'motherland': 'There are some things about Bangladesh that I did enjoy, like when everyone gets together ... everyone is sort of happy and it's fun.' However, despite this connection, the idea of being British is even more appealing to many third-generation Bangladeshis than the alternative. Visits to Bangladesh have reinforced Britain as 'home' and Bangladesh as a 'holiday' destination (Akbar) (Basit, 1997):

> I didn't enjoy my visit to Bangladesh. I was sick and did not enjoy the hot weather. I missed my mates in London. My family always talk of Bangladesh as home. My visit to Bangladesh made me realize that home for me was East London.
>
> (Saeed)

> I don't think that I would be able to adapt to the Bangladeshi way of life. Life is very different over there. The food, weather, drainage, culture, clothes, transport, electricity and too much poverty. I know how lucky I am. I am happy that they [grandparents] came here.
>
> (Sanjida)

The participants recall being called *Londonis* and *bideshis* (foreigners) by their Bangladeshi relatives. Some had been stared at and mocked: 'I was trying to speak Bengali and all they could do was laugh at me' (Sanjida). 'They just kept on staring at me. It was kinda weird' (Saeed). Disparities of wealth, class, culture, dress and language have positioned British-born Bangladeshis as tourists and foreigners in the country of ancestral origin. A consequence of non-acceptance in the country of birth and also in the motherland is that the participants are caught in the 'betwixt and between' phase of transmigration (Grillo, 2001).

The importance of birthplace and childhood memories in determining home and a national identity is highlighted by Sanjida:

> I have hazy memories of visits to Bangladesh. There is no comparison. I loved my childhood in East London. My friends, my area, going to the park … sometimes I think that my *dada* [grandfather] preferred Bangladesh than here and I think, Why? But then I think that if I had grown up in Bangladesh then I probably would think the same way.

However, a British national identity has many facets:

> Sometimes I am a proper Muslim, like during Ramadan when I am fasting. Sometimes I am Bengali, like when I go round my auntie's with my family and we have to dress up and eat lots of food. Er, and sometimes I am British when I am out with my mates going out for a meal or to the pictures.

> I guess I'm proud to be a Muslim, but with British it doesn't really come into anything [pause] it's not like I have a history

of living here, I just live here [pause] I am basically Bangladeshi [pause] I'm all three, I guess.

(Zeyba)

I am British because I was born here. But I am also so many other things – Bangladeshi, Muslim and a girl [pause] It's all rather confusing.

(Sanjida)

Commentators such as Geaves (2005: 75) have suggested that the exertion of more than one identity for the younger generation of Muslims is an example of their 'flexible' identities – the ability to adapt to different contexts and situations – which they are able to exert at ease while remaining secure in their primary identities of being Muslim and British. Their 'mobile identities' allow them to negotiate their multiple identities on a daily basis (Begum and Eade, 2005: 179). Ward (2004: 170) argues that there are 'tensions in all multiple identities, but that does not make multiple identities fundamentally incompatible'.

The primacy of particular identities may change, so that a third-generation Bangladeshi from Tower Hamlets might feel more 'Islamic' than Bangladeshi – or the reverse, depending on the situation and context. Nilufer Ahmed (2005: 200) calls this process 'shifting' and 'situational' identities. This is true of Zeyba, who feels like a 'Muslim' during Ramadan, feels 'Bengali' when she is at her auntie's home and 'British' when she is socializing with her friends. The different identities denote different communities of belonging. These complex narratives from the participants of this study reflect the experiences of the wider British-Bangladeshi community. A documentary by Selway (2010) highlighted how British Bangladeshis are constantly negotiating the 'three me's' of being a 'Muslim, British Westerner and Bangladeshi'. This strengthens Sen's (2006) argument that there is often an 'illusion' of a unique identity whereas the reality is that human beings have multiple identities.

However, the equation of home and a national British identity, with a place of birth, childhood memories and a sense of community, is not as clear cut as my participants claim. In the world post 9/11 and 7/7, where Islam and Islamic values have been presented in right-wing and mainstream political circles as a threat to peace and order and constructed as anti-Western and against the British way of life, there is serious tension and much debate over whether you can be both Muslim and British (Bunting, 2004; Omaar, 2007). As we have seen, the racial, ethnic and religious identities of third-generation

119

Bangladeshis from Tower Hamlets have become situated outside of what it means to be British, even though all six individuals viewed themselves as 'British'. Thus, the notion of Britishness is being actively contested and reconstructed to become inclusive in contemporary society. This concept requires further exploration.

The complexity of Britishness

Amid allegations of a 'Trojan Horse' takeover of schools in Birmingham by a group of conservative Muslims in 2014, the Department for Education (DfE) felt the need to reassert Britishness, partly in reaction to the alleged takeover and partly because the term is ambiguous and required definition. The DfE set up Islam and Islamic values as oppositional to what it means to be British. 'Fundamental British values' were constructed around the tenets of 'democracy, the rule of law, individual liberty, mutual respect and the tolerance of those of different faiths and beliefs' (DfE, 2014). Is this Britishness? Or is Britishness centred around iconic symbols such as HP Sauce, the Union Jack, the royal family (CRE, 2005: 20–21), 'roast beef and roast potatoes' (Bagguley and Hussain, 2005: 215), red buses and fish and chips? Is it more about everyday British traits and values such as respect, fairness, decency, talking about the weather and queuing in an orderly fashion? Or is it, as Azad states, 'all about supporting the English football team' or, as Sanjida says, 'the British are like ... always staying up partying, drinking ...[and eating with] knives and forks'? Britishness is, I believe, all the above and much more. And not everybody can claim Britishness for themselves and not everyone wants to be associated with it. Power relations, some of which are related to ethnicity, religion, class, age, generation and gender, are fundamentally involved in the definition and maintenance of the notion of Britishness (CRE, 2005), constructing it somewhat as an exclusive as opposed to an inclusive component of identity.

Britishness is a constantly evolving and complex theoretical concept. British historian Paul Ward has examined the definition and redefinition of national identities within the UK since the 1870s. Being British, he argues, is a complex issue as it is no longer viewed as innate, static or permanent (Ward, 2004: 1). Nations and national identities are not permanent and unchanging; they are the products of constant renegotiation, contest and debate. The idea of Britishness has been threatened, challenged, and in many respects has been in 'crisis' since the end of the Second World War, disrupted by historical events such as the end of empire, commonwealth immigration, 'Americanization', devolution, the weakening of the monarchy, European integration and the re-emergence of Celtic nationalisms (Ward, 2004: 171).

Mass non-white immigration into Britain since decolonization has challenged the racialized version of Britishness that rested on a myth of ethnic homogeneity and the slogan 'there ain't no black in the Union Jack' (Gilroy, 1987). This racialized Britishness has been presented as closed and exclusive by historic controversial political figures such as Enoch Powell (Heffer, 1998). Classifying the national identities of nearly 64 million people in one definition does not mirror the complexity and diversity of people's identities.

Historical debates about Britishness were associated with empire, imperialism, capitalism and Protestantism and seen as a hegemonic idea imposed upon lower classes and colonies – including Wales, Scotland and Ireland (Robbins, 1989; Colley, 1994; Weight, 2002; Ward, 2004). A more contemporary definition relates directly to the life experiences of the participants: the idea of Britishness as a concept that positively embraces cultural diversity (Alibhai-Brown, 2000; Parekh, 2000a). This definition illustrates the complex and fluid process of national identity and the notion of home discussed in this chapter. It suggests that the concept of liberal egalitarian multiculturalism lies at the core of contemporary Britishness. It is an open and inclusive version of Britishness that welcomes diversity as a core component of the British national character. It is an essentially optimistic view that sees Britishness as a diverse collective identity. As Ward (2004: 5) observes, throughout history, Britishness has more often than not been compatible with a huge variety of other identities. From this point of view, Britishness can surely manage to incorporate the ethno-religious identities of the third-generation Bangladeshis from Tower Hamlets. This concept of Britishness champions a civic, rather than ethnic, Britishness that recognizes and includes diversity rather than seeking to subordinate difference (Alibhai-Brown, 2000).

Furthermore, this concept of Britishness demands the decoupling of Britishness from racial connotations of whiteness, so that Black and Asian people in Britain do not feel excluded. It is, as Ward (2004: 138) argues, a 'different kind of British' and it promotes a form of Black Britishness (Parekh, 2000b). Britain and Britishness is a 'community of communities' (Parekh, 2000a) and as the poet Benjamin Zephaniah (n.d.) suggests, the ingredients of respect, tolerance, understanding and unity are necessary for this 'New Britain' to be realized. Kastoryano (2002) notes that many modern European nation states play an important role in adjusting policies and redefining the terms of citizenship so that minority communities are able to negotiate their identities within a nationalist discourse. Steeped within the politics of liberal egalitarian multiculturalism described above, such a process of negotiation of identities takes shape through British Islam for third-generation Bangladeshis, enabling them to be a part of both their nation and also their own communities.

The new British-Islamic identity embraces Ward's 'different kind of British'. It fits the rhetoric of the Labour government's desire in the early 2000s to establish a new Britain by positioning Black and Asian people more centrally within the British national identity. In what became known as the 'chicken tikka massala speech', MP Robin Cook outlined an inclusive version of Britishness that celebrated ethnic and cultural pluralism:

> Chicken Tikka Massala is now a true British national dish, not only because it is the most popular, but because it is a perfect illustration of the way Britain absorbs and adapts external influences. Chicken Tikka is an Indian dish. The Massala sauce was added to satisfy the desire of British people to have their meat served with gravy.
>
> (Cook, 2001)

This idealized plural and inclusive concept of Britishness has its limitations and has attracted resistance. Kenan Malik (2001) criticizes such a strand of multiculturalism by insisting that it helps segregate communities far more effectively than racism does. Farrukh Dhondy (2001) suggests that the focus should be not on 'multi-cultures', but rather on universal values such as freedom, respect and democracy. Prime Minister David Cameron lauched a scathing attack on this doctrine of state multiculturalism in 2011, calling it 'passive' and arguing that it has 'encouraged different cultures to live separate lives, apart from each other' (quoted in Kirkup, 2011: 1). Trevor Phillips (quoted in Baldwin, 2004), former chair of the Equality and Human Rights Commission, gave up on liberal multiculturalism declaring that, although it was useful once, it has run its course because it encourages difference as opposed to encouraging minorities to be truly British. Phillips famously observed that Britain is 'sleepwalking into segregation' on a scale already apparent in the United States (Casciani, 2005).

Towards a critical multiculturalism

> [Since the wave of mass immigration in the 1950s and 1960s from former colonies,] European nations have been looking for different ways to blend different people of different cultures into successful peaceful societies. All had the same goal: a society that gives equal opportunity and equal respect, regardless of race, creed, colour or faith. Forty years on, that society still doesn't

exist. But multiculturalism is with us to stay. So the question is how to make it work for Europe.

(Farouky, 2007: 18)

As a system of social and political governance, multiculturalism in Britain has emerged out of a history of race relations and immigration. The discourse, laws and policies governing racism in Britain in response to the mass immigration of the 1950s was heavily influenced by the Civil Rights Movement in the US, based on the assumption that discrimination was focused on colour and ethnicity. Colour racism was the dominant post-immigration perspective (Rex and Moore, 1967; CCCS, 1982; Jeffcoate, 1984; Gilroy, 1987; Solomos, 1992; Cornell and Hartmann, 1998; Bulmer and Solomos, 1999). After the initial welcoming of ethnic minorities onto the British shore as labourers needed to rebuild the British economy after the Second World War, competition for jobs, scarce resources and poverty has led to a backlash against black people. Hewitt (2005) notes how there was a 'white backlash' against the perceived equalities and multiculturalist practices of the local councils and other local agencies towards people of minority background. There was a perception that ethnic minorities were receiving too many privileges.

In what she refers to as the 'racialisation of immigration', Shain (2003: 1–2) observes that at various times since mass immigration from the commonwealth, black people have been positioned and represented as criminals, drug dealers, welfare cheats, single mothers and prostitutes (see also Layton-Henry, 1992; McLaren, 1994). Furthermore, the war on terror has postulated a view of Asian men as hot-headed, irrational terrorists. The constructed immigrant 'other' (*extracomunitari*) (Triandafyllidou, 2001), argues Shain (2003), has posed a threat to the 'British' way of life (Barker, 1981) – one of gentlemanly conduct, of honesty and of community. The negative representation of the immigrant 'other' has also revived the notions of 'in' and 'out' group rhetoric within nationalist discourse (Hagendoorm, 1993; Modood, 2006: 12).

Modood (2006: 38) argues that, with the physical assertiveness and mass public presence of Muslims in Britain, a more plural perspective is now needed that recognizes that discrimination can also be based on religious beliefs, rituals and practices. This echoes the earlier thinking of Barker (1981) and others such as Lawrence (1982), who argue that the 'new' shape of racism discriminates on the basis of values and culture and not exclusively on the colour of skin, although there is a complex relationship between biological and cultural racism (Goldberg, 1990).

Modood (2006: 41) agrees with Barker and suggests that racism has now moved away from the 'political blackness' period of the 1970s and 1980s, where the British population was largely divided into either 'black' or 'white'. Political blackness, argues Modood, did not offer an appropriate forum for the frustrations of South Asians. A more particular ethnic or religious identity, where culture and difference has taken on greater significance, is more appropriate for discussion in contemporary society.

The exertion of these public identities (black or Muslim) is a search for power, meaning, belonging, identity and visibility in a social system where many are invisible and remain marginalized. While the resistance of Asian youth to victimization has been well documented (Sivanandan, 1981; Castles and Miller, 1993), political blackness or the black identity movement of the 1970s and 1980s is important as it successfully raised questions of how British society had to change to accommodate new groups. It is this question of accommodation that most European states have tried, post-immigration, to tackle through their multicultural policies. The rhetoric and the objectives of justice, recognition and equality-seeking have remained the same even though the units of analysis for the Muslims of Britain have shifted from political blackness to Islamophobia.

It is within this socio-historical backdrop and context that the variations of multicultural theory have emerged. American social scientist David Theo Goldberg (1994: 1) argues that the 'multicultural condition' cannot be reductively defined; rather it can be described phenomenologically. Multiculturalism as a social and political condition of British society is both problematic and complex. Its historical backdrop is hegemonic monocultural white Britain and it has undergone a conflictual history of resistance, accommodation, integration and transformation. The various multiculturalisms discussed below are concerned with the notion of 'power'. The multicultural condition is a 'contest over power, over who mobilizes and expresses power, over how power is conceived and exercised, over who benefits or suffers the effects of power and its institutionalisation' (Goldberg, 1994: 30). There are many disparities between the principles and the practices of multicultural expression, and various multicultural theories.

With specific reference to American society in the 1980s and 1990s, sociologist Peter McLaren (1994) developed a typology of multiculturalism that provides a useful background to the current state of British egalitarian and political multiculturalism. McLaren observes that there are many theories of multiculturalism. First, he identifies conservative multiculturalism, which is deeply embedded in the colonial legacy of white supremacy. It rests on the notion that people of minority origin were savages and barbaric when white Europeans and North Americans were enlightened and civilized. The Bush/Blair rhetoric during the Iraq War of 2003 has reworked such terminology into the modern global geopolitical fabric, as a core rationale behind the war rested on notions of global security, exporting democracy and a civilizing mission (Rogers, 2002). These representations and images were also gendered: African women were seen as animalistic in terms of their sexuality and Arab women as exotic, guarding their sexuality behind the veil (Lawrence, 1982; Fryer, 1988; Banton, 1997).

The discourse that speaks of race, ethnicity and religion as backwards, argues Shain (2003), is a discourse of cultural pathology. This discourse implies that something is inherently inferior in the cultural and familial background of those people from minority-ethnic groups. This discourse problematizes such groups and positions them as inferior to the white-majority group. There is a clear relationship between Shain's cultural pathology argument and the conservative multicultural thinking whose rhetoric is located in evolutionary theories such as social Darwinism, US Manifest Destiny and Christian imperialism throughout the developing world, which position white Europeans as hegemonic, intellectual and morally superior.

Crucially, argues McLaren, its proponents pay lip service to the cognitive equality of all races in society and argue for a national common culture constructed with clear border lines. This form of multicultural theory has been heavily criticized by liberal opponents, mainly for its refusal to treat whiteness as a form of ethnicity and thus positioning whiteness as an invisible norm against which other ethnicities and cultures are measured. Conservative multiculturalism, furthermore, is essentially monolingual and asserts that English should be the only official language. English as a language of power has been elevated to 'truth-telling' status (McLaren, 1994: 50).

The liberal theory argues for a plural approach that recognizes multilingualism and advocates bilingual education. With a more progressive concept of freedom, justice, diversity and equality, liberal multiculturalism takes the view that all races and cultures are of equal moral and intellectual status and it is mainly due to structural inequalities in income, health and education and the competitive nature of the capitalist economy that an unequal stratified society exists. Liberal approaches to multiculturalism, while emphasizing the equality of all people, also acknowledges that there are important cultural differences between communities and people and that these are responsible for different behaviours, attitudes, values and social practices (McLaren, 1994). This presents a 'metropolitan paradox', especially in a city like London that is, on the one hand, a useful example of radical multicultre and yet, at the same time, is a site for hostile forms of racism (Back, 2009: 5–6).

What most concerns my study is what McLaren and others (Lott, 1994; Walzer, 1994) have termed 'critical' multiculturalism. This theory moves on from the conservative stress on sameness and the liberal preoccupation with difference, arguing that contemporary society needs to push for the politics of pluralism and to take note of the workings of 'power' and 'privilege' (McLaren, 1994: 54). Walzer (1994: 91) sees critical multiculturalism as a 'programme' for greater social and economic equality while, for Lott (1994), it is a form of resisting monoculturalism and cultural hegemony as well as socioeconomic exploitation and hardship. Through the expression of British Islam in public spaces, my participants are engaging in such a critical multiculturalism as they attempt to realize the ideal of what Modood and Kastoryano have termed egalitarian multiculturalism, where their ethno-religious identities are afforded space and respect in wider society equal to that of the dominant group:

> ...equality as not having to hide or apologise for one's origins, family or community, but requiring others to show respect for them and adapt public attitudes and arrangements so that the heritage they represent is encouraged rather than ignored or expected to wither away.
>
> (Modood and Kastoryano, 2006: 171)

Such equality recognizes and respects differences within the public and political arena, and affirms it (Modood, 2006).

John Rex's public/private precondition of a secular multicultural society

Sociologist John Rex casts valuable light on these theories of multiculturalism. Rex began with a version of multiculturalism in which being culturally different did not deny equal treatment to a person of whatever racial or ethnic background. He maintained that 'something has to be done to ensure the survival of a plurality of cultures. A fundamental human right … is the right to be culturally different' (Rex, 1986: 120). While still emphasizing that recognition of difference and diversity is a necessary condition for a multicultural society, Rex's thinking in his late writings dwells on the pivotal separation between the public and private space. For a multicultural world to be realized, Rex argued (1998), both public and private spaces need to be taken into account.

Rex advanced the definition of a multicultural society expressed in 1966 by then Home Secretary Roy Jenkins: 'integration [should be conceived] not as a flattening process of uniformity but as cultural diversity coupled with equal opportunity in an atmosphere of mutual tolerance' (Jenkins quoted in Rex, 2005: 240). Rex believed that there should be two separate domains for immigrant communities – the public sphere and the private, culturally diverse domain. In the public domain all individuals should be treated equally, whereas in the private domain individuals could practise their diverse cultures, speak their own languages, practise their religion and follow their own customs and family rituals. Rex (2005: 241) argues that this concept of a multicultural society recognizes the right of Muslims to practise their own religion in the private domain but not 'their right to have their religion made part of the public domain'.

Rex's public/private distinction sits comfortably within a secular polity. But it becomes problematic in its application to a group with a publicly assertive British-Islamic identity whose everyday beliefs, practices and lifestyle – their food choice, prayers, dress code – are very much part of a public identity. The six participants, along with countless others among the 2.7 million Muslims in Britain, will find it difficult to make a public/private distinction in their Islamic identity. As Zeyba declares: 'The hijab is a vital part of my personal and public identity. I feel secure and safe in my hijab and I want others to know that I am Muslim.' And Azad asserts: 'I had to quit my previous part-time job because they kept on giving me shifts on Friday afternoons despite me telling my boss that I needed to go to the mosque for prayers on Fridays.' Islam is thus a religion *in* and *of* the public space. It needs the public space in order to fulfil its goals, and its public existence is the prerequisite of many of the articulations required by the religion (Allievi, 2004: 187). This is acknowledged by Rex (2005: 242) when he observes that his notion of the private/public will be rejected by many Muslims who view Islam as a 'whole way of life'.

In a critique of Rex's multicultural precondition, Modood and Kastoryano (2006: 171) argue that people have the right to have their 'difference' recognized and supported in both public and private spheres. Political unity can be achieved without necessarily having cultural uniformity in public spaces (Abbas, 2005: 16). There is immense diversity among the people in Britain regarding their sociopolitical contexts, languages, ethnicities and religions. This is what Triandafyllidou *et al.* (2006) call the 'multicultural challenge' – how does the state deal with the assertion of religious, especially Muslim, identities in polities whose self-image is secular? The assertion of religious identities in public spaces, they argue, has reignited the multicultural debate and has also challenged the notion of secular Europe. The role of religious identities, especially regarding Islam, within contemporary secular British multicultural society merits discussion.

British Muslim assertiveness in public spaces: Multiculturalism redefined

One of the main obstacles in recognizing religion as a legitimate form of public identity is Britain's modern tradition of secularism. Secularism is an integral part of modern European history and is viewed as a defining feature and prerequisite to modernity. Secularism is complex and is built on the public/private boundary that Rex proposes, pushing forward the idea that belief and worship should be restricted to the private realm. In the 2011 census, 33.2 million (59.3 per cent of the population) defined themselves as Christians (ONS, 2012c). This figure and the development of a British-Islamic identity illustrates the growing importance of religion in Britain. Therefore, egalitarian and critical multiculturalism must incorporate Muslims and other religious communities, and this poses a challenge as it is built on the foundations of a secular space.

The scientific rationale of liberal European enlightenment of the eighteenth century challenged the Christian faith, the authority of the church and the promotion of religion by government. Religion was not compatible with some of the core tenets of liberalism such as humanism, individualism, scientific inquiry and freedom of thought (Locke, 1980 [1689]; Rousseau, 1968 [1762]). Political life, it was argued, must first remain secular as the state is concerned with the social reality of *this* world and not the afterlife. Social life should be centred around rationalism and reason. The emotive faith-based logic of religion can undermine scientific rationalism in public life (Parekh, 2006: 188). The French Revolution remains one of the most vehement examples of a shift from a religious to a political community in Western Europe.

The separation of church and state, of religion and politics, has become noted as a non-controversial and hegemonic feature of Western societies. But this separation is not so straightforward in the US (de Tocqueville, 1998 [1835]), which has no established church yet is still one of the most religiously observant countries in the world (Greely, 1995), even to the extent of deciding presidential elections. In Britain, the values of religion still have a strong presence in many public functions taken over by the state, such as education, family, the legal system, community and voluntary organizations (Parekh, 2006). And, as Modood and Kastoryano (2006: 169) note, there is no question of the public sphere being morally, ethically or religiously neutral, as religiously rooted 'folk' cultures have informed public civil society. The continued status of Sundays and Christmas as public holidays in many European states are obvious examples of the influence of Christianity continuing in public secular life. The separation between politics and religion is not clear cut, despite a public defence of secularism. At best, there is a reciprocal relationship – religious communities need the state to support their culture and the state looks towards religion to reinforce moral virtues such as truth-telling, civic volunteering and respect for property.

Modood and Kastoryano (2006: 162) and others (Bunting, 2004; Voas and Crockett, 2005; Khan, 2008) argue that the increasing visibility of and practice by young Muslims, and the public emergence of Islam (through the burning of *The Satanic Verses* in 1989 to the wearing of the hijab and the protests against the Danish cartoons in 2006), has challenged the very notion of a secular Europe, especially in countries such as the UK, France and Belgium (Bousetta and Jacobs, 2006; Kastoryano, 2006). Muslim assertiveness is also minority identity assertiveness. Modood (2006: 39) notes that in many countries around the world, minority-identity movements such as feminism, gay pride, Quebecois nationalism and the revival of Scottishness have become an important feature of social life. The assertiveness of such minority-identity movements within the public space has supported the idea of equality as 'difference' and for this 'difference' to be recognized and supported in the public arena as an equal to others (Modood, 2006: 39).

Modood (2006) argues that inclusion into a 'political community' (Parekh, 2000a) is not the same thing as immigrant communities readily accepting the rules of existing polity and its boundaries between the private and the public. Rather, public space is essentially created through ongoing discursive contestation and political struggles for 'recognition' from differing groups (Taylor, 1994).

In his essay, 'The politics of recognition', Canadian philosopher Charles Taylor (1994) argues that recognition in contemporary multicultural Western society is achieved through contestation, interaction and exchange with other members of society. Identity is essentially constructed through this recognition from others. As liberal multiculturalism has been unable to accommodate people of different cultural backgrounds, argues Taylor, there must now be a shift in emphasis to a politics of difference where there is a place for recognition and survival of minority cultures.

Crucially, Taylor argues that an important condition for this recognition to be of value to minority communities is for it to be underpinned by respect. Recognition for minority cultures must hold real value and cannot be viewed as tokenistic – it must originate out of genuine respect for minority cultures in multicultural societies. Minority communities must demand recognition as non-recognition or misrecognition can be harmful – a form of oppression that constructs certain groups as subhuman. Far from being settled, fixed and predetermined, the terms of politics in society are an object of debate (Benhabib, 1992). Muslim assertiveness and the emergence of a British-Islamic identity must be situated within the politics of recognition.

Muslim assertiveness has included the demand for government-funded faith schooling; the choice to wear Muslim clothing, especially the hijab, in public spaces; the implementation of Islamic sharia law in family matters; campaigning for religious discrimination to be against the law just like racial or gender discrimination; institutional representation; even-handedness among religions (for example, the high number of state-maintained Church of England schools compared to schools of other faiths) (Modood, 2006: 44); the demand for public holidays during Muslim festivals; the call to prayer being voiced through a loudspeaker to fellow community members during prayer times; and the availability of halal food in public places. British Muslims have succeeded in some areas of institutional and cultural reform. For example, many employers allow Muslim workers time off during the day to perform the daily prayers; many state schools in predominantly Muslim areas shut for the Islamic celebration of Eid twice a year; many Muslim workers get flexible working conditions during Ramadan; and the wearing of the hijab is now permitted in the Metropolitan Police Service (Anwar and Bakhsh, 2003).

However, despite these signs of progress gained by the demand for recognition (Taylor, 1994), there is still anxiety that Muslims are making 'politically exceptional, culturally unreasonable or theological alien demands upon European states' (Triandafyllidou *et al.*, 2006: 3). The 'Trojan Horse' affair of 2014 and the subsequent political and public response is one example of this anxiety. Bhikhu Parekh has highlighted other areas of European anxiety towards Muslims that have revived the argument of 'cultural separatism'. This rests on three interrelated factors. First, Muslims are culturally different to the majority population; second, Muslims living in the West are critical of the society they are a part of; and third, Muslim values and actions are anti-Western. From a critical perspective, Parekh (2006: 179–80) observes that:

- although Muslims have been present en masse for nearly five decades, they have failed to integrate

- Muslims show no commitment to the democratic traditions and institutions of the West and criticize its liberal freedoms
- Muslims do not feel at home in European societies, preferring to live among themselves, forming segregated communities and having minimum contact with wider society
- Muslims make unreasonable demands – implementation of Islamic sharia laws, funding for faith schools, particular forms of animal slaughter, time off for prayer during working hours and being allowed to wear Muslim clothing in public institutions – and they feel alienated and resentful when these demands are not met
- they increasingly view themselves as part of the global Muslim *umma* and do not view themselves as European citizens, being more concerned about the plight of their Muslim brothers and sisters around the globe
- many Muslims view themselves as morally superior to non-Muslims
- they are failing in Western education because they do not take it seriously – in one London primary school deeply conservative Muslim parents withdrew their children from music lessons because they believed that learning an instrument was forbidden in Islam (Ross, 2010: 9) – and they overburden their children with Islamic education after school and during the weekends
- they are failing economically because their educational attainment is poor and because they reject the culture of Western capitalism
- as a result of the above, they have remained an alienated community, 'in society but not of it', full of resentment and anger, so are a 'potential source of unrest and violence' (Parekh, 2006: 179).

The logic of such 'claims-making' is particularly European in context, assert Triandafyllidou *et al.* (2006: 3). The assertiveness of Muslims in public spaces challenges the 'taken for grantedness of secularism in most European societies' and also forces policymakers to rethink and reopen the secularist debate. The 'problem case' of Muslim assertiveness in Europe has not only challenged the many faces of multiculturalism but has also exposed the 'secular bias of the discourse and policies of multiculturalism in Europe' (Triandafyllidou *et al.*, 2006: 3). As a political condition of egalitarian multiculturalism, Muslims, like other faiths, cultures and immigrant communities in Britain, have just claims to difference, recognition and citizenship rights in public spaces. West/Muslim world-relations policy consultant H.A. Hellyer (2009) argues that Muslims across Europe should seize upon this pluralist European condition of egalitarian multiculturalism and strive harder to become an integral part of Europe.

Examination of these anxieties about Muslims exposes their limitations. Muslims continue to be viewed as perpetrators of their own misfortunes rather than as victims of hostile and racist structures. As Abbas (2005: 12–13) notes, 'It is easy to blame people and their values and to ignore processes and institutions.' Second, little evidence supports the claim that Muslims choose to stay isolated and that they are unassimilable within British public space. The reality, suggests Farouky (2007), is that Muslims make up only about 3 per cent of the total EU population, and that figure is expected to reach no more than 10 per cent by the year 2025. So Muslims are unlikely to become the majority population in Europe, as Bawer predicted in 2006. Third, fears of a culture clash and the view that British-born Muslims are rejecting their British identity is 'exaggerated' (Manning and Roy, 2010). The majority of Muslims living in the West are law-abiding and proud of their triple heritage: national, ethnic and religious. For example, research from the Institute for Social and Economic Research at the University of Essex (ISER, 2012), examining how British people feel about their nationality, found that 83 per cent of Muslims were proud to be British citizens compared to 79 per cent of the general public. Even when subjected to blatant discrimination such as being forbidden to build mosques in parts of Italy (Triandafyllidou, 2006), Muslims in Europe have either suffered quietly or protested peacefully. Rarely have they taken the law into their own hands.

There is also a push towards the reformation and modernization of Islam to be compatible with Western tradition and values (Gülen, 2006; Kamrava, 2006) and this has resulted in many overlaps between Islamic and Western values (Parekh, 2006; Thomas, 2009). A research study of 1,003 Muslims by the independent think tank Policy Exchange found that 62 per cent of 16- to 24-year-olds feel they have as much in common with non-Muslims as Muslims and 59 per cent would prefer to live under British law (Mirza *et al.*, 2007: 5). Parekh (2006: 184) observes that 'human dignity, equal human worth, equality of the races, civility, peaceful resolution of differences and reciprocity are all part of the Islamic tradition'. The fear and anxiety displayed towards British Muslims has prompted many commentators to suggest that Muslims are actually well integrated in Britain, 'but [that] no one seems to believe it' (Moosavi, 2012).

Muslims in Britain, especially in the past twenty years, have entered the public space through their demand for recognition and institutional representation. They have engaged constructively in democratic institutions, civic culture and pluralist dissent, mainly through alliances and coalitions with non-Muslim organizations and movements such as the Socialist

Workers' Party, the Stop the War Coalition and Runnymede, establishing 'moral communities' that transcend ethno-religious differences (Geaves, 2005: 73). The challenge for Britain, therefore, is how to govern a world religion such as Islam, which is very public in its expression, and to accept Muslims as equal social partners as a political condition of egalitarian multiculturalism despite some cultural and ideological differences.

Conclusion: Accepting British Islam in secular public spaces

> Fifteen years ago we [ethnic minorities] didn't care, or at least I didn't care, whether there was any black in the Union Jack. Now not only do we care, we must.
>
> (Hall, 1992: 259)

> ...so far it is we [Asian teenagers from Bradford, Brick Lane and Southall] who have had to make all the changes, now it is the turn of the British to accept our existence.
>
> (Modood, 1992: 264)

The narratives of the study's participants make an important contribution to contemporary egalitarian multicultural discourse for numerous reasons. First, what the six individuals say at the beginning of this chapter demonstrates that multiculturalism is in actuality a live experiment. Critical egalitarian multiculturalism provides the social tools for them to practise a version of British Islam that gives them meaning, belonging and acceptance, and which sits comfortably within the political condition of difference and diversity. As Parekh (2006: 199–200) argues, they have undergone a political journey from being Muslims 'in' Britain to Muslims 'of' Britain and consequently, many have become 'Britishized Muslims'.

Second, the narratives illustrate that Islam is compatible with British values and can thus coexist peacefully, so should not be viewed as a threat. There is no concrete evidence showing that British Muslims are not loyal to their country of settlement. The participants of this study, for example, viewed Britain as their 'home' by virtue of their birthright and childhood memories. The British Islam that is being developed by these participants demonstrates that they are willing to engage in a lifestyle centred around Western values of democracy, liberalism and human rights, albeit in an alternative Islamic halal way. Many young Muslims are still confronted with the question of what it means to be Muslim and British, whether you can be both or need to make a choice. This is the wrong question to ask.

A Muslim identity for the participants of this study is a core component of what it means to be British. Britishness, as a theoretical and political concept, is in need of definition. Britishness, as a layer of identity, is not fixed and is being contested by the participants:

> Just because I am a Muslim, it doesn't mean that I cannot be British as well.
>
> (Azad)

> I have a right to be British. I was born and raised here. No one can take that right away from me.
>
> (Saeed)

> As Bangladeshi Muslims, we are different to most British white people. But we can be different and also be British at the same time.
>
> (Taiba)

Muslims in Britain, therefore, need not to be viewed as the hostile 'other' but rather as part of the British plural and multicultural 'us'.

Third, and most important, the complex stories of my participants and their visible Islamic religiosity make the case that space should be allowed within the public arena for religious expression. This challenges the very core of secular Western societies, which allocate private spaces for religious worship and expression. A key argument of this chapter is that multiculturalism should incorporate religion as a form of diversity just like other forms of social identity such as race, ethnicity, ability and gender. The religious identities of my participants must be afforded equal status and recognition and receive institutional support and protection, just as the many other equality-seeking identities in society do today, such as feminism and gay pride.

Finally, liberal secularists must be able to handle criticism of their way of social organization. Like other minority groups, Muslims are among the biggest critics of the liberal Western lifestyle. Immigrant communities bring with them different values, customs and social organization. The Muslim cultural way of life offers an alternative model that does not necessarily place the same importance on liberal attitudes such as personal autonomy, individual choice and liberty. Liberals must be able to handle this difference and explore and debate the commonalities (see Lyon, 2005). British liberal society must view itself as a distinct cultural community just like the many communities that make up the multicultural society. It cannot present itself as the embodiment of universal values, a higher civilization, or position itself as a morally superior belief system. As Parekh (2006: 195–7) argues, liberal secularism is just one, and not 'the', way of social organization.

In forging and cementing a public space in multicultural Britain, one major obstacle the British-Bangladeshi Muslim community of East London must overcome is the perceived unequal treatment of women. This area of Islamic and Bangladeshi tradition and practice still sits uneasily within liberal Western discourse. This issue needs to be addressed to present a message of equality and human rights that is part of a modern and progressive Islamic school of thought and among the values of Western liberal democracies.

The next chapter explores the position of Bangladeshi women in Tower Hamlets and examines the emergence of a distinct gendered identity in the three female participants in my study.

Chapter 8

Third-generation Bangladeshi girls from Tower Hamlets

Introduction

At the beginning of the twenty-first century, the topic of Islam, fundamentalism, terrorism, extremism and women's position in Islam is on many people's minds, from the local bus driver to the specialist scholar. The discourse in the popular mind is one of the backwardness, violence and barbarity of Islam, Arabs and Muslims. *The oppression of women is a given.* This makes challenging the popular Western stereotype that the veil is a symbol of Muslim women's oppression an uphill battle, all the more so in light of certain late twentieth-century events in the Muslim world: Iran's imposition of the chador after Khomeini's revolution in 1979; the Taliban's imposition of the burqa after their accession to power in 1997; and the violence perpetrated by radical groups in the name of Islam in Egypt, Israel, Algeria and the like. Does not all this merely confirm that Islam is violent, intolerant and anti-women?

(Bullock, 2007: Introduction, 38, my italics)

This chapter is written against a sociopolitical backdrop of the oppression of Muslim women, locating the voices of the three women in this study within this wider local, national and international context. I argue, however, that far from being steeped in negativity as Bullock suggests, the women draw from their religion a positive sense of identity. The symbolism of the hijab and their membership, actual and ideological, of a religious community that is highly politicized and visible, gives them not only confidence but also belonging, recognition, sisterhood and voice. Contrary to being 'passive victims of oppressive cultures' and of a 'cultural pathology' that positions them as homebound, passive, docile, oppressed, lacking confidence and dominated by strict fathers, brothers and husbands (Shain, 2003: 14), my participants are actively adapting their culture and religion and establishing a positive British-Islamic identity for themselves.

British Islam is both resistance and 'negotiation' of Bangladeshi and Western patriarchy (Sanghera and Thapur-Björkert, 2007: 173–91) and at the same time combines elements of both cultures in an attempt to construct new syncretic meanings of what it means to be British, Bangladeshi, Muslim and female (Choudhury, 2008; Contractor, 2012). I subscribe to the view of patriarchy as a system of masculine dominance, power and control over women (Millet, 1970; Walby, 1990). Patriarchy can also be viewed as the maintenance of male privileges (Haw, 1998). The role of Islam in the lives of Bangladeshi Muslim women is important both symbolically and spiritually. They seek to make sense of Islam as a living entity relevant to their everyday lives inside and outside their home (N. Ahmed, 2005). Many Muslim women experience a form of triple oppression: of culture, community and religion.

Membership of British Islam is providing a platform to Sanjida, Taiba and Zeyba to resist the greater control to which they are exposed at home and within their communities (Sahin, 2005) and to challenge the aspects of traditional Bangladeshi and Muslim culture deemed to be oppressive towards women. The notion of the traditional Bangladeshi woman is being contested by the emergence of an Islamically and Western-oriented identity. Their identities are 'dynamic' rather than static (Basit, 1997).

This chapter is not a theological account of the status of women in Islam although I refer to the origins of the religion and to how, in the seventh century, Prophet Mohammed (PBUH) was trying to determine a more egalitarian theory of the position of women in Islamic societies. Lacking the knowledge or the expertise to make such an analysis, I must leave this for Islamic commentators and theologians to debate (Maqsood, 2003; Rippin, 2005; Channel 4, 2008). Here I embark on a sociological and ethnographic discussion of the evolving identities of British-born Bangladeshi females in which Islam has an important role as a social force.

A brief consideration of Muslim women and the veil is needed. Veiling is a generic and complex term that means covering. I use the words 'veil', 'veiling' and 'hijab' interchangeably, and all refer to a choice of women's dress code associated with the modest and loose covering of the full female body apart from the face and hands, unless specified otherwise. The term hijab also has a trilogy of meanings:

1. To conceal, hide and cover.
2. To lower the gaze with the opposite sex. This applies to men too – they must lower their gaze in the presence of unrelated women.
3. In recent times, hijab has become the common name given to the headscarf worn by Muslim women, pinned at the neck. There is a crucial

spiritual, ideological and cultural difference between those women just wearing the headscarf – with their faces showing – and those who wear the face veil – niqab. The reaction to the chosen dress code differs at both an intra-community (Muslim) and societal (non-Muslim) level.

Their choice of dress has become the most contested, visible and iconic symbol of Islam in Britain for Muslim women. It is impossible to untangle a discussion of third-generation Bangladeshi female identities, in which Islam plays a significant sociopolitical role, from a generic examination of the complexities of the hijab as discussed by feminists, sociologists, politicians and anthropologists (Mernissi, 1991, 2003 [1975]; El Guindi, 2000; Bullock, 2007; Tarlo, 2009; Gabriel and Hanan, 2011). A significant section of this chapter is devoted to the hijab as a focal point in our analysis. To develop the arguments above, this chapter is organized in order to:

- locate the voices of the three female participants in the wider discourse of gender roles within the Bangladeshi culture and Islamic religion
- discuss the status of women in Islam, which makes a key distinction between spiritual (scriptural) Islam and various cultural interpretations
- critically examine the role of the hijab as a symbol of either oppression or liberation
- promote the concept of a positive British-Islamic identity, which is allowing my participants to manage their multiple identities of being a British-born Bangladeshi Muslim woman.

The importance of Islam: Locating *their* voices within the wider debate

For Taiba, Sanjida and Zeyba, we see that their power and voice is strengthened by their increasingly important Islamic cultural way of life. What they said about their home, childhood memories, schooling, family life, culture and future aspirations showed a gendered perspective. Although they shared experiences of racism, language choice, the complexity of home and Britishness and memories of Bangladesh with the men in the study, the women were clearly involved in an additional battle of gender equality within both the private and public sphere. Islam, whether in practice or ideology, gave the women a vehicle through which to strive for greater gender equality or at least engage in the rhetoric of equality:

> ...er, I have to admit, I'm not the best of Muslims. I mean, I don't
> do anything bad like drinking or smoking and going out with
> boys. I'm just lazy. I should be praying much more and wearing

the headscarf all of the time … some of my friends are proper Muslims and I can see how Islam has benefited them. They are now much more expressive and confident and don't take crap.

(Sanjida)

I have a lot of time to read now that I am pregnant. I am reading lots and lots about my religion and the more I read, the more sense it makes to me … it is such a beautiful religion especially because it holds women with so much respect … it makes me sad to think that my *daadi* and mum hold such negative views about women.

(Taiba)

AH: What is it about Islam that you find most attractive?

Zeyba: Everything.

AH: You've gotta give me more than that … what do you mean by 'everything'?

Zeyba: Er, I mean the whole package – everything. It's so simple and beautiful especially how it treats women. It's not like how others view it.

AH: What do you mean – who is the 'other'?

[pause]

Zeyba: We Muslims get so much negative publicity by non-Muslims. Either we are terrorists or we don't like Britain. Like I said earlier, I am British, because I was born here and our fathers don't beat us up all of the time or force us to wear the hijab and, er, I personally don't know anyone who is a terrorist … I can do and be whatever I want. I am not oppressed.

These stories highlight both the diversity of Islamic practice (see Chapter 2) and the important role of religion in constructing a gendered identity for Sanjida, Taiba and Zeyba. Sanjida appears to mirror the concept of the 'lazy Muslim'. Although she is not engaged in the day-to-day practice of religion such as prayer, she is nonetheless ideologically committed to Islam and can see how it benefits women. Islam makes sense to Taiba because of its 'beaut[y]' and she is keen to use religion as a vehicle to strive for gender equality and also to challenge the traditional role of Bangladeshi women as observed by her grandmother and mother. Like Taiba, it is the simplicity and beauty, what she refers to as the 'whole package', of Islam that Zeyba finds most appealing. And like the others, she contests that the treatment of women in Islam is positive. However, her admission and keenness to maintain that she 'can do and be whatever [she] want[s]' and that she is 'not oppressed' suggests that her views are shaped by her family structure, her class position and her liberal values and lifestyle.

All three present a very positive account of the role of religion in their lives, especially concerning the treatment of women, with little critical vigour. Viewed from a feminist standpoint, however, the treatment of women in Islam is under debate. The contentious symbolism of the hijab and some of the stories told during the research, especially by Sanjida, suggest that patriarchy, tradition and culture still play a significant role in the shaping of Bangladeshi female identity despite the rhetoric of gender equality.

Women experience oppression and patriarchy in various ways. Experiences are ontologically fractured and there is no one single reality for women (Stanley and Wise, 1990). Class, income, geography and education all affect the practice of patriarchy in Bangladeshi households. There were gendered and class differences between the aspirations of Sanjida and Zeyba. Zeyba, whose background, income and family education mirrored a middle-class lifestyle, did not place much importance on motherhood, whereas Sanjida, who was steeped in a working-class lifestyle, wanted to maintain her 'culture' through marriage, language, children and domestic chores. So there are many complexities involved.

Taiba and Sanjida were actively resisting the 'backward' and 'old-fashioned' idea of the 'traditional Bangladeshi woman' – as homebound, family-oriented, quiet, passive and docile (Basit, 1997; Bhavani and Ahmad, 2006; Choudhury, 2008):

> I'm not like my mother and grandmother. If I don't agree with something then I will let others know. I am not a 'yes' person. I have my own mind, my own bank account and am in control of my own future.
>
> (Taiba)

> My cousin sister wanted a love marriage. I don't see anything wrong with that. It's her choice. Even though I am young, she approached me to approach her parents. That's because she knows I speak my mind and don't beat around the bush. I do

respect my elders but if something needs to be said then I don't hold back.

(Sanjida)

So even though their cultural values are similar to their mothers', girls like Sanjida and Taiba are more willing to express some disagreement – what Archer *et al.* (2010) describe as working-class girls 'speaking [their] mind'. In the context of the South Asian gender problematic, this can be viewed as a form of 'coming out' against certain cultural and ethnic community practices (see Geaves, 2005: 75–6). There has been a growing body of controversial literature from younger Muslim women from across the world who are speaking out against their disadvantaged position as women in Islamic communities (see Manji, 2005; Amara, 2006; Ali, 2007).

This shift in attitude between the first/second generations of British-Bangladeshi women and the third/fourth generations can be explained by a number of factors:

- Mothers are more likely to encourage their daughters to access education and employment (Bhavani, 2006; Aston *et al.*, 2007; Choudhury, 2008).
- Enhancement in educational attainment and diversification in employment patterns have generated a younger professional class of women (Basit, 1997; Bunting, 2004; Equal Opportunities Commission, 2007). In her discussion with almost 2,000 Bangladeshis, Gavron (2005) found that active and increasing participation in employment and higher education has led to greater independence and more British-educated Bangladeshi women taking responsibility for their own careers or choice of partner. This professional class is illustrated in the aspirations of the participants: Taiba wants to go into youth work, Zeyba has aspirations to become a scientist and Sanjida hopes to become a teacher.
- Younger women are influenced by mainstream British culture, moving away from the domestic sphere and accessing social spaces such as youth clubs, going to university, travelling abroad, taking part in sporting activities, and going on social outings to restaurants, galleries and cinemas (Gavron, 2005; Din, 2006; Lewis, 2007). These changes are influencing the 'expression' of Islam in Europe (Roald, 2001: 300).
- More young women are ready to speak up against a perceived sense of injustice than their mothers. For example, Sanjida would like to 'spit back [and] slap' the man who spat at her father.

- Higher literacy levels among the third generation affords them access to a variety of literature about Islam. Many daughters of the second generation are far more devout in their interpretation of Islam, their dress and prayer than their mothers (N. Ahmed, 2005; Choudhury, 2008). Furthermore, they can display a literal version of spiritual Islam that pushes for gender equality instead of the Bangladeshi cultural version of Islam followed by their mothers that is mainly based on local rituals and tradition from rural villages of Bangladesh (Parekh, 2006).

These sociopolitical changes have made the younger generation of women more confident, vocal, visible and politically active. Nevertheless, as Abbas (2005) notes, there are still structural and cultural constraints that restrict many Bangladeshi women in their engagement with mainstream society. Barriers to engagement such as racism, sexism and anti-Muslim prejudice remain significant areas of concern (Equal Opportunities Commission, 2007; Malik, 2012; Dobson, 2014).

The increasing popularity of Islam in the lives of Taiba, Sanjida and Zeyba invites the question of whether they have rejected one patriarchal culture – Bangladeshi – only to enter another – Islamic – which, although it offers many rights to women, also chains them within a culture where men are still deemed the 'protector' and 'guardian' of 'their' women (Mernissi, 2003 [1975]: 12). The increased religiosity among women must be viewed within the context of a new British Islam that is synonymous with a modern lifestyle. It is an Islam that emphasizes women's rights, education, career and motherhood, fashion, banking and socializing within an Islamic halal framework (Scott, 2004; Kermani, 2006; Warburton, 2007). It is this version of Islam that Zeyba, Sanjida and Taiba are trying to embrace, resisting the persona of the homebound and powerless Bangladeshi woman:

> [before I was pregnant] I meet up with my girlfriends every Thursday evening and go to smoke shisha (flavoured tobacco) in Mile End. It's a chilled place and the owners have segregated seating which means that it's ok Islamically and we can also let our hair down and have fun without being harassed by boys for our phone numbers.
>
> (Taiba)

> I try as often as I can to take my mum along to Islamic talks in the East London Mosque. She needs to understand Islam better. There are certain things that she does – like the clothes that she

wears – which are un-Islamic. I try and correct her as much as possible.

(Zeyba)

Taiba's shisha-smoking sessions with her girlfriends may be considered controversial in Sylheti-Bangladeshi culture as it is a departure from the traditional image of Bangladeshi women and entails smoking in an arena associated with men. But Taiba thinks she is doing nothing wrong as she smokes where 'segregated seating' is provided, so it is 'ok Islamically'. Taiba tells me that her 'hijabi'-wearing friend Lipi, who is very religious, drives her to the shisha bar in a car with 'blacked-out' windows so that Lipi can maintain a sense of separation, or purdah, from men. This reflects the syncretism of modern youth culture with religious spirituality. Lipi drives a fast sports car, playing loud 'hip-hop music' while maintaining purdah. Also, Zeyba is critical of her mother's 'un-Islamic' dress choice and is keen to 'correct her as much as possible'. Both examples illustrate the increased religiosity and the trendy and modern British Islam in the lives of Zeyba and Taiba.

This negotiation of identities, however, remains a complex and painful process, illustrated in particular by the contradictory voice of Sanjida. The new liberated Bangladeshi woman remains a myth for many third-generation Bangladeshi girls. There is mounting tension between British-Islamic modernity and Bangladeshi tradition. For example, Taiba is critical of her gendered upbringing, which revolved around cooking, cleaning, no interaction with boys, a very strict father and the expectation that she was to marry 'one of her cousin brothers from Bangladesh'. She has resisted such a cultural lifestyle by moving out of the family home.

Sanjida's inner battle to reconcile her Bangladeshi culture and tradition with the fact that she is a British-born teenager with a different Western way of life is evident in the confusion of her gendered role and responsibilities. Sanjida feels that a 'good' Bangladeshi girl – what she also refers to as 'miss goody goody two shoes' – needs to be able to cook, clean, keep her husband happy and rear children; skills that, according to Archer (2002: 364), are viewed as 'normal' components of Muslim femininity:

> I want to have lots of children and look after them just like my mum but I also want to have a career. There is nothing wrong in doing both things but I reckon it will be hard [pause] I do want to get married and settle down as soon as I finish my studies and make my family proud … I don't mind being a housewife but I hope my future mother-in-law allows me to work.

(Sanjida)

143

Sanjida wants to pursue a teaching career but acknowledges that it will be difficult to be a career woman as well as a mother and daughter-in-law. Reiterating the importance of 'cooking' and the ability to rear children as important elements of a particularly rural Sylheti-Bangladeshi female culture, Sanjida jokingly says, 'Kids, cook, mark [pause] mark, kids, cook. It's gonna be hard.' Her reference to whether her 'future mother-in-law' will give her permission to work points to an important element of Bangladeshi culture – the continual matriarchal power struggle and attempt to control junior women in the family hierarchy in order to maintain tradition and pass down cultural values through the generations.

Sanjida's remark that she wants to 'keep her husband happy' reflects the importance of patriarchy within Bangladeshi culture and illustrates the famous Bangladeshi proverb: 'When you live in the water, you don't argue with the crocodiles' (White, 1992). Although White's anthropological study focused on illiterate rural Bangladeshi women, this proverb highlights the importance of power relations between men and women as a key feature of Bangladeshi culture. Sanjida's dilemma echoes one of the key findings from Basit's (1997) in-depth study of 24 British Muslim girls and their parents. She found that the girls wanted to 'hang on' to their Asian and Muslim roots while finding ways to adapt these identities within British society.

Maintaining Bangladeshi culture and tradition through language, gender roles and rituals was important for Sanjida. Despite the emergence of a seemingly gender-neutral British Islam, her defence of the 'good' Bangladeshi girl highlights the importance of the politics of patriarchy that still regulate local community affairs. There remains an unequal gender space within the community, which does not afford the same rights and liberties to female members. There is still great tension between progressive British Islam and traditional conservative Bangladeshi-Muslim patriarchy. The 'cultural pathology' argument (Shain, 2003) still holds weight and is a reality for Bangladeshi women despite the rhetoric of gender equality.

The status of women in Islam

It is important to make a distinction between the traditional Bangladeshi cultural view of women and what the religion of Islam advocates in order to understand the appeal of Islam to many second- and third-generation Bangladeshi women in Britain. Historically, there have been three main schools of thought in the discussion of women and Islam. First, there are those who defend what is believed to be the divinely ordained difference between the sexes (see Haddad, 1980; Stowasser, 1987). This essentialist view of women is also ingrained in religions such as Catholicism (John Paul

II, 1988; Manning, 1999). Such thinking pushes forward the 'different but equal' argument, although feminists such as Berktay (1993) and Keddie (1991) suggest, instead, that essentialism consigns women to being 'different and inferior'.

Second, some Muslim feminists suggest a more progressive interpretation of the Qu'ran and claim that Islam has a very special status for women (Al-Hibri, 1982; El Saadawi, 1982). In such a reading of Islamic history, women played an important role in early Muslim societies, especially in public spaces such as education, the labour market and politics. Syria and Egypt, for example, had prominent Muslim women landowners and businesswomen from the thirteenth century on (Meriwether, 1993; Marsot, 1996). Kabeer (1991: 78–115) points to the recent role of Bangladeshi women in the struggle for independence from West Pakistan in 1971. Many even took up arms against the West Pakistani army (Autograph ABP, 2008).

However, a school of thought is growing that Islam is intrinsically patriarchal and inimical to women's rights (see Sabbah, 1984; Ghassoub, 1987). Popular, conservative books such as *Bahishti Zewar* by Islamic scholar Maulana Ashraf Ali Thanvi (2004 [1333]) support the view that Islam is inherently misogynistic. The book proposes that women are subordinate to and are the possessions of men, and that the ideal for women is to stay at home, secluded from all but family and a few female friends (Metcalf, 1990). Traditional texts such as Imam Nawawi's *Riyadh us Saliheen* depict women as the property of men and advocate violence against women (quoted in Lewis, 2007: 98–9). The Taliban of Afghanistan were an obvious visual example of such a misogynist society in recent times, where women were denied education, confined to the home and barred from public life (see Zoya *et al.*, 2002; Skaine, 2002; Hosseini, 2007). In these examples, women have suffered injustices at the hands of their husbands, family, village and society.

The view that women are subordinate to men is ahistorical, deeply conservative and is located within certain cultural contexts. It does not correlate with the reality nor reflect the changes in the aspirations and attitudes of twenty-first-century Muslim women such as the three who took part in my study. Muslim feminists such as Ahmed (1992) and Mernissi (2003 [1975]; 1991) argue that women have started to take more prominent roles in public life since the start of modernizing and nation-building projects in many Muslim countries post independence. Ahmed (1992), however, maintains that throughout history women have been controlled, subordinated, economically marginalized and conceptualized as inferior to men. It was only in the last century that women attained civil and political rights and gained access to educational and professional life in some countries.

The position of Muslim women in Western European countries has evolved over the past ten years. Many women are rebelling against highly sexist cultural conventions and using Islam to push for gender equality. As a result, there are Muslim women voting in elections, standing for public office, going on to higher and further education, carving out professions and careers for themselves and resisting the patriarchal dominance of their fathers, husbands and brothers (Ameli and Merali, 2006; Bhavani and Ahmad, 2006; Equal Opportunities Commission, 2007; Sanghera and Thapur-Björkert, 2007). In 2014, four out of forty-five directly elected councillors in Tower Hamlets were Bangladeshi women (Tower Hamlets, 2014). At time of publication, the Labour MP for Bethnal Green and Bow, Rushnara Ali, is also a Bangladeshi woman.

Moroccan feminist Fatima Mernissi (2003 [1975]) has added weight to Ahmed's (1992) argument that, in many Muslim countries, the ingrained cultural view of women as active sexual beings has resulted in stricter regulation and control of women's sexuality because it is perceived as a threat to civilized society. However, the requisites of modernization in the Muslim world, argues Mernissi, are incompatible with traditional Muslim structures. Public desegregation of the sexes allows Muslim women to access the labour and education markets and this is needed in a capitalist economy. Such nation-building and modernization projects have thrust women out of the domestic sphere and into 'classrooms, offices and factories', challenging the ideology of male supremacy and, in turn, society's gender balance (Mernissi, 2003 [1975]: 15).

Mernissi argues that the need to modernize has not only modified the traditional Moroccan family into a nuclear rather than extended structure, but that the new financial autonomy among both men and women has also redefined the male–female relationship, so challenging traditional/ Arab systems of male dominance. A similar challenge to patriarchy took place in Egypt during the nineteenth and twentieth centuries, according to historian Margot Badran (1991). She argues that many Egyptian Muslim women did not submit readily to the strictures of religious fundamentalism as interpreted by men but were active in pursuing their own versions of the ways in which Islam might further their interests as women.

Mernissi notes that, contrary to what is often perceived, Islam does not assert women's inherent inferiority to men. Islam as a religion places women's rights at the core of its ideology, has an 'ethical vision which is stubbornly egalitarian' and advocates potential equality between the sexes (Ahmed, 2006: 198). The inequality, argues Mernissi (2003 [1975]), is created not by some biological, ideological or theological concept of women's inferiority, but by specific social institutions, led by men, that are designed to restrict the power of women through segregation and legal subordination through family laws. Drawing on the origins of Islam in the seventh century, Mernissi (1991) points out that women were initially granted full and equal citizenship. The women who migrated from tribal Makkah to Medina enjoyed the status of *sahabiyat* (full citizenship) and were involved in the democratic management of society, especially in military and political affairs. As examples, she cites the wife of the Prophet Mohammed (PBUH) A'isha, who led the armed opposition against the caliph who ruled at that time, and the socialite Sukayna. Both were important political figures during early Islam. Mernissi (1991: 8) argues:

> …we Muslim women can walk into the modern world with pride, knowing that the quest for dignity, democracy, and human rights, for full participation in the political and social affairs of our country, stems from no imported Western values, but is a true part of the Muslim tradition.

Those who have denied women equal rights over the past 1,400 years have done so because of 'profit' and 'self interest' (Mernissi, 1991: 7). It is the Muslim male elite who have deliberately constructed a misogynistic and patriarchal version of Islam, since the rights of women conflicted with their interests within both the domestic and public spheres. Islamic history and memory, therefore, has been deliberately 'supervised', 'managed' and manipulated by those in positions of power – the male elite (El Saadawi, 1980).

Sociologist Katherine Bullock (2007), herself a convert to Islam, builds on Mernissi's ideas. She is keen to emphasize the difference between the status of women in Islam and the status of women in a male-biased cultural practice of the faith. It is this distinction between cultural practices and religion that is attractive to my participants. Taiba argues.

> Most people in and outside of our community are ignorant about the Islamic history of women [pause] They should attend conferences, visit websites, read themselves and speak more to lots of young Muslim girls … they will find out that there is a difference between the Islamic view of women and the Bangladeshi backwards view. Us younger girls are different to

> our mums mostly because we are not afraid to speak out and because we have more knowledge about Islam.

The media present a pejorative image of Muslim women. They portray the women covered from head to toe in public, women being stoned to death, family law that is heavily biased towards men, women's total obedience to their husbands, sexual segregation, easy divorce for men, polygamy and the enslavement and seclusion of women. While this may be the case in certain cultures and societies across the world, Bullock (2007) argues that Islam, as opposed to the cultural interpretation of it, places women in a position of dignity, respect and equality.

One of the key difficulties with the complex issue of the status of women in Islam is the problem of interpretation. There is a strong tradition within Islam of the sanctity of Qu'ranic verses and the stories and actions of the Prophet Mohammed (PBUH) and his companions (the hadith). There is complex debate among Islamic scholars as to their meaning and interpretation. This tradition of interpretation lays Islam open to manipulation and blurs important matters. Differences of opinion between Islamic scholars over the hijab, for example, remain a marked feature of Islam (Roald, 2001). Bullock (2007) notes that many Muslim women across the globe are following an unveiling trend, convinced that the hijab is not religiously required dress. They argue that the Qu'ran does not specifically refer to a head cover, but asks women to dress modestly by covering their chests. This interpretation refutes the widely held belief that modesty requires women to cover their hair as well as their shoulders and torso. This example of the complexities of interpretation makes it clear that all Muslim women cannot be branded as oppressed. Within the British Muslim communities alone, conservative followers of Islam are critical of those who do not wear the hijab and the modern progressives denounce women who wear the niqab (face mask). There is much complexity.

The importance of the hijab

The case of Shabina Begum from Luton who, in 2005, took her school to the High Court over her right to wear her religious dress to school was given much coverage in the media. So was MP Jack Straw's criticism in 2006 over a constituent who wore the niqab during meetings. Classroom assistant Aishah Azmi was fired from her job in the same year for refusing to remove her face veil in the classroom. The French banned the hijab and other religious symbols being worn in public schools in 2004. All this has brought the issue of the hijab, the veil and the status and rights of women in Islam generally into public, media and political prominence.

As an obvious visual symbol, the hijab 'communicate[s] meaningfully with others … a crucial part' of female, Bangladeshi-Muslim identity (Hall, 1990: 222, 1997: 29). The hijab is the 'most visible marker of 'otherness' and denotes 'difference' and 'subordination' (Ask and Tjomsland, 1998: 48). Therefore, the symbolism of the hijab and a discussion of Bangladeshi women in general is inevitably located within otherization and orientalist theory, as discussed in Chapter 2. White (1992: 4) argues that the discourse of Bangladeshi women as a visible 'other' is not neutral but arises from and reproduces certain relations of power. Such thinking has helped the West to maintain its hegemony and legitimize existing systems of political domination and subordination.

The symbolism and practicality of the hijab were both important to Sanjida, Zeyba and Taiba. Zeyba viewed the hijab as a 'public statement' of her 'inner faith'. She has worn the hijab since the age of 11 and views it as 'the most important' part of her identity. She says: 'It is much more than a piece of cloth to me … my personality, spirituality, my faith … it gives me confidence, direction, pride … The hijab means everything to me.' Taiba understands the role of the hijab as a statement of both her gender and her faith. She aspires to wear the hijab permanently when she feels spiritually ready to do so. Like Taiba, Sanjida is aware of the hijab's importance, but takes a more flexible approach – wearing it mainly at family events and weddings but abandoning it when she is 'out with her mates'. Depending on how she feels, she sometimes wears the hijab to school. Her attitude towards the hijab is governed by her 'deep faith' as well as her desire to bring 'respectability' upon her family.

A ferocious debate rages among feminists, sociologists and politicians over the hijab. One school of thought, to which the feminist Mernissi (2003 [1975], 1991) subscribes, is that the 'veiling' of Muslim women is a symbol of female oppression and subjugation and is forced upon women by men in a patriarchal system. But the other school of thought argues that the veil liberates women (Bullock, 2007; El Guindi, 2000) and that there are 'multiple meanings' behind the wearing of the veil (Bullock, 2007). Although this polemic is far more complex, historical and multi-layered than a simplistic opposition between oppression and liberation (Bullock, 2007: 136–82), I outline below some of the core themes of this debate.

In a critique of Mernissi, Bullock (2007: 85–135) claims that there are multiple meanings behind a woman's choice to wear the veil and that the veil liberates Muslim women from the male gaze. In a more anthropological analysis, El Guindi (2000) argues that Muslim women covered themselves as an affirmation of cultural identity. Importantly, the veil performs a dual symbolic resistance: historically, against colonial penetration of Muslim lands (El Guindi, 2000) and against today's consumer capitalist culture (Bullock, 2007).

In the modern British sociopolitical climate, views of the veil are negative, as they are underpinned by a historic Western colonial/oriental desire to unveil women as a symbol of liberation and modernity (Bullock, 2007; Al-Din, 1990 [1928]). That veiling is not a choice. Rather, it is a cultural and religious practice that is barbaric and outdated and forced upon women predominantly by the men of their societies. Unveiling thus liberates women from the chains of patriarchy, culture and community and gives them agency and freedom. Using the example of America's desire to liberate Afghan women, Ayotte and Husain (2005: 117) argue that the idea of unveiling as liberation can be viewed as a form of 'colonial feminism'.

In her 1996 in-depth study of 16 Muslim women in Toronto, Canada who wore the hijab, Bullock (2007) challenges popular Western notions about the veil and about Muslim women being subjugated. The idea that the veil is a symbol of Muslim women's oppression forced upon them by men, asserts Bullock (2007: 25), is a 'constructed' image that does not represent the experience of all those who wear it. She is highly critical of liberal Muslim feminists such as Mernissi who argue that the choice to cover is 'un-liberating'. Bullock contests that the notion of the veil as oppressive is based on liberal Western understandings of 'equality' and 'liberty' that preclude other ways of thinking about these concepts.

Bullock maintains that the veil is a symbol of resistance to the Western consumer capitalist culture that commodifies and exploits the female body in the name of profit. The hijab liberates women from this and empowers them to resist the 'beauty myth' and the ideal of the slim woman (Bordo, 1993), and counters the 'male gaze' which, according to radical feminists such as Dworkin (1995) and MacKinnon (1995), dehumanizes and objectifies the female body. Sanjida, jokingly, backs this up: 'There is always a pressure to look nice … Sometimes, I just cannot be bothered with make-up and nice clothes. I just throw the headscarf over my head and go out' [laughing].

Bullock proposes three ways of analysing the status of women and the role of the hijab in Islamic societies. One is the *mainstream pop culture* view, in which Muslim women are utterly subjugated by men and the veil is a symbol of this subjugation. This simplistic view is steeped in colonial and orientalist discourse and imagery and pushed by the media. Western politicians exploit such imagery when imposing their views on the Muslim world in a declared attempt to liberate and civilize them and also to justify colonization, intervention and invasion (see Rogers, 2002; Ayotte and Husain, 2005).

The second is the *liberal feminist* view. This attracts both Muslims and non-Muslims (Haw, 1998). Its proponents have a deep understanding of Islam and are committed also to the issue of women's rights. Imbued with liberal concepts such as individualism, liberty, equality, human rights and the meaning and nature of oppression, they believe that Islam, like all patriarchal religions, subordinates and holds misogynistic views of women (Daly, 1985 [1968]; Holm, 1994; Hamington, 1995; Manning, 1999). Farley's (2009) study of 92 Muslim girls and their teachers in Luton examined whether a state school should offer the hijab as part of the school uniform for Muslim students. Many of the teachers saw the hijab as a symbol of oppression and a way of constantly reminding the girls of their cultural obligations. One teacher regarded the hijab as repressive and a form of 'control' exerted by parents.

Ramazanoglu (1986), however, highlights a point of tension in this stance. On the one hand, Muslim women cannot be judged to be oppressed when they are simply celebrating the Muslim way of life by wearing the hijab. On the other hand, Western feminists argue that they know Muslim women are oppressed even if *they* do not, because they are subject to the universal criterion of oppression, external to Islam, which identifies veiling as oppressive. Central to this stance is the idea that the hijab is forced upon women by men as a form of control and thus takes away their agency and choice. It is the idea of women as possessions and as objects that need to guard their sexuality that is oppressive.

The third analysis is what Bullock calls the *contextual approach*, developed chiefly by anthropologists and historians. This line of argument problematizes the issue of veiling and the status of women in Islamic communities. It listens to the voices of veiled women and tries to understand the meaning of the social practice of veiling from the inside. The central question for Bullock and followers of this approach is whether the issues raised by Western feminists are universally applicable to all women (Fernea and Bezirgan, 1977; Wikan, 1982; Tucker, 1983; Fernea, 1989, 1998).

Lazreg (1988) observes that feminists from the East frequently adopt Western feminist categories without questioning their relevance and applicability to the lives of women in the East. This led to a movement in the 1990s for the construction of an indigenous rather than imported feminism, relevant to the lives of Muslim women (Ahmed, 1992; Yamani, 1996;

Karam, 1998). Although criticized for its cultural relativism as a banner under which the oppression of women is legitimized and therefore made to appear tolerable (Berktay, 1993), the contextual approach recognizes that women wear the veil for various reasons and are informed in their choices by context, local customs and rituals, social environment, political and economic climate and cultural lifestyle (El Saadawi, 1980).

Analysing the experiences of Sanjida, Taiba and Zeyba in terms of the contextual approach is a useful way of examining their identities. Although there are overlaps, their differing stories make it clear that Bangladeshi girls experience the hijab in different ways:

> I was forced to wear the hijab when I was young … I do not wear it any more. I will again, *inshallah*, when I am ready.
>
> (Taiba)

> My parents have never told me to wear it … I choose to wear the hijab. It's an important part of my identity as a Muslim female.
>
> (Zeyba)

> Sometimes I wear the headscarf when I am out. Other times I forget. It's important as it is a mark of respectability and deep faith.
>
> (Sanjida)

Farley (2009) confirms that what women feel about wearing the hijab is complex. Farley and others (El Guindi, 2000; Jawad and Benn, 2003; Iqbal, 2010) found that Muslim women wore the hijab for a variety of reasons: religion, culture, fashion, community, identity, privacy, space, protection, power, autonomy, respect, confidence and to prevent male harassment. The hijab is also a public expression of personal identity and a symbol of social status to many women (Watson, 1994; Franks, 2000; Bullock, 2007: 85–135). Farley (2009) found that Muslim women are conscious of practical reasons for wearing the hijab, including pleasing parents, lower costs for clothing and spending less time grooming their hair. Like Sanjida, many of Farley's participants were very flexible about when they wore it. Some wore the hijab only at school, some only during prayer time, whereas others wore it regularly, according to their personal, aesthetic, social, religious and political choices (Tarlo, 2009). Veiling as a social practice is therefore not fixed or unidirectional, but is a dynamic process.

That all Muslim women are oppressed and that the hijab is a symbol of this oppression, as the mainstream popular culture and liberal feminist arguments go, is simplistic. History, social class, context and social environment determine their experiences. There are, as Bullock (2007: 180) notes, 'sociological complexities of covering'. Just as the third-generation Bangladeshis in Tower Hamlets experience multiple identities, there are multiple meanings behind the concept of veiling. Of course, for the thousands of Muslim women around the globe who are living as second-class citizens, controlled and subjugated by men, the veil is not a choice but mandatory. Equally, however, there are thousands of Muslim women who, in the context of a British society that allows freedom of dress, have chosen to re-veil themselves for religious and personal reasons. There are also Muslim women who are deeply religious while choosing not to wear the veil. Muslim women, like the Muslim population, are not a homogeneous group (see Chapter 2). The women's conditions vary both within and across Muslim societies and they do not experience wearing the hijab in the same way. Bullock (2007: 38) usefully reminds us:

> Though Muslim women may share 'Islam', they come from a wide variety of class, race, and ethnic backgrounds. Muslim women wear hijab for different reasons ... [for example] the meaning of hijab for a woman in Iran can be completely different than the meaning of hijab for a woman in Toronto ... the point is not to assume that just because they look similar, they are similar.

Importantly, Bullock raises the possibility that some women may not find Islam or the veil restrictive or oppressive. This was the case for Zeyba who exerts the notion of choice:

> I am not oppressed and my father did not make me wear the headscarf [pause] In fact, he can't understand why me and sisters choose to wear hijab. He thinks that wearing the hijab will be bad for our careers.

At an intra-community level, she, Sanjida and Taiba represent the sociological complexities of the hijab. Only Zeyba wears it all the time, Sanjida wears it sometimes, depending on occasion, and Taiba, who is deeply rooted in her faith, does not wear it at all.

There are other issues concerning the hijab. For one thing, it does not necessarily remove the male gaze from the woman. In Western society, it has become something of a fashion statement: brightly coloured headscarves are worn with designer clothes, expensive footwear and make-up. This fusion of fashion and religion has helped construct the 'Hijabi Barbie' (Fanshawe,

2006). I discussed this with Zeyba, who admits that she can spend up to 'two hours' pinning her headscarf so that she can 'look good':

> *AH:* You said that the hijab is a 'public statement' of your 'inner faith' and you have also equated your choice of dress with words such as 'modesty' and 'covering'. However, I can see that you are wearing a very glamorous headscarf with beautiful jewellery and trendy clothes. Do you not find this a contradiction?
>
> *Zeyba:* Why can't I look good? Why can't I be fashionable and also be religious? Just because I wear the latest clothes, it doesn't mean that I am a bad Muslim girl.
>
> *AH:* I didn't mean to imply that you may be a 'bad Muslim girl' based on your choice of dress. But can you see how it may look to other people? If the religious objective is to be modest and not to attract attention, especially from men, then can you see how this may be viewed as a contradiction?
>
> *Zeyba:* I can see what you are trying to say [pause] I guess my reply to you is that my dress choice is my statement of faith and individuality. And, er, if men can't keep their grubby eyes off me because of it, then that's their problem.

Clearly, her dress choice is enabling Zeyba to negotiate the many identities of being a Westernized Muslim teenager. Her question: 'Why can't I be fashionable and also be religious?' is a valid one, and points towards the emergence of a trendy British-Islamic culture. This approach to her clothing can also be viewed as resistance against Bangladeshi 'patriarchal attempts to demand perfect reproductions of nation and culture' (Mani, 2002: 125). However, as well as looking attractive for themselves and wearing the hijab for spiritual and religious reasons, it suggests that these young women are giving in to the male gaze.

Second, it is not the case that women who veil themselves in public are less concerned about the female body ideal. A woman may be unhappy about the way she looks and have issues of low self-esteem despite the public expression of her personal identity via the hijab. Third, the wearing of the veil may oppose the flesh-exposing industry of Western advertising, film and pornography but that does not make veiling any less patriarchal. The patriarchal hegemonic desire for men to control women should not be confused with the issue of *choice* for women to veil themselves. In both the flesh-exposing West and the Muslim covering culture, it is still the men controlling women and the women internalizing and responding to the male gaze and desires via their dress (Parmer and Amos, 1981; Alibhai-Brown, 2006). Veiling is thus a choice made within a patriarchal framework (see Hessini, 1994).

Fourth, the idea that women adopt the hijab because all men are constantly dehumanizing women as sexual objects is to accept a generalized and essentialized view of men as nothing but sexual beings. Finally, the notion of choice is problematic. Do Muslim women really choose to cover themselves? Feminists such as Afshar (1991), Macleod (1991) and Helie-Lucas (1994) question whether Muslim women living mainly in the Middle East really do choose to cover or are culturally coerced and subtly brainwashed.

Notwithstanding these limitations with Bullock's positive theory of the veil, my study suggests that the visibility, sisterhood and self-consciousness that derives from the hijab helps British Muslim women cope with the ambiguities and contradictions they experience in British society. The hijab represents a symbol of resistance and helps forge a minority identity within Western society that has constructed them as the invisible other:

> ... in choosing the hijab, they are constructing a Muslim identity, a minority identity in the face of the dominant (Western) culture's message about women ... they use their Islamic heritage as a way to resist, rebel against and counter.
>
> (Bullock, 2007: 191)

One of the key findings of my study is that, whether veiled or not, these women's position as members of an actual, imagined and ideological British-Islamic identity enables them to construct a positive minority Muslim identity in British society. A female Muslim identity through the symbolism of the hijab has become a public expression of personal identity and must be located within the wider politics of recognition.

Young Bangladeshi women are engaged in a positive interpretation of Islam that enables them to further their gender interests and challenge traditional Bangladeshi patriarchal norms. Although gender equality remains an uncompleted and complex project, British Islam is steadily allowing women to counter the traditional Bangladeshi image of women as no more than child-bearers and home-makers and to claim public spaces as gender-neutral zones. Zeyba makes the point:

> My mum always walks behind my dad whenever they go out in public. I hate that about Bangladeshi culture. It's as if us women

> are inferior to men. Me and my sisters are always telling my mum off for doing it. Islam teaches us that we are equal to men. My mum should learn to stand up for herself more like my sisters do with their husbands.

British Islam allows women to feel part of a local and global community of sisterhood and has countered the identity conundrum that they belong to neither a Bangladeshi ethnic nor a British national community. For women who choose to cover themselves in a headscarf, jilbab (long dress) or face veil, the act of veiling has a triple role. First, for the vast majority of women, the hijab represents a spiritual journey providing them with dignity and respect. Second, the veil has become a symbol of 'resistance' and 'rejection' of the West (Ahmed, 1992: 235). And third, it enables women to resist and reject traditional patriarchal Bangladeshi cultural practices and parental regimes (El Guindi, 2000; Shain, 2003; Gupta, 2009). Many have, as a result, become visible in public spaces dominated by men (Mule and Barthel, 1992; Watson, 1994) and vocal and confident members of British society (Shain, 2003) – far removed from the orientalist construction of passivity and docility.

Conclusion

In summary, the visible female Muslim identity, and particularly the veil, is far from being a symbol of male patriarchy. It has become instead a symbol of choice, sisterhood, visibility and power, as shown by the women in my study. Despite some internal conflict, especially for Sanjida, between the traditional 'good Bangladeshi girl' and the modern girl who likes to speak her 'mind', the women in my study represent a poststructuralist generation that defines feminism for themselves by incorporating their own identities into the belief system. This progressive feminism accommodates diversity and change in modern society (Tong, 2009) and recognizes that an Islamic identity, far from being passive and docile, empowers them to contest, resist and speak out against oppressive structures.

The visible female Muslim identity represents a journey from tradition to modernity. It is a resistance against internal community patriarchal authority and wider societal patriarchal norms. The visibility is a political statement against the wider systemic issues of marginalization and otherization, of racist images and Islamophobia. This visible identity gives these women a sense of belonging and acceptance. Crucially, it allows them to negotiate and manage the complexity of being Muslim, British, Bangladeshi and female in public spaces.

Part Four

Conclusions

4

Chapter 9

A way forward for British Islam

A summary of *their* stories

The sociopolitical components of identity of the six British-born third-generation Bangladeshis from East London were examined using a phenomenological ethnographic approach. The research explored the role of language, race, religion, nation and gender in the construction of their identities. The many complex sub-themes that emerged from their self-narratives – about home, racism, multiculturalism, Britishness and the hijab – highlight the complex, contradictory, overlapping and fluid nature of identity. I was personally affected by many of the complex issues discussed, and an element of self-exploration made it difficult at times to disentangle myself from the research process.

The main conclusion I drew is that the religion of Islam, in its spiritual, visible and political context, provides a sense of belonging and acceptance to these third-generation Bangladeshis as they struggle against years of systemic and institutional isolation, racism and poverty. Islam also provides a safety net against a Bangladeshi culture and way of life that is becoming increasingly alien and irrelevant to the everyday lives of this community. For these young people, their country of parental origin has little emotional or even cultural meaning, and its place has been taken by religion (Parekh, 2006). The struggle for the third generation in Britain has shifted from striving for racial and ethnic equality, as the first and second generations did, to searching for a globally oriented religious identity (Samad, 1992).

Many third-generation Bangladeshis have reclaimed their religious identity and rediscovered and redefined Islam as a modern and progressive form of British Islam. British Islam, therefore, can be considered as a publicly expressed *new* identity and form of ethnicity. This religiously based identity has been accelerated by the ability of the third generation to read and speak English, allowing them to research via textbooks, conferences and the internet in the dominant language. Coming also from a Muslim majority in Bangladesh to a Muslim minority situation in Britain, the ability to speak English has afforded the third-generation Bangladeshis a form of linguistic competence, and this enables migrants to translate anger into argument (Hoffman, 1991). This Islamic awakening has enabled them to redefine their ethno-religious roots. As a result, many have constructed an idealized form of Islam based on theology and ancient tales as against lived religion, often fused with Bangladeshi ethnic customs and traditions (Bagguley and Hussain, 2005).

British Islam is a social construction by which the multiple identities of being British-born Bangladeshi Muslims can be negotiated. It is a space where the complexity of personal and social identities of being British (born), Bangladeshi (ethno-racial) and Muslim (religious) can be managed; a space where young people can engage in a process of syncretism and discernment – picking and choosing different elements and taking the best out of the multiple cultures they are a part of. British Islam does not conflict with what it means to be British. Although Britishness remains an exclusive, fluid and contentious concept, the idea of being British has not weakened and the participants' ties and commitment to Britain remain strong, based mainly on their birthright. British Islam reflects the British Western capitalist lifestyle, with its emphasis on banking, socializing, education, business, fashion, career professionalism, women's rights and democracy.

This British-Islamic identity, has not, however, emerged without struggle. It has developed through contest and protest, externally within the mainstream political arena and internally through the shake-up of Bangladeshi traditions, values and rituals. It is a visible identity that has demanded representation within public spaces. British Muslims continue to be marginalized, alienated, *misrecognized* as immigrants, second class, and *othered* as violent terrorists, barbaric and backward. It needs, therefore, to be located within the politics of 'recognition' (Taylor, 1994; Mandair, 2006: 23): it is an 'equality seeking movement' (Modood, 2005b: 10) (see Figure 1, p. 111).

Many third-generation Bangladeshis do still maintain a strongly religious spiritual identity that revolves around prayer, piety, family, purdah and charity (Vertovec, 1998), although popular British Islam does not necessarily imply a strict adherence to Islam's everyday practices, norms and rituals. It is not spiritual or moral guidance that many are after. Rather, what attracts them to a politicized British Islam is the *idea* of resisting the dominant negative hegemony. Akhtar (2005: 169) argues that actual and ideological membership to Islam provides the:

> ...vehicle for political mobilisation in relation to economic
> exclusion, and group solidarity in connection with social

exclusion. In neither case does the turn to religion have to be accompanied by an acceptance of actual religious practice.

So, although some of the participants are not practising Muslims, it is the *idea* of Islam as a global sociopolitical identity of resistance that so attracts them. Consequently, their multifaceted British-Islamic identity continues to be the way they identify themselves, and also the way they want to be identified by others.

The task of social visibility and recognition is difficult for young Bangladeshis, especially as they have become entangled in the global war on terror, are on the receiving end of a backlash from a hostile, culturally racist and Islamophobic British society, and continue to be ranked as one of the most impoverished social groups in the country.

There is, I suggest, a way for the British Bangladeshis with their large youth demographic to travel from the periphery to the centre of public and political discourse (Giddens, 1984; Malik, 2004) and to move towards recognition, visibility, voice, equality, belonging and power.

A social programme for the British-Bangladeshi community

Drawing on my years of experience as a youth and community worker, academic researcher and journalist involved in issues of identity, community and religion, I propose a six-point social programme as a way out of a cycle of poverty for the British-Bangladeshi community:

1. Central to the way forward is education. The significant improvement by Bangladeshi students at GCSE level in recent years must be seized upon. Parents should be critically involved in their children's education, more teaching staff should reflect the school population, more investment is needed in underachieving schools and more local professional and peer mentors are needed to mentor pupils from a young age. Subject choice at degree level needs to diversify away from traditional subjects and more Bangladeshi students need to expand their horizons by choosing universities outside London. Drawing on the thoughts of Chandia (quoted in Lewis, 2007: 89–92), education is arguably the way out of the cycle of poverty.

2. Young Bangladeshis need to become more involved with local civic volunteering projects in order to become engaged and responsible community citizens. They need to become 'politically literate' (Crick, 2000), take ownership of community issues and show signs of community leadership.

3. Young Bangladeshis need to continue engaging in the process of syncretism and discernment whereby they do not totally abandon their history, language, religion, culture and heritage but rather take the best out of all. Of crucial importance is the preservation of the Sylheti mother tongue, while using English as the pragmatic language of communication for everybody and community languages such as Bengali as the languages of history and identity.

4. British Bangladeshis need to mature *politically* as a community and engage democratically in wider issues such as gender equality, foreign policy, minority rights, human rights, environmental campaigns, freedom of speech, voting and much more. They should also adopt a more universal humanitarian approach and lobby and campaign agaist *all* issues of oppression and injustice, not just those that involve Muslims. This is starting to happen, as the number of educated and professional young Bangladeshis grows. There also needs to be much more constructive internal self-criticism at an intra-community level.

5. There should be more accessible public role models for Bangladeshi youth in decision-making circles. Role models need to be both aspirational and inspirational.

6. British-born Bangladeshis need to dispense with a Manichaean mindset ('them' vs 'us') and see themselves as part of the plural British 'us'.

All the subsequent points will develop when point 1 – sustained educational advancement – is achieved. Education is the most pressing concern for policymakers, community leaders and parents. Educational qualifications will give young Bangladeshis greater social prestige and the ability to bargain and engage in upward social mobility, or what historical sociologists refer to as the process of 'embourgeoisement' (Bernard, 1957; Kerr *et al.*, 1962). Bourdieu (1971, 1974) argues that education can provide the 'cultural' and 'social' capital to succeed in life, that educational attainment can be translated into wealth, knowledge and power.

Bourdieu reminds us, however, of 'cultural reproduction': when children from privileged backgrounds prosper in the educational system, from their pre-school years on, because they have the skills and knowledge (habitus) to succeed. But, while education is presented as a *way out* of poverty, the structural, cultural and practical constraints of poverty affect the chances for young Bangladeshis to succeed in education. The disconnection persists between middle-class schooling spaces and working-class students, to the detriment of pupils' educational aspirations (Archer *et al.*, 2010).

Implications for community, education and policy

I hope my study will contribute interesting opinions, insights and commentaries to the ongoing debate about cultural, linguistic, racial, religious, national and gendered identities, and that my Bangladeshi community and people of ethnic-minority origin will read this book. It might offer parents and community leaders who have a disconnection from the youth an insight into the conflicting and complex identities that young British-born Bangladeshi Muslims are experiencing. Many of the issues raised in the book – notions of community and home, Britishness, the 'other', foreign policy, the modernization of Islam, the role of race and racism, Islamophobia, gender inequality, the intergenerational linguistic and cultural gap, and others – invite constructive discussions and debates between parent and child, grandparent and grandchild, teacher and student, youth worker and young person, and among friends. These issues are live and evolving, providing the Bangladeshi community of East London with an opportunity to determine the shape of these important sociopolitical issues to their advantage.

The book is also intended for teachers, educationalists and other professionals working with young people in inner-city centres across Britain, and especially in the London Borough of Tower Hamlets. It argues for the incorporation of their students' alternative histories, viewpoints and identities into the school curriculum, youth workshop or training sessions. The book seeks to give such professionals insight into the effect of religion, social environment and home culture on people's construction of identity.

The book also aims to help educators and policymakers become more aware of the sociopolitical climate in which young people in inner-city areas are growing up. No one lives in a social vacuum and there should be no distinction between wider society and the educational world – young people do not leave their culture behind as they enter the school gates. Although practical issues arise when providing for mixed classes of bilingual and monolingual pupils – such as those in richly diverse multicultural cities like London – an inclusive multicultural curriculum has many educational advantages for all children. Understanding *their* social world and reflecting it within the school curriculum particularly benefits bilingual and bicultural pupils, as it:

- enhances children's cognitive development
- exposes children to a variety of languages and cultures
- prepares children for a modern multicultural and multiracial society

- enables the expression of cultural identities
- prepares young people to compete economically in a global society.

Consequently, children are better integrated, happier and perform better academically if value and importance are attributed to their languages (Bengali and Arabic) and home culture. But schools need to do more. Local issues such as those identified in this study should inform the pedagogy in schools, especially an exploration of identity, ancestry and heritage and a history of immigration in the local area. British history needs to be rewritten to be inclusive of its ethnic minorities and acknowledge their important contribution to the development of the British national story (Phillips, 2007). Miller (1983: 11) rightly calls for a 'curriculum for all children' in which language diversity remains central – a multicultural curriculum for a multicultural society.

There is plenty of research that explores how teachers and educators can act as mediators between language, community, culture and the school (see for example Gregory, 1997). Much of this research focuses on children aged 3 to 11, although there are examples of studies on pupils of secondary-school age (see Travers and Klein, 2004; Archer *et al.*, 2010). It stresses the need for teachers to develop culturally responsive programmes based on an awareness of the knowledge children bring from home and the community (Miller, 1983; Gregory, 1997; Nieto, 1999; Kenner, 2004; Went, 2004). As Conteh (2003: 24) argues:

> …the most effective teaching and learning happens when teachers and learners share values and views about how it should be done, when teachers can see things through their learners' eyes and understand their viewpoints.

Although my study has focused on people of secondary-school and college age – so that their learning patterns and cognitive development differ from those of younger learners – many of the issues are the same. My participants also have differing, complex and competing bilingual and bicultural identities. Both younger and older pupils may suffer what Cummins and Skutnabb-Kangas (1988: 5) call 'educational violence': the 'shame' of being a 'minority' within education felt by Azad and Zeyba, who developed negative attitudes towards their Bangladeshi culture and language as a result.

The sociocultural model of learning pioneered by Vygotsky (1978, 1986), further developed by educators such as Nieto (1999), suggests that learning is socially situated within educational environments and develops from the relationships between teachers/learners and learners/learners.

This means that, as well as a culturally responsive teaching programme, teachers should view bilingualism as an asset. There is a plethora of evidence showing, confidently, that children who are bilingual do well in school and in employment (Miller, 1983; Cummins, 1996; Conteh, 2003; Kenner, 2004). Conteh (2003) argues that when the skills of bilingual and bicultural learners are recognized and valued in the classroom, pupils move confidently and successfully between community, culture and school. The personal and social benefits of bilingualism far outweigh the nationalist and anti-immigration campaigns across Europe and the favouring of monolingualism in countries such as France and The Netherlands. Learning through different languages provides significant cognitive benefits and also enhances multilingual identities and provides a gateway into other cultural worlds (see Kenner and Hickey, 2008).

Considering the importance of bilingual education in richly diverse areas such as Tower Hamlets, schools need to adopt skills and strategies that allow the space for culture and language to develop within their teaching pedagogy.

Biliteracy is a prime strategy. Bilingual children can learn to write in different language scripts and live in two or more 'simultaneous [linguistic] worlds' (Kenner, 2004: 107). Literacy in the first language is known to help the learner to develop literacy in a second (Gravelle, 1996; Kenner, 2000; Sneddon, 2009).

In many instances, young children who speak more than one language syncretize their languages into a new language. Examples of verbal biliteracies are what I call Bang*lish* and Arab*inglish*, discussed earlier. My participants used their spoken languages creatively, much like the biliteracies developed in Kenner's (2004) study of 6-year-olds from London. Third-generation Bangladeshis have created a new language drawing on structures and vocabulary from English, Bengali and colloquial Arabic. As 'talk' is an essential part of learning, because it supports cognitive development and enhances skills that underpin literacy (Wells and Chang-Wells, 1992), Bang*lish* and Arab*inglish* have become new ways of communicating with peers who share the same language and cultural background (see Mor-Sommerfeld, 2002; Murshad, 2002).

In recognition of the importance and complexity of identity, culture and language, schools should adopt a flexible approach to language teaching and learning. Champions of bilingual education such as García and Kleifgen (2010) and Creese and Blackledge (2010) push forward *translanguaging* as a pedagogic teaching method for learners who speak more than one language. Traditional rigid monolingual instruction should be replaced by teaching bilingual children using bilingual instructional strategies. Where possible, two or more languages are used alongside each other. In some instances, the learner reads in one language and speaks and writes in another. Creese and Blackledge (2010) have observed the interdependence of skills and knowledge across languages and assert that community and mainstream languages complement each other.

Bilingual learners are empowered when schools positively value their history, culture, heritage, community and language within the school curriculum and teaching pedagogy. Cummins and Skutnabb-Kangas (1988) push this notion further, arguing that the right to speak and maintain the mother tongue is not only a 'human right' but also 'empowers' learners to challenge existing power relations in wider society. As well as challenging the status quo, the empowering process also fosters the critical consciousness – what Freire (1985) calls 'conscientization' – within bilingual learners. This enables them to become aware, analyse what has been done to them (alienation, discrimination, exclusion, social and political marginality) and thus begin the struggle for identity, self-respect, self-determination and representation. Unless the systemic issues of power, representation and marginality are challenged, school structures will mirror the imbalance of power in wider society and linguistic minorities will continue to experience academic difficulties.

If schools encourage students to discuss cultural, social and religious identities with their peers in an educational setting, this will motivate and affirm them and encourage them to try to understand each other's 'map[s] of meaning' (Hall, 1990: 222). An open and trusting school ethos encourages personal and academic achievement.

For policymakers, the message is to work closer with minority communities such as the East London Bangladeshis and to take account of the historical and contemporary structural and institutional constraints revolving around issues of poverty, discrimination, inequality and marginalization that have shaped their complex identities. The stories of a few of them, documented in this book, provide a useful way to start. It is vital that policymakers listen to and engage in constructive dialogue with those for whom policy is written. And they should be aware that, in the modern globalized world with its fast-evolving technology and communications, feelings of resentment and injustice in a neighbourhood are determined by global as well as local events, especially where foreign policy involves interventions or wars against Muslim countries.

Above all, the public expression of British Islam should be seen to be positive as it enables its members to negotiate and manage their multifaceted identities. Space should be afforded for recognizing religious identities in secular multicultural public spaces. With its emphasis on democratic values and a Western cultural lifestyle, the dynamic and modern British Islam should not sit outside a national British identity but be viewed positively as a 'different kind of British' (Ward, 2004: 138). Akbar sums it up:

> I'm just as British as the next man. I have a different skin colour, wear different clothes sometimes, speak a different language, have a beard on my face, pray to a different god and eat food with my hands. So what? I was born here, I speak English, I eat chicken and chips, have cried when England have lost a football game, I pay my taxes and I'm a pretty chilled-out family-orientated guy who respects the law … I'm just as British as the next man.

References

Abbas, T. (2005) 'British South Asian Muslims: State and multicultural society'. In Abbas, T. (ed.) *Muslim Britain: Communities under pressure*. London: Zed Books.

— (ed.) (2007) *Islamic Political Radicalism: A European perspective*. Edinburgh: Edinburgh University Press.

Adams, C. (1987) *Across Seven Seas and Thirteen Rivers*. London: Tower Hamlets Art Project Books.

Adichie, C. (2009) 'The danger of a single story'. TEDGlobal. Online. www.ted. com/talks/chimamanda_adichie_the_danger_of_a_single_story?language=en (accessed 9 December 2014).

Afshar, H. (1991) 'Fundamentalism and its female apologists'. In Prendergast, R. and Singer, H.W. (eds) *Development Perspectives for the 1990s*. London: Macmillan.

Ahmad, W.I.U. (1996) 'Family obligations and social change among Asian communities'. In Ahmad, W.I.U. and Atkin, K. (eds) *'Race' and Community Care*. Buckingham: Open University Press.

Ahmed, L. (1992) *Women and Gender in Islam: Historical roots of a modern debate*. Newhaven, CT: Yale University Press.

— (2006) 'Women and the rise of Islam'. In Kamrava, M. (ed.) *The New Voices of Islam: Reforming politics and modernity (A reader)*. London: I.B. Tauris.

Ahmed, M. (2004) 'Islam's new followers: How teens and trendies are being drawn to the Muslim faith'. *Eastern Eye*, 12 March.

Ahmed, N. (2005) 'Tower Hamlets: Insulation in isolation'. In Abbas, T. (ed.) *Muslim Britain: Communities under pressure*. London: Zed Books.

Ahmed, T. (2005) 'The Muslim "marginal man"'. *Policy*, 21 (1), 35–41.

Ahmed, T.S. (2005) 'Reading between the lines: Muslims and the media'. In Abbas, T. (ed.) *Muslim Britain: Communities under pressure*. London: Zed Books.

Ahsan, M.M., and Kidwai, A.R. (1991) *Sacrilege Versus Civility: Muslim perspectives on the Satanic Verses affair*. Leicester: Islamic Foundation.

Akhtar, P. (2005) 'Re(turn) to religion and radical Islam'. In Abbas, T. (ed.) *Muslim Britain: Communities under pressure*. London: Zed Books.

Alasuutari, P. (1995) *Researching Culture: Qualitative method and cultural studies*. London: Sage.

Alderson, P., and Morrow, V. (2011) *The Ethics of Research with Children and Young People*. 2nd ed. London: Sage.

Al-Din, N. (1990 [1928]) 'Unveiling and veiling: On the liberation of the woman and social renewal in the Islamic world'. In Badran, M., and Cook, M. (eds) *Opening the Gates: A century of Arab feminist writing*. Bloomington: Indiana University Press.

Alexander, C. (2006) 'Imagining the politics of BrAsian Youth'. In Ali, N., Kalra, V.S. and Sayyid, S. (eds) *A Postcolonial People: South Asians in Britain*. London: Hurst.

Al-Hibri, A. (1982) 'A study of Islamic herstory'. In al-Hibri, A. (ed.) *Women and Islam*. Oxford: Pergamon.

Ali, A.H. (2007) *The Caged Virgin*. London: Pocket Books.

Ali, T. (2003) *The Clash of Fundamentalisms: Crusades, jihad and modernity*. London: Verso.

Alibhai-Brown, Y. (2000) *Who Do We Think We Are?: Imagining new Britain*. London: Penguin.

— (2006) 'This is not about a woman's right of dress, it is about the values of our secular society'. *The Independent*, 16 October, 29.

Alladina, S., and Edwards, V. (eds) (1991) *Multilingualism in the British Isles: The older other tongues and Europe*. London: Longman.

Allen, C. (2005) 'From race to religion: The new face of discrimination'. In Abbas, T. (ed.) *Muslim Britain: Communities under pressure*. London: Zed Books.

— (2010) *Islamophobia*. Farnham: Ashgate.

Allen, C., and Nielsen, J. (2002) *Summary Report on Islamophobia in the EU after 11 September 2001*. Vienna: European Monitoring Centre on Racism and Xenophobia.

Allievi, S. (2004) 'Public space, global media and local umma'. In Malik, J. (ed.) *Muslims in Europe: From the margin to the centre*. Berlin: LIT.

Al-Yafai, F., and Hakim, F. (eds) (2010) *Women, Islam and Western Liberalism*. London: CIVITAS.

Amara, F. (2006) *Breaking the Silence: French women's voices from the ghetto*. Translated by Helen Harden Chenut. Berkeley: University of California Press.

Ameli, S.R., and Merali, A. (2006) *British Muslims' Expectations of the Government: Hijab, meaning, identity, otherization and politics: British Muslim women*. London: Islamic Human Rights Commission.

Amin, A. (2003) 'Unruly strangers? The 2001 urban riots in Britain'. *International Journal of Urban and Regional Research*, 27 (2), 460–3.

Anderson, B. (1983) *Imagined Communities*. London: Verso.

Anderson, L. (1997) 'State policy and Islamic radicalism'. In Esposito, J. (ed.) *Political Islam: Revolution, radicalism or reform?* London: Lynne Rienner.

Ansari, H. (2004) *'The Infidel Within': Muslims in Britain since 1800*. London: Hurst.

— (2005) 'Attitudes to jihad, martyrdom and terrorism among British Muslims'. In Abbas, T. (ed.) *Muslim Britain: Communities under pressure*. London: Zed Books.

Anwar, M. (1979) *The Myth of Return: Pakistanis in Britain*. London: Heinemann.

— (1995) 'New Commonwealth migration to the UK'. In Cohen, R. (ed.) *The Cambridge Survey of World Migration*. Cambridge: Cambridge University Press.

— (2005) 'Issues, policy and practice'. In Abbas, T. (ed.) *Muslim Britain: Communities under pressure*. London: Zed books.

Anwar, M., and Bakhsh, Q. (2003) *British Muslims and State Policies*. Coventry: University of Warwick Centre for the Research in Ethnic Relations.

Apple, M.W. (1982) *Education and Power*. Boston: Routledge and Kegan Paul.

— (1993) *Official Knowledge: Democratic education in a conservative age*. New York: Routledge.

Archer, L. (2002) 'Change, culture and tradition: British Muslim pupils talk about Muslim girls' post-16 "choices"'. *Race, Ethnicity and Education*, 5 (4), 359–76.

Archer, L., Hollingworth, S., and Mendick, H. (eds) (2010) *Urban Youth and Schooling*. Maidenhead: Open University Press.

Arksey, H., and Knight, P.T. (1999) *Interviewing for Social Scientists: An introductory resource with examples*. London: Sage.

Armstrong, K. (2004) *Islam: A short history*. London: Phoenix.

Aronson, J.D. (2001) 'The communications and internet revolution'. In Baylis, J. and Smith, S. (eds) *The Globalization of World Politics: An introduction to world politics*. 2nd ed. Oxford: Oxford University Press.

Asghar, M.A. (1996) *Bangladeshi Community Organisations in East London*. London: Bangla Heritage.

Ask, K., and Tjomsland, M. (eds) (1998) *Women and Islamization: Contemporary dimensions of discourse on gender relations*. Oxford: Berg.

Aston, J., Hülya, H., Page, R., and Willison, R. (2007) *Pakistani and Bangladeshi Women's Attitude to Work and Family*. London: Department for Work and Pensions.

Atkinson, P. (1992) 'The ethnography of a medical setting: Reading, writing and rhetoric'. *Qualitative Health Research*, 2 (4), 451–74.

Autograph ABP (2008) *Bangladesh 1971: An exhibition*. London: Autograph ABP.

Ayotte, K.J., and Husain, M.E. (2005) 'Securing Afghan women: Neocolonialism, epistemic violence, and the rhetoric of the veil'. *NWSA Journal*, 17 (3), 112–33.

Babb, P., Butcher, H., Church, J., and Zealey, L. (2006) *Social Trends*. No. 36. London: Office for National Statistics.

Back, L. (2009) 'Researching community and its moral projects'. *21st Century Society: Journal of the Academy of Social Sciences,* 4 (2), 201–14.

— (2010) 'Whiteness in the dramaturgy of racism'. In Hill Collins, P., and Solomos, J. (eds) *The Sage Handbook of Race and Ethnic Studies*. London: Sage.

Back, L., and Solomos, J. (2000) 'Introduction: Theorising race and racism'. In Back, L. and Solomos, J. (eds) *Theories of Race and Racism: A reader*. London: Routledge.

Badran, M. (1991) 'Competing agenda: Feminists, Islam and the state in 19th and 20th century Egypt'. In Kandiyoti, D. (ed.) *Women, Islam and the State*. Philadelphia: Temple University Press.

Bagguley, P., and Hussain, Y. (2005) 'Flying the flag for England? Citizenship, religion and cultural identity among British Pakistani Muslims'. In Abbas, T. (ed.) *Muslim Britain: Communities under pressure*. London: Zed Books.

Baker, C. (1993) *Foundations in Bilingual Education and Bilingualism*. Clevedon: Multilingual Matters.

Bakhtin, M. (1981) *The Dialogic Imagination*. Austin: University of Texas Press.

Baldwin, T. (2004) 'I want an integrated society with a difference'. *The Times*, 3 April. Online. www.thetimes.co.uk/tto/news/uk/article1905038.ece (accessed 11 December 2014).

Ball, S.J. (1990) 'Self-doubt and soft data: Social and technical trajectories in ethnographic fieldwork'. *International Journal of Qualitative Studies in Education*, 3 (2), 157–71.

Ballard, R. (1990) 'Migration and kinship: The differential effect of marriage rules in processes of Punjabi migration to Britain'. In Clarke, C., Peach, C. and Vertovec, S. (eds) *South Asians Overseas: Migration and ethnicity*. Cambridge: Cambridge University Press.

— (1994) 'The emergence of Desh pardesh'. In Ballard, R. (ed.) *Desh Pardesh: The South Asian Presence in Britain*. London: Hurst.

Banton, M. (1967) *Race Relations*. London: Tavistock.

— (1979) 'Analytical and folk concepts of ethnicity'. *Ethnic and Racial Studies*, 2 (2), 127–38.

— (1997) *Racial Theories*. Cambridge: Cambridge University Press.

Bari, M.A. (2002) 'Muslim identity in Britain today'. In Hamid, A.W. and Sherif, J. (eds) *The Quest for Sanity: Reflections on September 11 and the aftermath*. London: Muslim Council of Britain.

Barker, M. (1981) *The New Racism*. London: Junction.

Barrett, M., Eade, J., Cinnirella, M., and Garbin, D. (2006) *New Ethnicities Among British Bangladeshi and Mixed-heritage Youth*. Final report to the Leverhulme Trust. Online. http://epubs.surrey.ac.uk/1359/1/fulltext.pdf (accessed 11 December 2014).

Bartlett, S., and Burton, D. (2012) *Introduction to Education Studies*. 3rd ed. London: Sage.

Basit, T.N. (1997) *Eastern Values; Western milieu: Identities and aspirations of adolescent British Muslim girls*. Aldershot: Ashgate.

Bawer, B. (2006) *While Europe Slept: How radical Islam is destroying the West from within*. New York: Doubleday.

Baylis, J., and Smith, S. (2001) 'Introduction'. In Baylis, J. and Smith, S. (eds) *The Globalization of World Politics: An introduction to world politics*. 2nd ed. Oxford: Oxford University Press.

BBC News (2008) 'Ethnic clothes mental health link'. Online. http://news.bbc.co.uk/2/hi/health/7347092.stm (accessed 12 February 2009).

Becker, H.S. (1970) *Sociological Work*. New Brunswick, NJ: Transaction Books.

Begum, H., and Eade, J. (2005) 'All quiet on the eastern front? Bangladeshi reactions in Tower Hamlets'. In Abbas, T. (ed.) *Muslim Britain: Communities under pressure*. London: Zed Books.

Benhabib, S. (1992) *Situating the Self*. New York: Routledge.

Berg, B.L. (1989) *Qualitative Research Methods for the Social Sciences*. Boston: Alleyn and Bacon.

Berktay, F. (1993) 'Looking for the "other" side: Is cultural relativism a way out?' In de Groot, J. and Maynard, M. (eds) *Women's Studies in the 1990s: Doing things differently?* London: Macmillan.

Berman, P. (2004) *Terror and Liberalism*. New York: Norton.

Bermant, C. (1975) *Point of Arrival: A study of London's East End*. London: Methuen.

Bernard, J. (1957) *Social Problems at Mid Century*. New York: Holt, Rinehart and Winston.

Bethnal Green and Stepney Trades Council (1978) *Blood on the Streets: A report by Bethnal Green and Stepney Trades Council on racial attacks in East London*. London: Bethnal Green and Stepney Trades Council, September.

Bhabha, H.K. (1994) *The Location of Culture*. London: Routledge.

— (1995) 'Freedom's basis in the indeterminate'. In Rajchman, J. (ed.) *The Identity in Question*. London: Routledge.

— (1996) 'Culture's in-between'. In Hall, S. and du Gay, P. (eds) *Questions of Cultural Identity*. London: Sage.

Bhatia, M. (dir.) (2006) *Brick Lane*. Documentary film. BBC2, 25 March.

Bhavani, R. (2006) 'Ahead of the game: The changing aspirations of young ethnic minority women'. Manchester: Equal Opportunities Commission.

Bhavani, R., and Ahmad, W. (2006) *Inter-generational Change and Minority Ethnic Women in the Labour Market*. London: Social Policy Research Centre.

Biddiss, M. (1979) *Images of Race*. Leicester: Leicester University Press.

Birt, J. (2005) 'Lobbying and marching: British Muslims and the state'. In Abbas, T. (ed.) *Muslim Britain: Communities under pressure*. London: Zed Books.

Blumer, H. (1969) *Symbolic Interactionism: Perspective and method*. Berkeley: University of California Press.

BNP (British National Party) (2002) *The Truth about ISLAM: Intolerance, slaughter, looting, arson and molestation of women*. Wigton: BNP.

Bogdan, R., and Taylor, S.J. (1975) *Introduction to Qualitative Research Methods: A phenomenological approach*. New York: Wiley.

Bordo, S. (1993) *Unbearable Weight: Feminism, Western culture, and the body*. Berkeley: University of California Press.

Bottomore, T.B., and Rubel, M. (eds) (1963) *Karl Marx: Selected writings in sociology and social philosophy*. Harmondsworth: Penguin.

Boulding, C., and Oborne, P. (2008) 'It shouldn't happen to a Muslim'. *Dispatches: War on Terror*. Channel 4, 7 July.

Bourdieu, P. (1971) 'Intellectual field and creative project' and 'Systems of education and systems of thought'. In Young, M. (ed.) *Knowledge and Control: New directions for the sociology of education*. London: Collier-Macmillan.

— (1974) 'The school as a conservative force: Scholastic and cultural inequalities'. In Eggleston, J. (ed.) *Contemporary Research in the Sociology of Education*. London: Methuen.

— (1991) *Language and Symbolic Power*. Cambridge, MA: Harvard University Press.

— (1994) 'Structures, habitus and practices'. In Polity (ed.) *The Polity Reader in Social Theory*. Oxford: Polity Press.

Bousetta, H., and Jacobs, D. (2006) 'Multiculturalism, citizenship and Islam in problematic encounters in Belgium'. In Modood, T., Triandafyllidou, A. and Zapata-Barrero, R. (eds) *Multiculturalism, Muslims and Citizenship: A European approach*. London: Routledge.

Bowen, I. (2014) *Medina in Birmingham, Najaf in Brent: Inside British Islam*. London: Hurst.

Bowling, B. (1996) 'The emergence of violent racism as a public issue in Britain, 1945–81'. In Panayi, P. (ed.) *Racial Violence in Britain in the Nineteenth and Twentieth Centuries*. Revised ed. London: Leicester University Press.

Brown, M. (2000) 'Religion and economic activity in the South Asian population'. *Ethnic and Racial Studies*, 23 (6), 1035–61.

Bullock, K. (2007) *Rethinking Muslim Women and the Veil: Challenging historical and modern stereotypes*. 2nd ed. London: International Institute of Islamic Thought.

Bulmer, M., and Solomos, J. (1999) 'General introduction'. In Bulmer, M. and Solomos, J. (eds) *Racism*. Oxford: Oxford University Press.

Bunting, M. (2004) 'Young, Muslim and British'. *The Guardian*, 30 November. Online. www.theguardian.com/uk/2004/nov/30/islamandbritain.madeleinebunting (accessed 12 December 2014).

Burr, V. (2003) *Social Constructionism*. 2nd ed. Hove: Routledge.

Butler, J.P. (1990) *Gender Trouble: Feminism and the subversion of identity*. London: Routledge Classics.

— (1993) *Bodies That Matter*. London: Routledge.

Byrne, B. (2004) 'Qualitative interviewing'. In Searle, C. (ed.) *Researching Society and Culture*. 2nd ed. London: Sage.

Cantle, T. (2001) *Community Cohesion: A report of the independent review team*. London: Home Office.

Carr, D. (1986) *Time, Narrative and History*. Bloomington: Indiana University Press.

Casciani, D. (2005) 'Analysis: Segregated Britain?' BBC News. Online. http://news.bbc.co.uk/1/hi/uk/4270010.stm (accessed 28 June 2007).

Castles, S., and Kosack, G. (1973) *Immigrant Workers and the Class Structures in Western Europe*. London: Institute of Race Relations and Oxford University Press.

Castles, S., and Miller, M.J. (1993) *The Age of Migration: International population movements in the modern world*. London: Macmillan.

CCCS (Centre for Contemporary Cultural Studies) (1982) *The Empire Strikes Back: Race and racism in 70s Britain*. London: Hutchinson.

Channel 4 (2008) *Islam Unveiled*. Online. www.youtube.com/watch?v=Fh3MdoNFfCc and www.youtube.com/watch?v=KhIoBSj8ikU (accessed 10 December 2014).

Charlesworth, S.J. (2000) *A Phenomenology of Working Class Experience*. Cambridge: Cambridge University Press.

Choudhury, G.W. (1974) *The Last Days of United Pakistan*. London: Hurst.

Choudhury, S. (2008) 'The Cultural Identities of Second and Third Generation Bangladeshi Women from Tower Hamlets: Similarities and divergence'. Unpublished BA diss., Goldsmiths College, University of London.

CILT (2010) Online. www.cilt.org.uk (accessed 5 February 2010).

Clifford, J. (1988) *The Predicament of Culture: Twentieth-century ethnography, literature and art*. Cambridge, MA: Harvard University Press.

Coffey, A., and Atkinson, P. (1996) *Making Sense of Qualitative Data*. Thousand Oakes, CA: Sage.

Cohen, R. (1994) *Frontiers of Identity: The British and the others*. Harlow: Longman.

Colley, L. (1994) *Britons: Forging the nation 1707–1837*. London: Pimlico.

Collins, G. (2010) 'Dole kids run out of hope'. *East London Advertiser*, 12 August, 1.

Conteh, J. (2003) *Succeeding in Diversity: Culture, language and learning in primary classrooms*. Stoke-on-Trent: Trentham Books.

Contractor, S. (2012) *Muslim Women in Britain: De-mystifying the Muslimah*. Abingdon: Routledge.

Cook, R. (2001) 'Robin Cook's chicken tikka masala speech'. *The Guardian*, 19 April. Online. www.guardian.co.uk/world/2001/apr/19/race.britishidentity (accessed 4 January 2007).

Cornell, S., and Hartmann, D. (1998) *Ethnicity and Race: Making identities in a changing world*. Thousand Oaks, CA: Pine Forge Press.

Cox, O.C. (1970 [1948]) *Caste, Class and Race*. New York: Monthly Review Press.

CRE (Commission for Racial Equality) (2005) *Citizenship and Belonging: What is Britishness?* London: ETHNOS Research and Consultancy.

Creese, A., and Blackledge, A. (2010) 'Translanguaging in the bilingual classroom: A pedagogy for learning and teaching?' *The Modern Language Journal*, 94 (1), 103–15.

Crick, B. (2000) *Essays on Citizenship,* London: Continuum.

Cummins, J. (1996) *Negotiating Identities: Education for empowerment in a diverse society*. Ontario, CA: California Association for Bilingual Education.

— (2000) *Language, Power and Pedagogy: Bilingual children in the crossfire*. Clevedon: Multilingual Matters.

Cummins, J., and Skutnabb-Kangas, T. (eds) (1988) *Minority Education: From shame to struggle*. Clevedon: Multilingual Matters.

Dahrendorf, R. (1987) 'The erosion of citizenship and the consequences for us all'. *New Statesman*, 12 June, 12–15.

Dahya, B. (1974) 'The nature of Pakistani ethnicity in industrial cities in Britain'. In Cohen, A. (ed.) *Urban Ethnicity*. London: Tavistock.

Daly, M. (1985 [1968]) *The Church and the Second Sex*. Boston: Beacon Press.

Davies, C.A. (1999) *Reflexive Ethnography: A guide to researching selves and others*. London: Routledge.

Davies, L. (1985) 'Ethnography and status: Focusing on gender in educational research'. In Burgess, R. (ed.) *Field Methods in the Study of Educational Research*. London: Falmer.

Davison, R.B. (1964) *Commonwealth Immigrants*. London: Oxford University Press.

De Houwer, A. (1998) 'Environmental factors in early bilingual development: The role of parental beliefs and attitudes'. In Extra, G. and Verhoeven, L. (eds) *Bilingualism and Migration*. Berlin: Mouton de Gruyter.

Denham Report (2002) *Building Cohesive Communities: A report of the Ministerial Group of Public Order and Community Cohesion*. London: Home Office.

Denscombe, M. (2010) *The Good Research Guide: For small-scale social research projects*. 4th ed. Maidenhead: Open University Press.

Department for Education (2012) *GCSE and Equivalent Attainment by Pupil Characteristics in England, 2010/11*. SFR 03/2012. Online. www.gov.uk/government/uploads/system/uploads/attachment_data/file/219306/sfr03_2012_001.pdf (accessed 30 June 2014).

— (2014) 'Consultation on promoting British values in schools'. Online. www.gov.uk/government/news/consultation-on-promoting-british-values-in-school (accessed 12 December 2014).

Desai, R. (1963) *Indian Immigrants in Britain*. Oxford: Oxford University Press.

De Tocqueville, A. (1998 [1835]) *Democracy in America*. Ware: Wordsworth.

Dhondy, F. (2001) 'Our Islamic fifth column'. *City Limits*, 11(4). Online. www.city-journal.org/html/11_4_our_islamic.html (accessed 7 January 2015).

Din, I. (2006) *The New British: The impact of culture and community on young Pakistanis*. Aldershot: Ashgate.

Dobson, R. (2014) 'British Muslims face worst discrimination of any minority group, according to research'. *The Independent*, 30 November. Online. www.independent.co.uk/news/uk/home-news/british-muslims-face-worst-job-discrimination-of-any-minority-group-9893211.html (accessed 16 January 2015).

Docherty, S., and Sandelowski, M. (1999) 'Focus on qualitative methods: Interviewing children'. *Research in Nursing and Health*, 22 (2), 177–85.

Dodd, V. (2001) 'Blunkett's blame game'. *The Guardian*, 11 December. Online. www.theguardian.com/world/2001/dec/11/race.politics (accessed 12 December 2014).

— (2010) 'Media and politicians "fuel rise in hate crimes against Muslims"'. *The Guardian*, 28 January. Online. www.theguardian.com/uk/2010/jan/28/hate-crimes-muslims-media-politicians (accessed 12 December 2014).

Dosanjh, J., and Ghuman, P. (1996) *Child Rearing in Ethnic Minorities*. Clevedon: Multilingual Matters.

Du Bois, W.E.B. (1995 [1903]) *The Souls of Black Folk*. New York: Signet Classics.

Duke, O., and Brett, N. (1978) 'Black Monday'. *The Express*, 22 July, 30–31.

Dworkin, A. (1995) 'Pornography is a civil rights issue'. In Stan, A.M. (ed.) *Debating Sexual Correctness: Pornography, sexual harassment, date rape, and the politics of sexual equality*. New York: Delta.

Dwyer, S.C., and Buckle, J.L. (2009) 'The space between: On being an insider-outsider in qualitative research'. *International Journal of Qualitative Methods*, 8 (1), 54–63.

Dyer, R. (1993) *The Matter of Images: Essays on representation*. London: Routledge.

Eade, J. (1998) 'The search for wholeness: The construction of national and Islamic identities among British Bangladeshis'. In Kershen, A.J. (ed.) *A Question of Identity*. Aldershot: Ashgate.

Eade, J., Peach, C., and Vamplew, T. (1996) 'The Bangladeshis: The encapsulated community'. In Peach, C. (ed.) *Ethnicity in the 1991 Census, Volume 2: The ethnic minority populations of Britain*. London: Office for National Statistics.

Easterly, W. (2007) *The White Man's Burden: Why the West's efforts to aid the rest have done so much ill and so little good*. Oxford: Oxford University Press.

East London Advertiser (1993) 'Family offer up prayers as son fights for life'. *East London Advertiser*, 16 September.

Economist, The (2013) 'Ethnic-minority pupils are storming ahead, thanks partly to tutors', 16 November. Online. www.economist.com/news/britain/21589874-ethnic-minority-pupils-are-storming-ahead-thanks-partly-tutors-road (accessed 23 December 2014).

El Guindi, F. (2000) *Veil: Modesty, privacy and resistance*. New York: Berg.

Ellen, R.F. (ed.) (1984) *Ethnographic Research: A guide to general conduct*. London: Academic Press.

Ellison, R. (1965 [1952]) *Invisible Man*. Harmondsworth: Penguin.

El Saadawi, N. (1980) *The Hidden Face of Eve*. Boston: Beacon Press.

— (1982) 'Women and Islam'. In al-Hibri, A. (ed.) *Women and Islam*. Oxford: Pergamon.

Ely, P., and Denney, D. (1987) *Social Work in a Multi-racial Society*. Aldershot: Gower.

Equal Opportunities Commission (EOC) (2007) *Moving on up? The way forward: Report of the EOC's investigation into Bangladeshi, Pakistani and Black Caribbean women at work*. Manchester: European Social Fund.

Esposito, J.L. (ed.) (1997) *Political Islam: Revolution, radicalism, or reform*. Boulder, CO: Lynne Rienner.

— (1999) 'Clash of civilisations? Contemporary images of Islam in the West'. In Munoz, G.M. (ed.) *Islam, Modernism and the West*. London: I.B. Tauris.

Ethnologue (n.d.) 'Statistical summaries: Summary language by size'. Online. www.ethnologue.com/ethno_docs/distribution.asp?by=size (accessed 13 April 2011).

Fanon, F. (1967) *Towards the African Revolution*. New York: Monthly Review Press.

Fanshawe, S. (2006) 'The millions of reasons to see Islam in a new light'. *The Guardian*, 15 November 2006, 6. Online. www.theguardian.com/society/2006/nov/15/comment.guardiansocietysupplement (accessed 12 December 2014).

Farley, J. (2009) 'Should English State Schools Offer a Regulation Headscarf as a Part of the Uniform for Muslim girls? A review and re-evaluation of the wearing of the headscarf at an all-girl's comprehensive school in Luton, Bedfordshire'. Unpublished MA diss., Goldsmiths College, University of London.

Farouky, J. (2007) 'The many faces of Europe'. *Time Magazine*, 26 February, 16–23.

Fernandes, K. (1978) 'The labour movement must mobilise to smash the fascists'. *Militant*, 18 August, 3.

Fernea, E.W. (1989) *Guests of the Sheikh: An ethnography of an Iraqi village*. 2nd ed. New York: Anchor Books.

— (1998) *In Search of Islamic Feminism: One woman's global journey*. New York: Anchor Books.

Fernea, E.W., and Bezirgan, B (eds) (1977) *Middle Eastern Women Speak*. Austin: University of Texas Press.

Fishwick, C. (2015) 'Fox News man is "idiot" for Birmingham Muslim comments – David Cameron'. *The Guardian*, 12 January. www.theguardian.com/media/2015/jan/12/fox-news-expert-ridiculed-over-birmingham-is-totally-muslim-city-claims (accessed 17 January 2015).

FOSIS (The Federation of Student Islamic Societies) (2014) 'FOSIS horrified by murder of female Muslim student'. Press release, 18 June. Online. http://media.fosis.org.uk/press-releases/1596-fosis-condemns-horrific-murder-of-female-muslim-student (accessed 17 June 2014).

Foucault, M. (1980) *Power/Knowledge: Selected interviews and other writings, 1972–1977*. Brighton: Harvester Press.

Francis, H. (1993) 'Advancing phenomenography: Questions of method'. *Nordisk Pedagogik*, 2, 68–75.

Franks, M. (2000) 'Crossing the borders of whiteness? White Muslim women who wear the hijab in Britain today'. *Ethnic and Racial Studies*. 23 (5), 917–29.

Fredrickson, G.M. (1981) *White Supremacy: A comparative study in American and South African History*. New York: Oxford University Press.

Freire, P. (1985) *The Politics of Liberation: Culture, power and liberation*. South Hadley, MA: Bergin and Garvey.

Frith, M. (2004) 'Ethnic minorities feel strong sense of identity with Britain, report reveals'. *The Independent*. Online. www.independent.co.uk/news/uk/this-britain/ethnic-minorities-feel-strong-sense-of-identity-with-britain-report-reveals-578503.html (accessed 16 December 2009).

Fryer, P. (1985) *Staying Power: The history of Black people in Britain*. London: Pluto Press.

— (1988) *Black People in the British Empire*. London: Pluto Press.

Fulat, S. (2005) 'Caught between two worlds: How can the state help young Muslims?' In Bunting, M. (ed.) *Islam, Race and Being British*. London: *The Guardian* in association with Barrow Cadbury Trust.

Gabriel, T., and Hannan, R. (eds) (2011) *Islam and the Veil: Theoretical and regional contexts*. London: Continuum.

Garbin, D. (2005) 'Bangladeshi Diaspora in the UK: Some observations on socio-cultural dynamics, religious trends and transnational politics'. Paper presented at the Human Rights and Bangladesh Conference, School of Oriental and African Studies, University of London. Online. www.surrey.ac.uk/cronem/files/BE04B01Ed01.pdf (accessed 7 January 2015).

García, O., and Kleifgen, J. (2010) *Educating Emergent Bilinguals: Policies, programs, and practices for English language learners*. New York: Teachers College Press.

Gardner, K. (1993) 'Desh-Bidesh: Sylheti images of home and away'. *Man: The Journal of the Royal Anthropological Institute*, 28 (1), 1–17.

— (1995a) *Global Migrants, Local Lives: Travel and transformation in rural Bangladesh*. Oxford: Clarendon Press.

— (1995b) 'International migration and the rural context in Sylhet'. *New Community*, 18, 579–90,

— (1998) 'Women and Islamic revivalism in a Bangladeshi community'. In Jeffrey, P. and Basu, A. (eds) *Appropriating Gender: Women's activism and political religion in South Asia*. London: Routledge.

— (2002) *Age, Narrative and Migration: The life course and life histories of Bengali elders in London*. Oxford: Berg.

Gardner, K., and Shukur, A. (1994) 'I'm Bengali, I'm Asian and I'm living here: The changing identity of British Bengalis'. In Ballard, R. (ed.) *Desh Pardesh: The South Asian presence in Britain*. London: Hurst.

Gavron, K. (2005) 'Migrants to citizens: Bangladeshi women in Tower Hamlets, London'. *Revue européene des migrations internationals*, 21 (3), 69–81.

Geaves, R. (2005) 'Negotiating British citizenship and Muslim identity'. In Abbas, T. (ed.) *Muslim Britain: Communities under pressure*. London: Zed Books.

Geertz, C. (2000a) *Available Light*. Princeton: Princeton University Press.

— (2000b [1973]) *The Interpretation of Cultures: Selected essays by Clifford Geertz*. New York: Basic Books.

Gergen, M., and Gergen, K. (1984) 'The social construction of narrative accounts'. In Gergen, M. and Gergen, K. (eds) *Historical Social Psychology*. Hillsdale, NJ: Lawrence Erlbaum Associates.

Ghassoub, M. (1987) 'Feminism or the eternal masculine – in the Arab world'. *New Left Review*, 161, 3–13.

Ghuman, P. (1995) 'Acculturation, ethnic identity and community languages: A study of Indo-Canadian adolescents'. In Jones, B. and Ghuman, P. (eds) *Bilingualism, Education and Identity*. Cardiff: University of Wales Press.

Giddens, A. (1973) *The Class Structure of the Advanced Societies*. London: Hutchinson.

— (1984) *The Constitution of Society: Outline of the theory of structuration*. Berkeley: University of California Press.

— (1991) *Modernity and Self-identity: Self and society in the late modern age*. Cambridge: Polity Press.

Gillborn, D., and Mirza, H.E. (2000) *Educational Inequality: Mapping race, class and gender, a synthesis of research evidence*. London: Office for Standards in Education.

Gilman, S.L. (1991) *The Jew's Body*. New York: Routledge.

Gilroy, P. (1987) *There Ain't no Black in the Union Jack: The cultural politics of race and nation*. London: Hutchinson.

Githens-Mazer, J., and Lambert, R. (2010) *Islamophobia and Anti-Muslim Hate Crime: UK case studies 2010*. Exeter: European Muslim Research Centre, University of Exeter. Online. http://tinyurl.com/o4g58wp (accessed 12 December 2014).

Glassner, B., and Loughlin, J. (1987) *Drugs in Adolescent Worlds: Burnouts to straights*. New York: St Martin's Press.

Glover, J. (2001) 'Blair backs Blunkett over race'. *The Guardian*, 10 December. Online. www.guardian.co.uk/politics/2001/dec/10/immigrationpolicy.race (accessed 23 November 2007).

Glynn, S. (2002) 'Bengali Muslims: The new East End radicals?' *Ethnic and Racial Studies*, 25 (6), 969–88.

Gmelch, G. (1980) 'Return migration'. *Annual Review of Anthropology*, 9 (1), 135–59.

Goldberg, D.T. (ed.) (1990) *Anatomy of Racism*. Minneapolis: University of Minnesota Press.

— (1993) *Racist Culture: Philosophy and the politics of meaning*. Oxford: Blackwell.

— (1994) *Multiculturalism: A critical reader*. Oxford: Blackwell.

Goldthorpe, J.H. (1987) *Social Mobility and Class Structure in Modern Britain*. 2nd ed. Oxford: Oxford University Press.

Goodson, I., and Sikes, P. (2001) *Life History Research in Educational Settings*. Buckingham: Open University Press.

Gordon, M. (1964) *Assimilation in American life: The role of race, religion and national origins*. New York: Oxford University Press.

Gottschalk, P., and Greenberg, G. (2008) *Islamophobia: Making Muslims the enemy*. Lanham, MD: Rowman and Littlefield.

Gove, M. (2006) *Celsius 7/7*. London: Weidenfeld and Nicolson.

Graddol, D. (2006) *English Next: Why global English may mean the end of 'English as a foreign language'*. London: British Council.

Gramsci, A. (1973) *Selections from the Orison Notebooks*. London: Lawrence & Wishart.

Gravelle, M. (1996) *Supporting Bilingual Learners in Schools*. Stoke-on-Trent: Trentham Books.

Gray, C., and Macblain, S. (2012) *Learning Theories in Childhood*. London: Sage.

Greater London Authority (2011) 'Population by ethnicity and age: Tower Hamlets'. 2010 Round Ethnic Group Population Projections, SHLAA scenario. London: Greater London Authority.

Greely, A. (1995) 'The persistence of religion'. *Cross Currents*, 45, 24–41.

Gregory, E. (ed.) (1997) *One Child, Many Worlds: Early learning in multicultural communities*. London: David Fulton.

Grillo, R.D. (2001) 'Transnational migration and multiculturalism in Europe'. A working paper on the Transnational Communities Programme website (www.transcomm.ox.ac.uk/). Online. http://tinyurl.com/nnae4gc (accessed 12 December 2014).

Grosjean, F. (1982) *Life with Two Languages*. Cambridge, MA: Harvard University Press.

Gubrium, J.A., and Holstein, J.F. (2000) *The Self We Live By: Narrative identity in a postmodern world*. Oxford: Oxford University Press.

— (2004) 'The active interview'. In Silverman, D. (ed.) *Qualitative Research: Theory, method and practice*. 2nd ed. London: Sage.

Gubrium, J.A., Holstein, J.F., and Buckholdt, D. (1994) *Constructing the Life Course*. Dix Hills, NY: General Hall.

Gülen, F. (2006) 'A comparative approach to Islam and democracy'. In Kamrava, M. (ed.) *The New Voices of Islam: Reforming politics and modernity*. London: I.B. Tauris.

Gupta, A.S. (2009) *What Fatima Did*. Hampstead Theatre, October.

Haddad, Y.Z. (1980) 'Traditional affirmations concerning the role of women as found in contemporary Arab Islamic literature'. In Smith, J.I. (ed.) *Women in Contemporary Muslim Societies*. New Brunswick, NJ: Associated University Presses.

Hagendoorm, L. (1993) 'Ethnic categorization and outgroup exlusion: Cultural values and social stereotypes in the construction of ethnic hierarchies'. *Ethnic and Racial Studies*, 16 (1), 26–51.

Hai, Y. (2008) 'First person'. *The Guardian*, 5 April. Online. www.theguardian. com/lifeandstyle/2008/apr/05/familyandrelationships.family1 (accessed 16 June 2009).

Hall, S. (1980) 'Race articulation and societies structured in dominance'. In UNESCO (ed.) *Sociological Theories: Race and colonialism*. Paris: UNESCO.

— (1990) 'Cultural identity and diaspora'. In Rutherford, J. (ed.) *Identity: Community, culture, difference*. London: Lawrence and Wishart.

— (1991) 'Old and new identities'. In King, A.D. (ed.) *Culture, Globalisation and the World System*. New York: Macmillan.

— (1992) 'New ethnicities'. In Donald, J. and Rattansi, A. (eds) *'Race', Culture and Difference*. London: Sage/Open University.

— (1993a) 'Cultural identity in question'. In Hall, S., Held, D. and McGrew, T. (eds) *Modernity and its Futures*. Cambridge: Polity Press.

— (1993b) 'Culture, community, nation'. *Cultural Studies*, 7 (3), 349–63.

— (1996) 'Who needs "identity"?' In Hall, S. and du Gay, P. (eds) *Questions of Cultural Identity*. London: Sage.

— (ed.) (1997) *Representation: Cultural representation and signifying practices*. London: Sage.

Halliday, F. (1992) *Arabs in Exile: Yemini migrants in urban Britain*. London: I.B. Tauris.

Hamington, M. (1995) *Hail Mary? The struggle for ultimate womanhood in Catholicism*. New York: Routledge.

Hammersley, M., and Atkinson, P. (2007) *Ethnography: Principles in practice*. London: Routledge.

Hammersley, M., and Traianou, A. (2012) *Ethics and Educational Research*. London: British Educational Research Association. Online. www.bera.ac.uk/wp-content/uploads/2014/03/Ethics-and-Educational-Research.pdf (accessed 12 December 2014).

Hankiss, A. (1981) 'Ontologies of the self: On the mythological rearranging of one's life-history'. In Bertaux, D. (ed.) *Biography and Society: The life history approach in the social sciences*. Beverly Hills, CA: Sage.

Hannerz, U. (1992) *Cultural Complexity: Studies in the social organisation of meaning*. New York: Columbia University Press.

Harding, E., and Riley, P. (1986) *The Bilingual Family: A handbook for parents*. Cambridge: Cambridge University Press.

Harding, S. (1986) *The Science Question in Feminism*. Milton Keynes: Open University Press.

Hatch, A.J., and Wisniewski, R. (1995) 'Life history and narrative: Questions, issues and exemplary works'. In Hatch, A.J. and Wisniewski, R. (eds) *Life History and Narrative*. London: Falmer Press.

Hatt, A., and Issa, T. (2012) *Language, Culture and Identity in the Early Years*. London: Bloomsbury Academic.

Haw, K. (1998) *Educating Muslim Girls: Shifting discourses*. Buckingham: Open University Press.

Heffer, S. (1998) *Like the Roman: The life of Enoch Powell*. London: Weidenfeld and Nicolson.

Helie-Lucas, M.A. (1994) 'The preferential symbol for Islamic identity: Women in Muslim personal laws'. In Moghadam, V. (ed.) *Identity Politics and Women: Cultural reassertions and feminisms in international perspective*. Boulder, CO: Westview Press.

Hellyer, H.A. (2009) *Muslims of Europe: The 'other' Europeans*. Edinburgh: Edinburgh University Press.

Henzell-Thomas, J. (2002) 'Embracing the challenge of a connected world'. In Hamid, A.W. and Sherif, J. (ed.) *The Quest for Sanity: Reflections on September 11 and the aftermath*. London: Muslim Council of Britain.

Hepple, B., and Choudhury, T. (2001) *Tackling Religious Discrimination: Practical implications for policy makers and legislators*. London: Home Office.

Herding, M. (2014) *Inventing the Muslim Cool: Islamic youth culture*. New York: Columbia University Press.

Heritage, J. (1984) 'Conversational analysis and institutional talk: Analysing data'. In Atkinson, J.M. and Heritage, J. (eds) *Structures of Social Action*. Cambridge: Cambridge University Press.

Hessini, L. (1994) 'Wearing the hijab in contemporary Morocco: Choice and identity'. In Göçek, F.M. and Balaghi, S. (eds) *Reconstructing Gender in the Middle East: Tradition, identity and power*. New York: Columbia University Press.

Hewitt, R. (2005) *White Backlash and the Politics of Multiculturalism*. Cambridge: Cambridge University Press.

Hill, M. (1997) 'Introduction: Vipers in Shangri-la: Whiteness, writing, and other ordinary terrors'. In Hill, M. (ed.) *Whiteness: A critical reader*. New York: New York University Press.

Hiro, D. (1971) *Black British, White British*. New York and London: Monthly Review Press.

Hoffman, E. (1991) *Lost in Translation: A life in a new language*. London: Vintage.

Holiday, A., Hyde, M., and Kullman, I. (2004) *Inter-cultural Communication: An advance resource book*. London: Routledge.

Holm, J. (1994) 'Introduction: Raising the issues'. In Holm, J. and Bowker, J. (eds) *Women in Religion*. London: Pinter.

Holmes, C.A. (1988) *John Bull's Island: Immigration and British society, 1871–1971*. Basingstoke: Macmillan.

hooks, b. (1981) *Ain't I a woman: Black women and feminism*. Boston: South End Press.

Hope, C. (2014) 'Trojan Horse Report: All schoolchildren to be taught British values from September, says Michael Gove'. *Daily Telegraph*. Online. http://tinyurl.com/m3uywpy (accessed 12 December 2014).

Hoque, A. (2003) 'Long-distance nationalism: The case of the Bagir Ghatis from East London'. Unpublished MSc diss. London: School of Oriental and African Studies (SOAS).

— (2004a) *The Tower Hamlets A–Z Guide to Working With Young People*. London: Tower Hamlets College.

— (2004b) 'Islamic pride and prejudice'. *The Independent*, 12 April, 4–5.

— (2004c) 'Islamic pride'. BBC Radio 1Xtra, 14 April.

— (2005) 'Long-distance nationalism: A study of the Bagir Ghati community in East London'. *eSharp Journal*, 5: Borders and Boundaries. Online. www.gla.ac.uk/media/media_41168_en.pdf (accessed 12 December 2014).

— (2006) 'Inner city Islam'. BBC Radio 1Xtra. September.

— (2011) 'The development of a Br-Islamic identity: Third generation Bangladeshis from East London (Tower Hamlets)'. Unpublished PhD thesis, Goldsmiths College, University of London.

Horsman, R. (1981) *Race and Manifest Destiny*. Cambridge, MA: Harvard University Press.

Hosseini, K. (2007) *A Thousand Splendid Suns*. London: Bloomsbury.

Huda [Christine Hude Dodge] (2015) 'Arabic language in Islam: Why do many Muslims strive to learn Arabic?' *About Religion*. Online. http://islam.about.com/od/arabiclanguage/a/arabic.htm (accessed 6 January 2015).

Humphrey, C. (2007) 'Insider-outsider: Activating the hyphen'. *Action Research*, 5 (1), 11–26.

Huntington, S.P. (1993) 'The clash of civilisations'. *Foreign Affairs*, 72 (3), 22–49.

Husain, E. (2007) *The Islamist: Why I joined radical Islam in Britain, what I saw inside and why I left*. London: Penguin.

Inglis, D. (2005) *Culture and Everyday Life*, London: Routledge.

Institute of Race Relations (2012) 'Poverty statistics'. Online. www.irr.org.uk/research/statistics/poverty/ (accessed 18 June 2014).

Iqbal, N. (2010) 'Beyond the veil'. *London Evening Standard*, 5 November, 24–5.

ISER (2012) 'Ethnic minorities living in the UK feel more British than white Britons'. Online. www.iser.essex.ac.uk/2012/06/30/ethnic-minorities-living-in-the-uk-feel-more-british-than-white-britons (accessed 26 June 2014).

Islam, M. (1987) 'Bangladesh migration: An impact study'. In Islam, M. (ed.) *Overseas Migration from Rural Bangladesh: A micro study*. Chittagong: University of Chittagong.

Islam, N. (2008) 'At the heart of the community'. *East End Life*, 1–7 December, 6.

Issa, T. (2005) *Talking Turkey: The language, culture and identity of Turkish speaking children in Britain*. Stoke-on-Trent: Trentham Books.

James, A. (2007) 'Giving voice to children's voices: Practices and problems, pitfalls and potentials'. *American Anthropologist*, 109 (2), 261–72.

Jawad, H., and Benn, T. (eds) (2003) *Muslim Women in the United Kingdom and Beyond: Experiences and images*. Boston: Brill.

Jayaratne, T., and Stewart, A. (1995) 'Quantitative and qualitative methodology in the social sciences: Feminist issues and practical strategies'. In Holland, J., Blair, M. and Sheldon, S. (eds) *Debates and Issues in Feminist Research and Pedagogy*. Clevedon: Multilingual Matters and Open University Press.

Jeffcoate, J. (1984) *Ethnic Minorities and Education*. London: Harper and Row.

Jenkins, R. (1996) *Social Identity*. London: Routledge.

Jocelyn, C. (2006) 'Muslims in Western Europe after 9/11: Why the term Islamophobia is more a predicament than an explanation'. Challenge: Liberty and Security. Online. www.libertysecurity.org/article1167.html (accessed 18 June 2009).

John Paul II (1988) *Mulieris Dignitatem: On the dignity and vocation of women*. Vatican City: Liberia Editrice Vaticana. Online. www.vatican.va/holy_father/john_paul_ii/apost_letters/documents/hf_jp-ii_apl_15081988_mulieris-dignitatem_en.html (accessed 16 May 2009).

Jones, P.N. (1978) 'The distribution and diffusion of the coloured population in England and Wales, 1961–1971'. *Transactions of the Institute of British Geographers*, 3, 515–33.

Jones, S. (2006) *Antonio Gramsci (Routledge Critical Thinkers* series). Abingdon: Routledge.

Jorda, M. (1978) 'Search goes on to find new clues to murders'. *East Ender*, 20 May.

Jordan, W.D. (1968) *White over Black: American attitudes towards the Negro 1550–1812*. New York: Norton.

— (1974) *The White Man's Burden: Historical origins of racism in the United States*. New York: Oxford University Press.

Joseph Rowntree Foundation (2007a) *Experiences of Poverty and Educational Disadvantage*. Online. www.jrf.org.uk/sites/files/jrf/2123.pdf (accessed 12 December 2012).

— (2007b) 'Poverty twice as likely for minority ethnic groups: Education fails to close gap'. Online. www.jrf.org.uk/media-centre/poverty-twice-likely-minority-ethnic-groups-education-fails-close-gap (accessed 12 October 2009).

Kabeer, N. (1991) 'The quest for national identity: Women, Islam and the state of Bangladesh'. In Kandiyoti, D. (ed.) *Women, Islam and the State*. Philadelphia: Temple University Press.

Kachru, B.B. (ed.) (1992) *The Other Tongue: English across cultures (English in the global context)*. 2nd ed. Urbana: University of Illinois Press.

Kamrava, M. (ed.) (2006) *The New Voices of Islam: Reforming politics and modernity*. London: I.B. Tauris.

Karam, A.M. (1998) *Women, Islamisms and the State: Contemporary feminisms in Egypt*. London: Macmillan.

Kastoryano, R. (2002) *Negotiating Identities: States and immigrants in France and Germany*. Princeton: Princeton University Press.

— (2006) 'French secularism and Islam: France's headscarf affair'. In Modood, T., Triandafyllidou, A. and Zapata-Barrero, R. (eds) *Multiculturalism, Muslims and Citizenship: A European approach*. London: Routledge.

Kearney, C. (2003) *The Monkey's Mask: Identity, memory, narrative and voice*. Stoke-on-Trent: Trentham Books.

Keddie, N. (1991) 'Introduction: Deciphering Middle Eastern women's history'. In Keddie, N. and Baron, B. (eds) *Women in Middle Eastern History: Shifting boundaries in sex and gender*. New Haven, CT: Yale University Press.

Kenner, C. (2000) *Home Pages: Literacy links for bilingual children*. Stoke-on-Trent: Trentham Books.

— (2004) *Becoming Biliterate: Young children learning different writing systems*. Stoke-on-Trent: Trentham Books.

Kenner, C., and Hickey, T. (eds) (2008) *Multilingual Europe: Diversity and learning*. Stoke-on-Trent: Trentham Books.

Kenner, C., and Ruby, M. (2012) *Interconnecting Worlds: Teacher partnerships for bilingual learning*. Stoke-on-Trent: Trentham Books.

Kepel, G. (1997) *Allah in the West: Islamic movements in America and Europe*. Cambridge: Polity Press.

— (2003) *Jihad: The trial of political Islam*. London: I.B. Tauris.

Kermani, F. (2006) 'Women only Jihad'. *Dispatches*. Channel 4, 28 October.

Kerr, C., Dunlop, J., Harbison, F., and Myers, C. (eds) (1962) *Industrialism and Industrial Man*. London: Heinemann.

Kershen, A.J. (ed.) (1998) *A Question of Identity*. Aldershot: Ashgate.

— (2000) 'Mother tongue as a bridge to assimilation? Yiddish and Sylheti in East London'. In Kershen, A.J. (ed.) *Language, Labour and Migration*. Aldershot: Ashgate.

— (2007) *Strangers, Aliens and Asians: Huguenots, Jews and Bangladeshis in Spitalfields, 1660–2000*. London: Frank Cass.

Keval, H.C. (2009) 'Negotiating constructions of "insider"/"outsider" status and explaining the significance of dis/connections'. *Enquire*, 4, 51–72.

Khalil, S. (2010) 'Halal holidays in the sun'. *FastTrack*. BBC. Online. http://news.bbc.co.uk/1/hi/programmes/fast_track/8901976.stm (accessed 20 November 2010).

Khan, N.A (n.d.) 'The importance of Arabic language'. Online. www.youtube.com/watch?v=VGMQtAfhC6M (accessed 6 January 2015).

Khan, S. (2008) Interview with the author at the London Muslim Centre, 4 December.

— (2010) Interview with the author at the London Muslim Centre, 12 March.

— (2014) Interview with the author at the London Muslim Centre, 27 June.

Kibria, N. (2006) 'The "New Islam" and Bangladeshi youth in Britain and the US'. Paper presented at the annual meeting of the American Sociological Association, Montreal, Canada, 11 August.

Kimber, J., and Cooper, L. (1991) *Victim Support: Racial harassment project*. Final report. London: Community Research Advisory Centre.

Kirkup, J. (2011) 'Muslims must embrace core British values, says Cameron'. *Daily Telegraph*, 5 February, 1.

Kroeber, A.L., and Kluckhohn, C. (1963) *Culture: A critical review of concepts and definitions*. New York: Vintage Books.

Kureishi, H. (1990) *The Buddha of Suburbia*. Harmondsworth: Penguin Books.

Kvale, S., and Brinkman, S. (2008) *InterViews: Learning the craft of qualitative research interviewing*. Thousand Oaks, CA: Sage.

Laclau, E. (1990) *New Reflections on the Revolution of our Time*. London: Verso.

Lamont, N. (2002) 'Down with multiculturalism, book-burning and fatwas'. *The Telegraph*, 8 May. Online. www.telegraph.co.uk/comment/personal-view/3576323/Down-with-multiculturalism-book-burning-and-fatwas.html (accessed 15 October 2007).

Lavery, B. (2006) *Churchill's Navy: The ships, men and organisation*. London: Conway.

Lawler, S. (2013) *Identity: Sociological perspectives*. 2nd ed. Cambridge: Polity Press.

Lawrence, E. (1982) 'Just plain common sense: The roots of racism'. In Centre for Contemporary Cultural Studies, *The Empire Strikes Back: Race and racism in the 70s*. London: Hutchinson.

Layton-Henry, Z. (1992) *The Politics of Immigration*. Oxford: Blackwell.

Lazreg, M. (1988) 'Feminism and difference: The perils of writing as a woman on women in Algeria'. *Feminist Studies*, 14 (1), 82.

Lee, D.J., and Turner, B.S. (1996) 'Introduction: Myths of classlessness and the "death" of class analysis'. In Lee, D.J. and Turner, B.S. (eds) *Conflicts About Class*. Harlow: Longman.

Leech, K. (1993) 'Civil war in the East End'. *East London Advertiser*, 9 September.

Lees, L.H. (1979) *Exiles of Erin: Irish migrants in Victorian London*. Manchester: Manchester University Press.

Leiken, R.S. (2012) *Europe's Angry Muslims: The revolt of the second generation*. New York: Oxford University Press.

Le Quesne, N. (2001) 'Islam in Europe: A changing faith'. *Time*, 24 December, 50–56.

Lewis, P. (2002) *Islamic Britain. Religion, politics and identity among British Muslims*. 2nd ed. London: I.B. Tauris.

— (2007) *Young, British and Muslim*. London: Continuum.

Lewis, R. (ed.) (2013) *Modest Fashion: Styling bodies, mediating faith*. London: I.B. Tauris.

Lister, R. (1990) 'Concepts of poverty'. *Social Studies Review*, 6 (5), 192–5.

Locke, J. (1980 [1689]) 'Second treatise of government'. In Macpherson, C.B. (ed.) *John Locke: Second treatise of government*. Indianapolis, IN: Hackett.

Lorimer, D. (1978) *Colour, Class and Victorians*. Leicester: Leicester University Press.

Lott, T.L. (1994) 'Black vernacular representation and cultural malpractice'. In Goldberg, D.T. (ed.) *Multiculturalism: A critical reader*. Oxford: Blackwell.

Luard, T. (2005) 'Chinese diaspora: Britain'. BBC News. Online. http://news.bbc.co.uk/1/hi/world/asia-pacific/4304845.stm (accessed 25 March 2014).

Lyon, J., and Ellis, N. (1991) 'Parental attitudes towards the Welsh language'. *Journal of Multilingual and Multicultural Development*, 12 (4), 239–51.

Lyon, S. (2005) 'In the shadow of September 11: Multiculturalism and identity'. In Abbas, T. (ed.) *Muslim Britain: Communities under pressure*. London: Zed Books.

MacKenzie, J.M. (1984) *Propaganda and Empire: The manipulation of British public opinion 1880–1960*. Manchester: Manchester University Press.

— (ed.) (1986) *Imperialism and Popular Culture*. Manchester: Manchester University Press.

MacKinnon, C.A. (1995) 'Sexuality, pornography and method: "Pleasure under patriarchy"'. In Tuana, N. and Tong, R. (eds) *Feminism and Philosophy: Essential readings in theory, reinterpretation and application*. Boulder, CO: Westview Press,

Mackinnon, I. (1993) 'Asian anger simmers after racist assault'. *The Independent*, 10 September, 8.

Macleod, A.E. (1991) *Accommodating Protest: Working women and the new veiling in Cairo*. New York: Columbia University Press.

Macpherson, W. (1999) *The Stephen Lawrence Inquiry: Report of an inquiry by Sir William Macpherson of Cluny*. London: HMSO.

Maduro, O. (1982) *Religion and Social Conflicts*. New York: Orbis.

Mahmood, R.A. (1991) *Employment of Bangladeshis Abroad and Use of Their Remittances*. Bangladesh: Dhaka Planning Commission.

Male, L. (2006) 'The veil is a symbol of women's subjugation'. *Daily Mirror*, 16 October, 4.

Malik, J. (ed.) (2004) *Muslims in Europe: From the margin to the centre*. Berlin: LIT.

Malik, K. (2001) 'The real value of diversity'. *Connections*, Winter. London: Commission of Racial Equality.

Malik, M. (ed.) (2012) *Anti-Muslim Prejudice: Past and present*. Abingdon: Routledge.

Mandair, A. (2006) '(Im)possible intersections: Religion, (post)-colonial subjectivity and the ideology of multiculturalism'. In Ali, N., Kalra, V.S., and Sayyid, S. (eds) *Post Colonial People: South Asians in Britain*. London: Hurst.

Mani, B. (2002) 'Undressing the diaspora'. In Puwar, N., and Raghuram, P. (eds) *South Asian Women in the Diaspora*. Oxford: Berg.

Manji, I. (2005) *The Trouble with Islam Today: A wake-up call for honesty and change*. Edinburgh: Mainstream.

Manning, A., and Roy, S. (2010) 'Culture clash or culture club? National identity in Britain'. *Economic Journal*, 120 (542), F72–F100.

Manning, J. (1999) *Is the Pope Catholic? A Woman confronts her church*. Toronto: Malcolm Lester Books.

Mannoni, O. (1964) *Prospero and Caliban: The psychology of colonization*. New York: Praeger.

Maqsood, R.W. (2003) *Teach Yourself Islam*. London: Bookpoint.

Marranci, G. (2005) 'Pakistanis in Northern Ireland in the aftermath of September 11'. In Abbas, T. (ed.) *Muslim Britain: Communities under pressure*. London: Zed Books.

Marsot, A.L.A.S. (1996) 'Women and modernization: A re-evaluation'. In Sonbol, A.E.A. (ed.) *Women, the Family and Divorce Laws in Islamic History*. Syracuse, NY: Syracuse University Press.

Massey, D.S. (1997) 'Causes of migration'. In Guibernau, M. and Rex, J. (1997) *The Ethnicity Reader: Nationalism, multiculturalism and migration*. Cambridge: Polity Press.

Matar, N. (1998) *Islam in Britain: 1558–1685*. Cambridge: Cambridge University Press.

McLaren, P. (1994) 'White terror and oppositional agency: Towards a critical multiculturalism'. In Goldberg, D.T. (1994) *Multiculturalism: A critical reader*. Oxford: Blackwell.

McRoy, A. (2006) *From Rushdie to 7/7: The radicalisation of Islam in Britain*. London: Social Affairs Unit.

Meriwether, M.L. (1993) 'Women and economic change in nineteenth century Syria: The case of Aleppo'. In Tucker, J. (ed.) *Arab Women: Old boundaries, new frontiers*. Bloomington: Indiana University Press.

Mernissi, F. (1991) *The Veil and the Male Elite: A feminist interpretation of women's rights in Islam*. Trans. Lakeland, M.J. Cambridge, MA: Perseus Books.

— (2003 [1975]) *Beyond the veil: Male–female dynamics in modern Muslim society*, London: Saqi Books.

Metcalf, B.D. (tr.) (1990) *Perfecting Women: Maulana Ashraf Ali Thanawi's Bihishti Zewar* [Heavenly Ornaments]. Berkeley: University of California Press.

Miles, R. (1982) *Racism and Migrant Labour*. London: Routledge.

— (1984) 'Marxism versus the "sociology of race relations"?' *Ethnic and Racial Studies*, 7 (2), 217–37.

— (1989) *Racism*. London: Routledge.

Miliband, R. (1987) 'Class analysis'. In Giddens, A. and Turner, J. (eds) *Social Theory Today*. Cambridge: Polity Press.

Miller, J. (1983) *Many Voices: Bilingualism, culture and education*. London: Routledge and Kegan Paul.

— (2001) *One of the Guys: Girls, gangs and gender*. New York: Oxford University Press.

Miller, J., and Glassner, B. (2004) 'The "inside" and the "outside": Finding realities in interviews'. In Silverman, D. (ed.) *Qualitative Research: Theory, method and practice*. 2nd ed. London: Sage.

Millet, K. (1970) *Sexual Politics*. New York: Doubleday.

Mills, J. (2001) 'Being bilingual: Perspectives of third generation Asian children on language, culture and identity'. *International Journal of Bilingual Education and Bilingualism*, 4 (6), 383–402.

Mirza, M., Senthilkumaran, A., and Ja'far, Z. (2007) *Living Apart Together: British Muslims and the paradox of multiculturalism*. London: Policy Exchange.

Modood, T. (1992) 'British Asian Muslims and the Rushdie Affair'. In Donald, J. and Rattansi, A. (eds) *'Race', Culture and Difference*. London: Sage/Open University.

— (2005a) 'Foreword'. In Abbas, T. (ed.) *Muslim Britain: Communities under pressure*. London: Zed Books.

— (2005b) *Multicultural Politics: Racism, ethnicity, and Muslims in Britain*. Minneapolis: University of Minnesota Press.

— (2006) 'British Muslims and the politics of multiculturalism'. In Modood, T., Triandafyllidou, A. and Zapata-Barrero, R. (eds) *Multiculturalism, Muslims and Citizenship: A European approach*. London: Routledge.

— (2010) *Still Not Easy Being British: Struggles for a multicultural citizenship*. Stoke-on-Trent: Trentham Books.

Modood, T., Berthoud, R., Lakey, J., Nazroo, J., Smith, P., Virdee, S., and Beishon, S. (1997) *Ethnic Minorities in Britain: Diversity and disadvantage – the fourth national survey of ethnic minorities*. London: Policy Studies Institute.

Modood, T., and Kastoryano, R. (2006) 'Secularism and the accommodation of Muslims in Europe'. In Modood, T., Triandafyllidou, A. and Zapata-Barrero, R. (eds) *Multiculturalism, Muslims and citizenship: A European approach*. London: Routledge.

Moosavi, L. (2012) 'Muslims are well integrated in Britain – but no one seems to believe it'. *The Guardian*. Online. www.theguardian.com/commentisfree/belief/2012/jul/03/muslims-integrated-britain (accessed 26 June 2014).

Morrison, T. (1992) *Playing in the Dark: Whiteness and the literary imagination*. Cambridge, MA: Harvard University Press.

Mor-Sommerfeld, A. (2002) 'Language mosaic: Developing literacy in a second new language: A new perspective'. *Reading, Literacy and Language*, 36 (3), 99–105.

Mudimbe, V.Y. (1994) *The Idea of Africa*. Bloomington: Indiana University Press.

Mule, P., and Barthel, D. (1992) 'The return to the veil'. *Sociological Forces*, 7 (2), 323–32.

Mumford, K., and Power, A. (2003) *East Enders: Family and community in East London*. Bristol: Policy Press.

Munoz, G.M. (ed.) (1999) *Islam, Modernism and the West*. London: I.B. Tauris.

Murad, A.H. (2003) 'Muslim loyalty and belonging: Some reflections on the psychosocial background'. In Seddon, M. (ed.) *British Muslims: Loyalty and belonging*. Leicester: Islamic Foundation.

Murphy, K. (1978) 'Do the police really want to know?' *Evening News*, 5 July.

Murray, K. (1989) 'The construction of identity in the narratives of romance and comedy'. In Shotter, J., and Gergen, K.J. (eds) *Texts of Identity*. London: Sage.

Murshad, A. (2002) 'Tools for talking'. *Reading, Literacy and Language*, 36 (3), 106–12.

Muslim Council of Britain (2010) 'Tackling Islamophobia: Reducing street violence against British Muslims'. Online. http://thecordobafoundation.com/print_article.php?id=1&art=31&page=press.php (accessed 22 December 2014).

Newman, A. (ed.) (1981) *The Jewish East End: 1840–1920*. London: Jewish Historical Society.

Newsweek Staff (2006) 'My two lives'. *Newsweek*, 3 June. Online www.newsweek.com/id/46810 (accessed 22 June 2009).

Nieto, S. (1999) *The Light in their Eyes: Creating multicultural learning communities*. New York: Teacher's College Press.

Norris, P., and Inglehart, R. (2004) *Sacred and Secular: Religion and politics worldwide*. Cambridge: Cambridge University Press.

Nye, C. (2011) 'Converting to Islam – the white Britons becoming Muslims'. BBC News, 4 January. Online. www.bbc.co.uk/news/uk-12075931 (accessed 20 June 2014).

Oakley, A. (1981) *Subject Women*. Oxford: Martin Robertson.

O'Connor, K. (1974) *The Irish in Britain*. Dublin: Gill and Macmillan.

O'Donnell, D. (1999) *East is East*. Channel 4 Films.

Olney, J. (1972) *Metaphors of Self*. Princeton: Princeton University Press.

Omaar, R. (2007) *Only Half of Me: British and Muslim – the conflict within,* London: Penguin.

ONS (Office for National Statistics) (2012a) 'Census gives insights into characteristics of London's population'. Online. http://tinyurl.com/oaaxmg2 (accessed 26 December 2014).

— (2012b) *Ethnicity and National Identity in England and Wales*. Online. www. ons.gov.uk/ons/rel/census/2011-census/key-statistics-for-local-authorities-in-england-and-wales/rpt-ethnicity.html#tab-Ethnicity-in-England-and-Wales (accessed 6 January 2015).

— (2012c) *Religion in England and Wales 2011*. Online. www.ons.gov.uk/ons/ dcp171776_290510.pdf (accessed 23 December 2014).

Open Society Institute (2002) *Monitoring Minority Protection in the EU: The situation of Muslims in the UK*. Budapest: Open Society Institute. Online. http:// tinyurl.com/mgsrep2 (accessed 23 December 2014).

Paechter, C. (2013) 'Researching sensitive issues online: Implications of a hybrid insider/outsider position in a retrospective ethnographic study'. *Qualitative Research*, 13 (1) 71–86.

Pakulsi, J., and Waters, M. (1996) *The Death of Class*. London: Sage.

Panayi, P. (2003) 'Cosmopolis: London's ethnic minorities'. In Kerr, J. and Gibson, A. (eds) *London: From punk to Blair*. London: Reaktion Books.

Papastergiadis, N. (2000) *The Turbulence of Migration*. Cambridge: Polity Press.

Parekh, B. (2000a) *The Future of Multi-ethnic Britain*. Commission on Multi-ethnic Britain. London: Profile Books.

— (2000b) 'Why it is vital to change what it means to be British'. *The Telegraph*, 18 October. Online. www.telegraph.co.uk/comment/4255965/Why-it-is-vital-to-change-what-it-means-to-be-British.html (accessed 23 December 2014).

— (2006) 'Europe, liberalism and the "Muslim question"'. In Modood, T., Triandafyllidou, A., Zapata-Barrero, R. (eds) *Multiculturalism, Muslims and Citizenship: A European approach*. London: Routledge.

Park, R.E. (1928) 'Human migration and the marginal man'. *American Journal of Sociology*, 33, 881–93.

— (1950) *Race and Culture*. New York: Free Press.

Parker, A., Russo, M., Sommer, D., and Yaeger, P. (eds) (1992) *Nationalisms and Sexualities*. New York: Routledge.

Parker, L., and Lynn, M. (2002) 'What's race got to do with it? Critical race theory's conflicts with and connections to qualitative research methodology and epistemology'. *Qualitative Inquiry*, 8 (1), 7–22.

Parmer, P., and Amos, V. (1981) 'Resistance and responses: The experiences of black girls in Britain'. In McRobbie, A. and McCabe, T. (eds) *Feminism for Girls: An adventure story*. London: Routledge and Kegan Paul.

Parry, B. (1998) *Delusions and Discoveries: Studies on India in the British imagination 1880–1930*. London: Verso.

Payne, M., and Hunter, J. (eds) (2003) *Renaissance Literature: An anthology*. Malden, MA: Blackwell.

Peach, C. (2005) 'Britain's Muslim population: An overview'. In Abbas, T. (ed.) *Muslim Britain: Communities under pressure*. London: Zed Books.

Pennycook, A. (1994) *The World in English: The cultural politics of English as an international language*. London: Longman.

— (1998) *English and the Discourse of Colonialism*. London: Routledge.

Pew Forum on Religious and Public Life (2009) *Mapping the Global Muslim Population: A report on the size and distribution of the world's Muslim population*. Washington, DC: Pew Research Center. Online. www.pewforum.org/files/2009/10/Muslimpopulation.pdf (accessed 23 December 2014).

— (2011) *The Future of the Global Muslim Population*. Washington, DC: Pew Research Center. Online. www.pewforum.org/2011/01/27/the-future-of-the-global-muslim-population/ (accessed 30 June 2014).

Phillips, D. (1988) 'Race and housing in London's East End: Continuity and change'. *New Community*, 14 (3), 356–69.

Phillips, T. (2007) 'Include Muslims in British history'. *Muslim Weekly*, 28 September, 1.

Phillipson, R. (1988) 'Linguicism: Structures and ideologies in linguistic imperialism'. In Cummins, J. and Skutnabb-Kangas, T. (eds) *Minority Education: From shame to struggle*. Clevedon: Multilingual Matters.

— (1992) *Linguistic Imperialism*. Oxford: Oxford University Press.

Phinney, J.S., and Rotheram, M.J. (eds) (1987) *Children's Ethnic Socialization, Pluralism and Development*. Thousand Oaks, CA: Sage, in cooperation with the Society for Child Development.

Platt, J., Weber, H., and Ho, M.L. (1983) *Singapore and Malaysia (Varieties of English around the World)*. Amsterdam: John Benjamins.

Platt, L. (2005) 'The intergenerational social mobility of minority ethnic groups'. *Sociology*, 39 (3), 445–61.

Plummer, A. (1972) *The London Weavers' Company: 1600–1970*. London: Routledge and Kegan Paul.

Poston, L.A. (1991) 'Da'wa in the West'. In Yazbeck, Y. (ed.) *The Muslims of America*. Oxford: Oxford University Press.

Poverty Site, The (2010) 'Low income and ethnicity'. Online. www.poverty.org.uk/06/index.shtml (accessed 18 June 2014).

Power, A. (1979) 'Council estates caught in a vicious racial spiral'. *New Society*, 19 April, 140–1.

Pratt, M.L. (1992) *Imperial Eyes: Travel writing and transculturation*. London: Routledge.

Press Association (2013) 'UK anti-Muslim hate crime soars, police figures show'. *The Guardian*, 27 December. Online. www.theguardian.com/society/2013/dec/27/uk-anti-muslim-hate-crime-soars (accessed 23 June 2014).

Primary Languages (n.d.) Bengali–Tower Hamlets case study Online. www.primarylanguages.org.uk/teaching__learning/community_languages/key_stage_2_curriculum_models/bengali_case_study.aspx (accessed 10 December 2010).

Rabe, M. (2003) 'Revisiting "insiders" and "outsiders" as social researchers'. *African Sociological Review*, 7 (2), 149–61.

Rahman, Z.H. (2007) 'We need to ask difficult questions'. *East London Advertiser*, 10 May, 4.

Ramadan, T. (2004) *Western Muslims and the Future of Islam*. Oxford: Oxford University Press.

Ramazanoglu, C. (1986) 'Gender and Islam – the politics of Muslim feminism'. *Ethnic and Racial Studies*, 14 (1), 11–31.

Randall, W.L. (1995) *The Stories We Are: An essay on self creation*. Toronto: University of Toronto Press.

Religion and Society (2013) 'Loss, creativity, and social class shape young people's religious and spiritual encounters in deprived neighbourhoods'. Online. http://tinyurl.com/lsnu33q (accessed 6 January 2015).

Renton, D. (2006) *When we Touched the Sky: The Anti-Nazi league 1977–1981*. Cheltenham: New Clarion Press.

Rex, J. (1979) 'Black militancy and class conflict'. In Miles, R. and Phizacklea, A. (eds) *Racism and Political Action in Britain*. London: Routledge and Kegan Paul.

— (1983 [1970]) *Race Relations in Sociological Theory*. 2nd ed. London: Routledge and Kegan Paul.

— (1986) *Race and Ethnicity*. Milton Keynes: Open University Press.

— (1998) *Ethnic Minorities in the Modern Nation State*. Basingstoke: Macmillan.

— (2005) 'An afterword on the situation of British Muslims in a world context'. In Abbas, T. (ed.) *Muslim Britain: Communities under pressure*. London: Zed Books.

Rex, J., and Moore, J. (1967) *Race, Community and Conflict: A study of Sparkbrook*. London: Institute of Race Relations and Oxford University Press.

Rex, J., and Tomlinson, S. (1979) *Colonial Immigrants in a British City*. London: Routledge and Kegan Paul.

Richardson, J. and Lambert, J. (1985) *The Sociology of Race*. Ormskirk: Causeway Press.

Richardson, J.E. (2004) *(Mis)representing Islam: The racism and rhetoric of British broadsheet newspapers*. Amsterdam: John Benjamins.

Riessman, C.K. (1993) *Narrative Analysis*. Newbury Park, CA: Sage.

Rippin, A. (2005) *Muslims: Their religious beliefs and practices*. 3rd ed. London: Routledge.

Roald, A.S. (2001) *Women in Islam: The Western experience*. London: Routledge.

Robbins, K. (1989) *Nineteenth-century Britain: England, Scotland and Wales: The making of a nation*. Oxford: Oxford University Press.

Roberts, K. (2001) *Class in Modern Britain*. Basingstoke: Palgrave.

Robinson, R. (1986) *Transients, Settlers and Refugees: Asians in Britain*. Oxford: Clarendon Press.

Rogers, P. (2002) 'If it's good for America, it's good for the world'. *The Observer*, 27 January. Online. www.guardian.co.uk/world/2002/jan/27/usa.georgebush (accessed 8 September 2009).

Romaine, S. (1995) *Bilingualism*. Oxford: Blackwell.

— (1998) 'Early bilingual development: From elite to folk'. In Extra, G. and Verhoeven, L. (eds) *Bilingualism and Migration*. Berlin: Mouton de Gruyter.

Ross, A. (2000) *Curriculum: Construction and critique*. London: Falmer.

Ross, T. (2010) 'Muslim pupils taken out of music lessons "because Islam forbids playing an instrument"'. *Evening Standard (London)*, 1 July, 9.

Rousseau, J.J. (1968 [1762]) *The Social Contract*. Trans. Cranston, M. London: Penguin.

Roy, O. (2004) *Globalised Islam: The search for a new ummah*. London: Hurst.

Runciman, W. (1966) *Relative Deprivation and Social Justice: A study of attitudes to social inequality in twentieth-century England*. Berkeley: University of California Press.

Runnymede (1997) *Islamophobia: A challenge for us all*. London: Runnymede Trust.

— (2012) 'Briefing on ethnicity and educational attainment'. Online. www.runnymedetrust.org/uploads/Parliamentary%20briefings/ EducationWHdebateJune2012.pdf (accessed 23 December 2014).

Rushdie, S. (1982) 'The new empire within Britain'. *New Society*, 9 December.

— (1989) *The Satanic Verses*. New York: Viking Press.

Ryle, G. (1971) *Collected Papers*. London: Hutchinson.

Sabbah, F.A. (1984) *Women in the Muslim Unconscious*. New York: Pergamon Press.

Sabin, L. (2015) 'Moroccan man killed at home in front of wife in "horrible Islamophobic attack"'. *The Independent*, 17 January. Online. www. independent.co.uk/news/world/europe/moroccan-man-in-france-killed-at-home-in-front-of-wife-by-intruder-shouting-about-islam-9985072.html (accessed 17 January 2015).

Sacks, H. (1992) *Lectures on Conversation*. Vols 1 and 2. Oxford: Blackwell.

Saeed, A., Blain, N., and Forbes, D. (1999) 'New ethnic and national questions in Scotland: Post-British identities among Glasgow Pakistani teenagers'. *Ethnic and Racial Studies*, 22 (5), 821–44.

Sahin, A. (2005) 'Exploring religious life world and attitudes toward Islam among British Muslim adolescents'. In Francis, L.J. (ed.) *Religion, Education and Adolescence: International empirical perspectives*. Cardiff: University of Wales Press.

Said, E.W. (1979) *Orientalism*. Harmondsworth: Penguin. 2nd ed. (1995) *Orientalism: Western conceptions of the Orient*. Harmondsworth: Penguin.

— (1997) *Covering Islam: How the media and the experts determine how we see the rest of the world*. London: Vintage.

— (2001) 'The clash of ignorance'. *The Nation*, 22 October, 11–13.

Samad, Y. (1992) 'Book burning and race relations: Political mobilisation of Asians in Bradford'. *New Community*, 18 (4), 507–19.

Sampson, A., and Phillips, C. (1992) *Multiple Victimisation: Racial attacks on an East London estate*. London: Home Office Police Research Group.

Sanghera, G., and Thapur-Björkert, S. (2007) '"Because I am Pakistani … and I am Muslim … I am political" – Gendering political radicalism: Young femininities in Bradford'. In Abbas, T. (ed.) *Islamic Political Radicalism: A European perspective*. Edinburgh: Edinburgh University Press.

Sarup, M. (1994) 'Home and identity'. In Bird, J., Curtis, B., Mash, M., Putnam, T., Robertson, G. and Tickner, L. (eds) *Travellers' Tales: Narratives of home and displacement*. London: Routledge.

— (1996) *Identity, Culture and the Postmodern World*. Edinburgh: Edinburgh University Press.

Saunders, P. (1990) *Social Class and Stratification*. London: Routledge.

Savage, M., Barlow, J., Dickens, P., and Fielding, T. (1992) *Property, Bureaucracy and Culture: Middle-class formation in contemporary Britain*. London: Routledge.

Scott, S. (prod.) (2004) 'Covering up'. *Panorama*. BBC, 13 June.

Sedghi, A. (2013) 'UK Census: Religion by age, ethnicity and country of birth'. *The Guardian* Datablog. Online. www.theguardian.com/news/datablog/2013/may/16/uk-census-religion-age-ethnicity-country-of-birth (accessed 26 December 2014).

Selway, K. (dir.) (2010) *My Name is Muhammad*. BBC One, 28 February.

Sen, A. (2006) *Identity and Violence: The illusion of destiny*. New York: Norton.

Shah, N.M. (1998) 'Emigration dynamics in South Asia: An overview'. In Appleyard, R. (ed.) *Emigration Dynamics in Developing Countries, Vol II: South Asia*. Aldershot: Ashgate.

Shahid, O. (2014) 'Halalywood: The rise of the Islamic entertainment industry'. Aquila Style, April. Online. www.aquila-style.com/focus-points/halalywood/62379 (accessed 1 September 2014).

Shain, F. (2003) *The Schooling and Identity of Asian Girls*. Stoke-on-Trent: Trentham Books.

Shields, V.R., and Dervin, B. (1993) 'Sense-making in feminist social science research: A call to enlarge the methodological options of feminist studies'. *Women's Studies International Forum*, 16 (1), 65–81.

Siddiqui, A. (2004) 'Muslim youth in Britain: Cultural and religious conflict in perspective'. In Malik, J. (ed.) *Muslims in Europe: From the margin to the centre*. Berlin: LIT.

Silverman, D. (2005) *Doing Qualitative Research: A practical handbook*. 2nd ed. London: Sage.

Sivanandan, A. (1981) 'From resistance to rebellion: Asian and Afro-Caribbean struggles in Britain'. *Race and Class*, 23, 111–52.

Skaine, R. (2002) *The Women of Afghanistan Under the Taliban*. Jefferson, NC: McFarland.

Skutnabb-Kangas, T., García, O., and Torres-Guzmán, E.M. (2006) 'Weaving spaces and (de)constructing ways for multilingual schools: The actual and the imagined'. In Skutnabb-Kangas, T., García, O., and Torres-Guzmán, E.M. (eds) *Imagining Multilingual Schools: Languages in education and globalization*. Clevedon: Multilingual Matters.

Smith, A.D. (1986) *The Ethnic Origins of Nationalism*. Oxford: Blackwell.

Smith, G. (1999) 'East London is no longer secular: Religion as a source of social capital in the regeneration of East London'. *Rising East: The Journal of East London*, 4 (3), 128–57.

Sneddon, R. (2009) *Bilingual Books, Biliterate Children: Learning to read through bilingual books*. Stoke-on-Trent: Trentham Books.

SOAS (n.d.) 'Arabic at SOAS Language Centre'. SOAS. Online. www.soas.ac.uk/languagecentre/languages/arabic/ (accessed 24 September 2009).

Solomos, J. (1992) 'The politics of immigration since 1945'. In Braham, P., Rattansi, A. and Skellington, R. (eds) *Racism and Antiracism: Inequalities, opportunities and policies*. London: Sage.

Sonalwar, P. (2014) 'Hindujas stay ahead of Mittal to top UK Indian rich list'. *Hindustan Times*. Online. www.hindustantimes.com/news-feed/homepage-business/hindujas-stay-ahead-of-mittal-to-top-uk-rich-list/article1-1207772.aspx (accessed 22 June 2014).

Song, M. (2003) *Choosing Ethnic Identity*. Cambridge: Polity Press.

Stanley, L., and Wise, S. (1990) 'Method, methodology and epistemology in feminist research process'. In Stanley, L. (ed.) *Feminist Praxis: Research, theory and epistemology in feminist sociology*. London: Routledge.

— (1993) *Breaking Out Again: Feminist ontology and epistemology*. 2nd ed. Abingdon: Routledge.

STAR (Sylheti Translation and Research) (n.d.) 'Sylheti literature'. Online. www.sylheti.org.uk/page2.html (accessed 13 April 2011).

Stonequist, E.V. (1935) 'The problem of the marginal man'. *American Journal of Sociology*, July, 1–12.

Storry, M., and Childs, P. (eds) (2002) *British Cultural Identities*. 2nd ed. London: Routledge.

Stowasser, B.F. (1987) 'Liberated equal or protected dependent? Contemporary religious paradigms on women's status in Islam'. *Arab Quarterly Studies*, 9 (3), 260–3.

Strategy Unit (2003) *Ethnic Minorities and the Labour Market*. London: Cabinet Office.

Suleaman, N. (2010) 'The birth of halal holidays'. *The Guardian*, 28 August. Online. www.theguardian.com/travel/2010/aug/28/halal-holidays-turkey-muslim-women (accessed 23 December 2014).

Swain, J., Heyman, B., and Gillman, M. (1998) 'Public research, private concerns: Ethical issues in the use of open-ended interviews with people who have learning difficulties'. *Disability and Society*, 13 (1), 21–36.

Tanesini, A. (1999) *An Introduction to Feminist Epistemologies*. Oxford: Blackwell.

Tarlo, E. (2009) *Visibly Muslim: Fashion, politics and faith*. Oxford: Berg.

Taylor, C. (1994) 'The politics of recognition'. In Gutnam, A. (ed.) *Multiculturalism: Examining the politics of recognition*. Princeton: Princeton University Press.

Taylor, J. (2011) 'The intimate insider: Negotiating the ethics of friendship when doing insider research'. *Qualitative Research*, 11 (1), 3–22.

Taylor, M., and Dodd, V. (2006) 'Take off the veil, says Straw – to immediate anger from Muslims'. *The Guardian*, 6 October 2006, 1.

Thanvi, M.A.A. (2004 [1333]) *Bahishti Zewar: Heavenly ornaments*. Trans. Muhammed Masroor Khan Saroha. New Delhi: Abdul Naeem for Islamic Book Service.

Thomas, P. (2009) 'The last Britons? Young Muslims and national identity'. Online. http://eprints.hud.ac.uk/5404/1/Thomas.pdf (accessed 23 December 2014).

Thornton, E. (1983) *Brick Lane: A historical study of settlement*. London: Inner London Education Authority.

Tinker, H. (1974) *A New System of Slavery: The export of Indian labour overseas, 1830–1920*. London: Oxford University Press for the Institute of Race Relations.

— (1977) *The Banyan Tree: Overseas emigrants from India, Pakistan and Bangladesh*. Oxford: Oxford University Press.

Tollefson, J.W. (1989) *Alien Winds*. Westport, CA: Greenwood Press.

— (1995) *Power and Inequality in Language Education*. Cambridge: Cambridge University Press.

Tomlinson, S., and Hutchinson, S. (1991) *Bangladeshi Parents and Education in Tower Hamlets*. Lancaster: University of Lancaster Advisory Centre for Education.

Tong, R. (2009) *Feminist Thought: A more comprehensive introduction*. 3rd ed. New York: Westview Press.

Tower Hamlets (n.d.) 'Diversity'. Online. www.towerhamlets.gov.uk/lgsl/901-950/916_borough_profile/research_and_briefings/diversity.aspx (accessed 26 December 2014).

— (2014) 'Mayor and councillors'. Online. Moderngov.towerhamlets.gov.uk/mgMemberIndex.aspx?bcr=1 (accessed 28 June 2014).

Tower Hamlets Trade Council (1979) *Brick Lane 1978: A community under attack*. London: Tower Hamlets Trade Council.

Travers, P., and Klein, G. (eds) (2004) *Equal Measures: Ethnic minority and bilingual pupils in secondary schools*. Stoke-on-Trent: Trentham Books.

Travis, A. (2001) 'Blunkett in race row over culture tests'. *The Guardian*. Online. www.guardian.co.uk/society/2001/dec/10/asylum.raceequality (accessed 29 April 2007).

Triandafyllidou, A. (2001) *Immigrants and National Identity in Europe*. London: Routledge.

— (2006) 'Religious diversity and multiculturalism in Southern Europe: The Italian mosque debate'. In Modood, T., Triandafyllidou, A. and Zapata-Barrero, R. (eds) *Multiculturalism, Muslims and Citizenship: A European approach*. London: Routledge.

Triandafyllidou, A., Modood, T., and Zapata-Barrero, R. (2006) 'European challenges to multicultural citizenship: Muslims, secularism and beyond'. In Modood, T., Triandafyllidou, A., and Zapata-Barrero, R. (eds) *Multiculturalism, Muslims and Citizenship: A European approach*. London: Routledge.

Tucker, J.E. (1983) 'Problems in the historiography of women in the Middle East: The case of nineteenth century Egypt'. *International Journal of Middle East Studies*, 15 (3): 321–36.

Tylor, E.B. (1930 [1881]) *Anthropology: An introduction to the study of man and civilisation*. 2 vols. London: Watts.

Vertovec, S. (1998) 'Young Muslims in Keighley, West Yorkshire: Cultural identity, context and "community"'. In Vertovec, S. and Rogers, A. (eds) *Muslim European Youth: Reproducing ethnicity, religion, culture*. Aldershot: Ashgate.

Visram, R. (1986) *Ayahs, Lascars and Princes*. London: Pluto Press.

— (1993) 'South Asians in London'. In Merriman, N. (ed.) *The Peopling of London: Fifteen thousand years of settlement from overseas*. London: Museum of London.

Voas, D., and Crockett, A. (2005) 'Religion in Britain: Neither believing nor belonging'. *Sociology*, 39 (1), 11–28.

Volosinov, V.N. (1973) *Marxism and the Philosophy of Language: Studies in language*. New York: Academic Press.

Vygotsky, L.S. (1978) *Mind in Society: The development of higher psychological processes*. Cambridge, MA: Harvard University Press.

— (1986) *Thought and Language*. Edited by Kozulin, A. Cambridge, MA: MIT Press.

Walby, S. (1990) *Theorizing Patriarchy*. Oxford: Blackwell.

Wallerstein, I. (1991) 'The construction of peoplehood: Racism, nationalism, ethnicity'. In Balibar, E. and Wallerstein, I. (eds) *Race, Nation, Class*. London: Verso.

Walsh, M. (ed.) (2000) *Health and Social Care*. London: HarperCollins.

Walzer, M. (1994) 'Multiculturalism and individualism'. *Dissent*, Spring, 185–91.

Warburton, M. (2007) *Ramadan: She's a thoroughly modern Muslim*. BBC1, 12 September.

Ward, P. (2004) *Britishness Since 1870*. London: Routledge.

Warner, R.S. (1998) 'Approaching religious diversity: Barriers, byways and beginnings'. *Sociology of Religion*, 59, 193–216.

Watson, H. (1994) 'Women and the veil: Personal responses to global process'. In Ahmed, A. and Donnan, H. (eds) *Islam, Globalization and Postmodernity*. London: Routledge.

Watson, J.L. (1977) *Between Two Cultures: Migrants and minorities in Britain*. Oxford: Blackwell.

Weber, M. (1997) 'What is an ethnic group?' In Guibernau, M. and Rex, J. (eds) *The Ethnicity Reader: Nationalism, multiculturalism and migration*. Cambridge: Polity Press.

— (2001 [1930]) *The Protestant Work Ethic and the Spirit of Capitalism*. London: Routledge.

Weight, R. (2002) *Patriots: National identity in Britain 1940–2000*. Basingstoke: Macmillan.

Weller, P., Feldman, A., and Purdam, K. (2001) *Religious Discrimination in England and Wales*. London: Home Office.

Wells, G., and Chang-Wells, G.L. (1992) *Constructing Knowledge Together: Classrooms as centres of inquiry and literacy*. Portsmouth, NH: Heinemann.

Went, G. (2004) 'Roma asylum seekers – The double whammy: Additional issues faced by Roma pupils and effective school provision'. In Travers, P. and Klein, G. (eds) *Equal Measures: Ethnic minority and bilingual pupils in secondary schools*. Stoke-on-Trent: Trentham Books.

Werbner, P. (1994) 'Diaspora and millennium: British-Pakistani global–local fabulations of the Gulf War'. In Ahmed, A.S., and Donnan, H. (eds) *Islam, Globalization and Identity*. London: Routledge.

— (2004) 'The predicament of diaspora and millennial Islam: Reflections on September 11, 2001'. *Ethnicities*, 4 (4), 451–76.

West, C. (1995) 'A matter of life and death'. In Rajchman, J. (ed.) *The Identity in Question*. London: Routledge.

Westwood, S. (1995) 'Gendering diaspora: Space, politics and South Asian masculinities in Britain'. In van der Veer, P. (ed.) *Nation and Migration: The politics of space in the South Asian diaspora*. Philadelphia: University of Pennsylvania Press.

White, J. (1980) *Rothschild Buildings – Life in an East End Tenement Block: 1887–1920*. London: Routledge and Kegan Paul.

White, S.C. (1992) *Arguing with the Crocodile: Gender and class in Bangladesh*. London: Zed Books.

Wiegman, R. (1999) 'Whiteness studies and the paradox of particularity'. *Boundary 2*, 26 (3), 115–50.

Wikan, U. (1982) *Behind the Veil in Arabia: Women in Oman*. Baltimore: Johns Hopkins University Press.

Williams, E. (1944) *Capitalism and Slavery*. London: Andre Deutsch.

Williams, R. (1961) 'The analysis of culture'. In Bennet, T. (ed.) *Culture, Ideology and Social Process: A reader*. London: Batsford Academic and Educational in association with Open University Press.

— (1980) *Culture and Materialism: Selected essays*. London: Verso.

Wilson, W.J. (1973) *Power, Racism and Privilege*. New York: Macmillan.

Wintour, P. (2015) 'Cameron backs Pickles' letter to Muslim leaders'. *The Guardian*, 19 January. Online. www.theguardian.com/uk-news/2015/jan/19/david-cameron-backs-eric-pickles-letter-muslim-leaders (accessed 19 January 2015).

Wolf, E. (1982) *Europe and the People without History*. Berkeley: University of California Press.

Woodward, K. (ed.) (2004) *Questioning Identity: Gender, class, ethnicity*. 2nd ed. London: Routledge and Open University Press.

Wynne, D. (1998) *Leisure, Lifestyle and the New Middle Class*. London: Routledge.

Wynne-Jones, J. (2010) 'Britons are suspicious towards Muslims, study finds'. *Daily Telegraph*. 9 January. Online. www.telegraph.co.uk/news/newstopics/religion/6958571/Britons-are-suspicious-towards-Muslims-study-finds.html (accessed 9 July 2010).

Yamani, M. (1996) 'Introduction'. In Yamani, M. (ed.) *Feminism and Islam: Legal and literary perspectives*. Reading: Garnet.

Zephaniah, B. (n.d.) 'The British (serves 60 million) from "wicked world"'. Online. www.benjaminzephaniah.com/content/245.php (accessed 19 April 2009).

Zoya, with Follain, J., and Christofari, R. (2002) *Zoya's Story: An Afghan woman's struggle for freedom*. New York: Harper Perennial.

Zwick, J. (dir.) (2002) *My Big Fat Greek Wedding*. Beverly Hills, CA: Gold Circle Films.

Index